AMERICAN
TRADE POLICY,
1923–1995

AMERICAN TRADE POLICY, 1923–1995

Edward S. Kaplan

Contributions in Economics and Economic History,
Number 172

GREENWOOD PRESS
Westport, Connecticut • London

Library of Congress Cataloging-in-Publication Data

Kaplan, Edward S.
    American trade policy, 1923–1995 / Edward S. Kaplan.
        p.   cm.—(Contributions in economics and economic history,
    ISSN 0084–9235 ; 172)
    Includes bibliographical references and index.
    ISBN 0–313–29480–1 (alk. paper)
    1. United States—Commercial policy—History—20th century.
    2. Free trade—United States—History—20th century.   3. Canada.
    Treaties, etc. 1992 Oct. 7.   I. Title.   II. Series.
    HF1455.K26   1996
    382′.3′0973—dc20   95–42919

British Library Cataloguing in Publication Data is available.

Library of Congress Catalog Card Number: 95–42919
ISBN: 0–313–29480–1
ISSN: 0084–9235

First published in 1996

Greenwood Press, 88 Post Road West, Westport, CT 06881
An imprint of Greenwood Publishing Group, Inc.

Printed in the United States of America

The paper used in this book complies with the
Permanent Paper Standard issued by the National
Information Standards Organization (Z39.48–1984).

10 9 8 7 6 5 4 3 2 1

To my mother, Rose L. Kaplan

Contents

Preface

The Clinton administration's trade policy in the 1990s appears more protectionist oriented than that of any other president since Herbert Hoover more than sixty-five years ago. Clinton's U.S. Trade Representative Mickey Kantor has threatened any country that practices unfair trade with trade sanctions in the form of 100 percent tariff increases that would assure that the foreign goods affected will be unsalable in the United States. Japan, in the spring of 1995, already has been chosen as a Clinton administration target, and the Japanese trade officials have complained bitterly to the new World Trade Organization (WTO), the successor to the General Agreement on Tariffs and Trade (GATT) that the United States is practicing managed trade. Both the European Union (EU) and the Japanese government have declared that U.S. trade policy in 1995 has come full circle since the protectionist 1920s.

It is the purpose of this book to trace the history of American trade policy beginning in 1923 and concluding in 1995 and to show how that policy has evolved. Beginning in the 1920s, during the administrations of Republican presidents Harding, Coolidge, and Hoover, the United States maintained a system of high protective tariffs as witnessed by both the Fordney-McCumber and the Hawley-Smoot tariffs in 1922 and 1930, respectively. However, protectionism was denounced with the election of Franklin D. Roosevelt to the presidency in 1932 and his appointment of Cordell Hull as secretary of state. Congress passed the Reciprocal Trade Agreements Act in 1934, authorizing the reduction of tariff rates up to 50 percent by means of bilateral trade agreements with foreign nations. These agreements contained an unconditional most-favored-nation clause so that all concessions made by either party to third countries would freely apply to the trade of the other party to an agreement.

After World War II the United States became part of the General Agreement on Tariffs and Trade, a liberal, multilateral system of world trade. The American government worked with foreign nations to accord nondiscriminatory most-favored-nation treatment to all other members with respect to import and export duties, customs regulations, and other matters pertaining to trade and commerce. All presidents from Lyndon Johnson to Bill Clinton took advantage of the GATT to reduce tariff and nontariff barriers in the Kennedy, Tokyo, and Uruguay rounds from 1963 to 1994.

In 1988 America's trade policy began to change with the passage of the Omnibus Trade and Competitiveness Act (OTCA) and its major provision "Super 301." The United States, while still involved in the Uruguay Round calling for multilateral trade reductions and joining the WTO to resolve trade disputes, had decided that it would attack unfair trade unilaterally in order to reduce its large trade deficit. In the 1990s it appears that the United States is moving from a multilateral trade approach within the WTO to a unilateral one under which it threatens countries like Japan with tariff increases for failing to open their markets ("Super 301"). This policy could lead to the destruction of the WTO and hasten a return to the protectionist days of the Hawley-Smoot Tariff.

I would like to thank the librarians at New York City Technical College of the City University of New York, SUNY Purchase of the State University of New York, and the White Plains and Harrison public libraries, whose help was indispensable in acquiring the materials for my research. Special thanks are owed my wife and my mother, who both encouraged me in this undertaking.

ESK

AMERICAN TRADE POLICY, 1923–1995

1

Background to the Hawley-Smoot Tariff

On September 21, 1922, President Warren Harding signed the Fordney-McCumber Tariff Act into law. He praised it as one of the greatest tariff acts in the history of the United States and declared that it would contribute to the already-growing prosperity in the nation. In truth, this bill set the highest tariff rates known up to that time, and unlike the president, most economic historians criticized the bill, claiming that it would do more harm than good for both the national and international economy.[1] The purpose of this chapter is to discuss the effects of the Fordney-McCumber Tariff on the economy and the events leading up to the Hawley-Smoot Tariff.

THE FORDNEY-McCUMBER TARIFF AND THE AGRICULTURAL DEPRESSION

Though the 1920s were prosperous for the country as a whole, the American farmer suffered, for the most part, through this decade. In fact, the depression for the American farmer began almost ten years prior to that for everyone else. During World War I agriculture enjoyed high prices as the American farmer fed Europe. After 1910 farmers had increased total acreage harvested by almost 15 percent, and the war encouraged the continuation of production. The recession of 1920-1921 marked the end of prosperity for the American farmer because Europe had recovered sufficiently from the ravages of war and no longer required large quantities of American agricultural products. The surplus of farm goods could not be absorbed in the national market, and agricultural prices dropped rapidly in the United States. Gross agricultural income fell from $17.7 billion in 1919 to $10.5 billion in 1921. From June to July 1920 the index of farm prices dropped ten points, and by August it fell another thirty points. As prices fell, the burden of taxation and debt grew. The number of farm foreclosures per thousand told the harrowing story of the farmer's plight. From 1913 to 1920 it averaged only 3.2 per thousand farms, increasing to 10.7 per thousand from 1921 to 1925 and 17.0 per thousand from 1926 to 1930. The decline in the value of farm products best measured the disaster that befell American agriculture. In 1919 the total value of farm products was $21.4 billion, but in 1929 it was only $11.8 billion.[2]

In the 1920s the tariff became a major issue in agricultural America. Farmers either supported the Republican administration's contention that the tariff would create prosperity for them by raising farm prices or they blamed the tariff for their economic woes. In 1920, when prices of wheat, corn, meats, and cotton declined one-third of their wartime values due to overproduction, many farmers believed that a protective tariff would resolve the problem and supported the Emergency Tariff Act of 1921. The farm bloc, made up of bipartisan members of the House and Senate, did much to alert agricultural interests to the advantages of representation. It supported many features of the Fordney-McCumber Tariff, including taking hides off the free list and imposing a duty of 15 percent ad valorem on them. Senator Edwin Ladd of North Dakota, a leader of the farm bloc, threatened to fight any attempt to lower agricultural rates, including the duty on hides.[3]

President Harding, in a speech before the Southern Tariff Association in Houston, Texas, in January 1922, claimed that the tariff was necessary to protect all sections of the country, including the farmer.[4] Senator Arthur Capper of Kansas in 1922 stated, "Under the policy of protection we have built a great industrial nation and the same protection cannot now be withheld from agriculture if we would preserve the balance between industrial and agricultural growth."[5]

President Harding's secretary of commerce, Herbert Hoover, was an ardent protectionist. He claimed that there was "no measure in the whole economic gamut more vital to the American workingman and the farmer today than the maintenance of a protective tariff."[6] In October 1923 Hoover tried to demonstrate that the Fordney-McCumber Tariff did not cause higher prices for farmers by keeping imports out of the country. He claimed that increasing percentages of U.S. imports were entering duty free, and that imports were higher in October 1923 than at the same period in 1921. This was probably due to the fact that many shipments were rushed into the country to beat the tariff deadline and were not received until October 1923.[7]

Many farmers and their supporters blamed the Fordney-McCumber Tariff for the agricultural depression. Democratic Senator Oscar W. Underwood of Alabama, a possible candidate for the nomination to the presidency in 1924, spoke to a joint session of Congress in late July 1923. He lashed out at the Republicans for erecting a tariff barrier against Europe. He asserted that western farmers had realized the need of having foreign countries absorb the surplus farm goods in the United States. He claimed that the tariff had strangled the agricultural industry to death.[8]

The former secretary of the Treasury in the Woodrow Wilson administration, William G. McAdoo, another possible Democratic candidate in 1924, called the Fordney-McCumber Tariff "an economic abortion." It fostered isolation in international markets and soaked the American farmer by keeping prices low for farm goods that must be sold abroad while keeping prices high for manufactured goods that farmers must buy. He clearly made his point by claiming that farmers needed less credit and more markets.[9]

Hoover was never very popular among the farmers because as secretary of commerce in the 1920s, he appeared unsympathetic to their plight. He insisted that the tariff did not increase the cost of living and decrease foreign trade. He claimed that only 4 to 6 percent of imports came under the influence of the Fordney-McCumber Tariff. H. E. Miles, chairman of the Fair Tariff League and an opponent of the Fordney-McCumber bill, ridiculed Hoover after the secretary of commerce blamed the shortage of sugar on its high price. Miles pointed to Cuba as having all the sugar the United States needed, but claimed that the high tariff imposed to protect the Great Western sugar refinery made it unprofitable for Cuba to sell its sugar in the United States. Consequently, the sugar tariff raised the price of sugar 2 cents a pound, for a total increase of $200 million a year in 1923.[10]

The American Farm Bureau Federation, founded in 1919, lobbied actively for farm legislation to benefit the farmer. It opposed the Fordney-McCumber Tariff, claiming that it raised prices for all consumers and specifically pointing to the tariff on raw wool that cost the public $91 million a year and farmers as consumers $27 million. It blamed the agricultural recession on the tariff that reduced many farmers to a state of poverty, causing them to dress in the winter in a rag shoddy overcoat, which was a garment consisting of 60 percent cotton, 20 percent wool shoddy, and 20 percent defective wool. The high price of artificial silk yarns, controlled by a few sellers, was no longer affordable to the general public due to the tariff. The American Farm Bureau Federation contended that the high tariff prevented foreign countries from selling their goods in the United States, and this, in turn, prevented them from buying the agricultural surplus that was depressing farm prices.[11]

Sir Arthur Balfour, president of the Associated Chamber of Commerce in Great Britain, commented on the effects of the Fordney-McCumber Tariff after a four-week business trip to the United States. Balfour pointed to the tariff as the primary reason for the high cost of living and production in the United States. He asserted that wages, rents, and prices were too high in the United States, and that farmers had to pay $800 million more there for their machinery and general farm requirements. He noted that farm prices were falling rapidly, and noted that Great Britain could easily compete with America in the world export trade market.[12]

In January 1924 John W. Davis of West Virginia, the eventual Democratic nominee for the presidency that year, called the Fordney-McCumber Tariff a gift to certain interests in return for their political contributions. Davis and the Democratic party promised the farmer tariff relief by reducing the tariff on calcium arsenate (used to fight the boll weevil) and farm tools. The Democrats promised to make the tariff an issue in the 1924 election if the Republicans refused to cooperate.[13]

The Republicans, led by Calvin Coolidge, who became president after Harding's death in August 1923, continued to defend the Fordney-McCumber Tariff. Coolidge pointed out that the tariff created as much as $550 million a year in new revenue, and that it was the lowest tariff since the McKinley bill in 1890. He declared that foreign trade had increased and criticized farmers for not realizing that most of the things used in the business of farming were not subject to the tariff because they remained on the free list. Coolidge's statement that the Fordney-

McCumber Tariff was the lowest since 1890 was inaccurate.[14]   The fact remained that the president cared less about agriculture than industry and said as much in October 1924 when he claimed that the tariff was necessary for the prosperity of American industry, for American wages to be paid, and for the American standard of living to be maintained.[15]

Senator David Walsh, Democrat of Massachusetts, challenged the Republican claim that the tariff helped the farmer by protecting his market at home while raising his prices. He contended that the farmer did not need tariff protection, and that protection would not raise farm prices because the farmer was now a net exporter of goods and depended on foreign markets in order to sell his surplus. Walsh declared that the tariff only protected big business and did nothing for the farmer, wage earners, and the salaried class. In fact, he pointed out, in its first year of existence, it raised the cost of living higher than in any other year except during the war.   In every one of the thirty-two cities covered by the survey of the Department of Labor, there had been an increase in the cost of living since the Fordney-McCumber Tariff had become effective. For example, the senator showed that food costs increased in one year 8.9 percent in Norfolk, Virginia, 16.5 percent in Chicago, 9.4 percent in New York, and 14.4 percent in Detroit. Clothing prices increased 5.5 percent in Buffalo, New York, and 10.2 percent in Chicago.[16]

Though many farmers and their supporters continued to criticize the tariff, some looked for a way to make use of it. In January 1924 Senator Charles McNary of Oregon and Congressman Gilbert N. Haugen introduced the McNary-Haugen bill into Congress. Though the House defeated the bill that year, it was reintroduced in 1927 and 1928 and passed both times by Congress, thanks to the farm bloc, but vetoed by President Coolidge on both occasions. Though this bill never became law, it was the most popular American scheme for raising agricultural prices that depended on tariffs.[17]

George N. Peek, a manufacturer of agricultural machinery, developed the McNary-Haugen plan. He realized that the trouble with American agriculture was that especially in wheat and cotton, as well as in other commodities, the nation produced more goods than the American market could absorb. There was always an exportable surplus offered for sale on the world market at whatever price it would bring. Increased agricultural production throughout the world in the 1920s caused a glutted market and low prices. If the United States produced less of any given item than it consumed, then the tariff would apply and raise the American price above the world price. But if the United States produced more than it consumed, the price of the exportable goods would determine the price both at home and abroad.[18] Farmers did not understand this. They knew that manufacturers profited from the tariff. For example, an increase in the tariff on pig iron and aluminum helped to raise the prices of those products, so why should not an increase in the tariff on wheat and meat do the same thing? Politicians, who knew better, easily persuaded the farmer that they would benefit him when they raised tariff rates on such products as wheat and meat. However, as Peek pointed out, what farmers failed to understand was that manufacturers could control production, whereas farmers did not. Continued low farm prices convinced the farmer that he had to produce more each year to maintain a decent living.[19]

Could the government do for the farmers the equivalent of what it was doing through the protective tariff for the manufacturers? For example, what about dumping farm surplus abroad for whatever price it would bring? Manufacturers, sometimes due to tariff rates, could dump goods abroad at lower prices than they would sell them for in the United States and still make a profit. However, even if manufacturers took a loss by selling abroad, they disposed of their surpluses, and the losses abroad were offset by the profits from the protected price at home. Peek wanted to do the same thing for the farmer, but the difficulty came in trying to get the farmers to work as a unit. Probably only a government agency could bring the farmers together.[20]

Peek proposed what he thought was the solution to the agricultural problem by using tariffs to boost certain farm prices. He wanted the government to buy up the surplus American wheat and cotton, arguing that because of the additional demand, the domestic prices of these crops would rise to the limit of whatever tariffs were placed on them. The government would then sell the surpluses abroad for whatever it could get. To recover its losses on these foreign sales, the government would levy a tax called an equalization fee on domestic producers. Coolidge vetoed the bill twice, as mentioned earlier. He considered the bill both unconstitutional and unsound. It was unconstitutional because the government should not get into the business of farming by directly helping the farmer to sell his goods. This made little sense since the government already was helping business and industry through the passage of the tariff act. However, the bill was unsound because higher prices would only encourage the farmer to produce more that the government would have to buy, and eventually it would lead to a greater equalization fee. Furthermore, the McNary-Haugen bill would have resulted in antidumping laws and other trade restrictions by foreign nations.[21]

The failure of the Congress to pass the McNary-Haugen bill in 1924 led to continued farm protest against the tariff. In June 1924 Frank W. Murphy, head of the Minnesota Farm Bureau and a longtime Republican, blamed the tariff for the agricultural depression. He insisted that "the world price of farm products is not depressed. It is an increase in the things farmers have to buy." Murphy claimed that the price of staples was fixed in the markets where they were sold, such as in Liverpool, England. It was the export price that determined the domestic American price. However, when the farmer bought his supplies, he found himself burdened by a chain of tariff-protected domestic monopolies that included the shingles on his barn, his reaper, and his household utensils and clothes.[22]

The agricultural depression caused the closing of numerous textile mills in Massachusetts in the summer of 1924. Massachusetts Congressman John J. Rogers was hard pressed to explain the downturn in the state economy. He admitted to his constituents that he had originally supported the Fordney-McCumber Tariff in 1922 because he had believed that it would mean higher wages and prosperity for his constituents. However, the reverse had happened, as unemployment in the mills had soared and those lucky enough to have jobs were experiencing wage reductions. Rather than admit that the tariff was a mistake and work for its reduction, Rogers blamed the recession in his state on cloth and cotton importations. Consequently, he wanted to raise cotton rates even higher. This brought a sharp retort from Frederic Shipley, president of the National Council of American Importers and Traders. Shipley was willing to have the Tariff Commission investigate cotton importations into the United States, but he stated unequivocally that importations only amounted to 3 percent of the domestic output and were not the problem. In fact, the existing tariff on cotton and cloth kept clothing prices high and the demand for clothing low. Since an increase in the tariff rate on cotton would not help the farmer, the Tariff Commission refused to recommend it to President Coolidge. This was one of the few intelligent decisions made on the tariff in the 1920s.[23]

The Tariff Commission played an advisory role to the president. Woodrow Wilson established the bipartisan commission in 1916 partly as a concession to business demands. After the passage of the Fordney-McCumber Tariff Act, the Tariff Commission helped the president implement the new flexible tariff provisions. It aided the president in determining the differences in the cost of production at home and abroad. On the commission's recommendation, the president might raise or lower any duty by as much as 50 percent if he desired to close the gap between American and foreign costs. The protectionist Republican presidents of the 1920s, Harding, Coolidge, and Hoover, chose the members of the bipartisan commission who made it more protectionist as low-tariff holdovers were not reappointed. For example, the first new member after the Republicans took over was T. O. Marvin, the longtime secretary of the Home Market Club of Boston and editor of a journal known as the *Protectionist*. W. S. Culbertson, another low-tariff supporter, was offered a diplomatic post for his seat on the commission. Harding and Coolidge together instituted only thirty-seven changes in tariffs, of which thirty-two called for higher rates.[24]

President Coolidge did not always take the advice of his Tariff Commission. For example, in 1924, when the sugar duty was costing American citizens $224 million a year, the Tariff Commission recommended to the president a reduction in the sugar tariff of 0.5 cents a pound. Coolidge refused to implement the recommendation even though it would have benefitted millions of housewives in the upcoming preserving season. Clem L. Shaver, chairman of the Democratic National Committee, attacked Senator Reed Smoot, chairman of the Senate Finance Committee, former Congressman Joseph Fordney, author of the Fordney-McCumber Tariff, and the president as caring more about the sugar-beet farmers than saving American housewives $145,000 a day. Smoot felt the sting of the attack when it was revealed that he owned four hundred shares of stock in the Utah-Idaho Company, which operated fifteen beet-sugar factories in Utah, Idaho, and Washington State, a fact that the senator did not deny.[25]

John W. Davis, the Democratic presidential candidate in 1924, continued to blame the Fordney-McCumber Tariff for the agricultural depression. In September, two months before the election, Davis mocked the Republican assertion that the tariff benefitted the farmer. He declared that the Republican statement that prosperity for protected industry assured a large demand for what the farmers had to sell was nonsense.   This was like a trickle-down theory where improved economic conditions for the farmer would have to wait upon the prosperity of protected industry. In other words, the farmer should ignore the foreign market and depend upon eventual domestic consumption.[26]

In October 1924, with the election less than a month away, Republican Congressman W. R. Green, chairman of the House Ways and Means Committee, the committee responsible for writing new tariff bills in the House, shocked some of his colleagues when he echoed Davis's statement that the tariff did hurt the farmer by keeping nonfarm prices high and farm prices low. Green stated that prices of farm goods were fixed by free competition abroad, and unfortunately, the farmer was protected against "buying cheaply but not against selling cheaply."[27] Green came from the farm state of Iowa and was concerned about his constituents and reelection, not necessarily in that order. He admitted that he had supported the Emergency Tariff in 1921 that had quickly been followed by the farm depression, and that he had hoped that the Fordney-McCumber Tariff would benefit his constituents. However, Green acknowledged that the statistics of the Bureau of Research of the American Farm Bureau showed that farmers had lost more than $300 million annually as a result of the tariff.[28]

Though the tariff was an issue in the 1924 election, it was not enough of one to help either Davis or Robert M. La Follette, the Progressive party candidate. Prosperity was the greatest handicap facing both of Coolidge's major opponents. Except for the farmers, there were few economic problems facing the nation, and that guaranteed Coolidge's election.[29]

In February 1925, three months after Coolidge won election, there was a movement among low-tariff revisionists to eradicate the flexible tariff provisions that gave the president the power to raise or lower rates on the recommendation of the Tariff Commission. The critics of the flexible tariff claimed that the president seldom paid attention to his own commission and exercised absolute power. For example, the Tariff Commission wanted the sugar tariff reduced, but Coolidge refused. At other times, the commission wanted half a dozen rates lowered, but the president raised them. The bottom line was that the flexible tariff gave the president control over tariff rates until a new tariff law could be written by Congress. Coolidge saw nothing wrong with the Fordney-McCumber Tariff and supported its flexible tariff provisions.[30]

In June 1925 Coolidge decided to take a trip to the northwestern farm belt. He wanted to talk to the farmers and assure them that the government was doing everything to help them short of revising the tariff. Once again, the president praised the tariff as the major cause of the prosperity in the nation and said that he hoped that it would eventually benefit agriculture.[31] The farmers were not satisfied with Coolidge's speeches. They wanted to know how to raise cotton and wheat prices and how to afford the high prices they had to pay for nonfarm goods. Coolidge was concerned that Republicans from wheat states would join with Democrats to reduce tariff schedules unless the price of wheat was raised. Benjamin Marsh, managing director of the Farmers' National Council located in Washington, D.C., and a leading spokesman for the farmers, attacked the tariff as the "worst gold brick ever sold to the farmers." He urged Coolidge and the Congress to help the farmer secure lower costs of production, including cheaper rent, credit, and goods.[32]

In October 1925 the Census Bureau made available figures that showed the severe depression in the farm belt. The farm census revealed that over 75,000 farms throughout the country had been abandoned since 1920.[33] Cordell Hull, a Democratic member of the House of Representatives from Tennessee, a state mired in the farm depression, and a supporter of low tariffs, denounced Coolidge for his insensitivity to the American farmer. Hull pulled no punches when he claimed that the only purpose of the Fordney-McCumber Tariff was to raise prices, but not farm prices. Hull declared that the president was wrong when he told the farmers that their only tariff losses were on a few imports that came in over high tariff walls. Hull, who would later become secretary of state in the Franklin Roosevelt administration and the architect of various reciprocal trade agreements, blamed the tariff law for retaliation by other nations against American agriculture. He certainly understood the economic importance of a low tariff.[34]

As Hull became one of the chief spokesmen against the tariff for the farmers in the House, Senator Pat Harrison of Mississippi did the same for them in the Senate. He criticized the president for failing to understand the seriousness of the farm problem. In January 1926 Harrison mocked Coolidge for the speech he had made in Chicago in early December 1925 when the president had claimed that the tariff hardly affected the farmer, as it accounted for only 2 to 3 percent of his purchases. Harrison argued that the tariff caused a disparity between the purchasing power of the farmers' dollar and that of other industries and imposed a serious burden for agriculture because it placed a tax on everything used, from the dynamite to clear the stumps from the fields and the fertilizer used for the crops to the medicine taken by a farmer's family.[35]

On January 30, 1926, Hull promised that he would offer a bill to reduce the tariff downward on a number of items, including iron and steel products and household goods. If Hull could get the Congress to lower the tariff on iron and steel products, he would help the farmer in getting lower prices for all goods he bought that were made out of iron and steel. Hull's main objective was to lower production and living costs for the farmer as well as to provide him with suitable outlets for his goods. Hull's bill never really had a chance because not only the president opposed it, but also John H. Kirby, the president of the Southern Tariff Association. Kirby claimed to speak for southern farmers when he declared that the Fordney-McCumber Tariff was a prosperity producer for the South.[36]

The dairy farmers complained bitterly about the high tariff on butter and how it affected the demand for butter in the United States. The Fordney-McCumber Tariff placed a duty of eight cents per pound on butter, a good 25 to 50 percent higher than ever before. The duty did nothing to help dairy farmers, as imports amounted to only 1.5 percent of total butter production in the United States. All the tariff did was raise the domestic price of butter to where it was no longer competitive with oleomargarine, its substitute.[37] In March 1926 the Tariff Commission, in its infinite wisdom, decided to recommend to Coolidge another increase in the tariff on butter, from eight to twelve cents per pound. What was the reason for the increase in the tariff on butter? Since the cost of production in Denmark was lower than in the United States, the Tariff Commission called for the costs to be equalized using the provisions of the flexible tariff. Obviously, Coolidge and the Tariff Commission thought that the tariff was such a good thing for the farmer's prosperity that they hoped to make him more prosperous.[38]

By the summer of 1926 three different opinions on the tariff were being voiced. Most of the Democrats wanted a downward revision of the Fordney-McCumber Tariff to help the farmer, while the Republicans remained divided on its effectiveness. For example, Coolidge and many Republican protectionists believed that the present tariff would help agriculture because it brought a general prosperity to the nation as a whole, and eventually agriculture would reap benefits from the overall prosperity. Even certain congressional representatives from the farm states, ardent supporters of Coolidge, accepted this view. Congressman Will R. Wood of Indiana praised the president and the Fordney-McCumber Tariff, claiming that it had proven to be the best and most practical tariff law enacted in the twentieth century.[39] On the other hand, many Republican protectionists, mostly from the farm belt, remained critical of the Fordney-McCumber Tariff because it failed to protect the farmer adequately. Senator Arthur Capper of Kansas, a leader of the farm bloc in the Senate, had long been a proponent of protection. As already noted in 1922, he had stated that protection for agriculture was necessary to preserve the balance between agricultural and industrial growth.[40] In the summer of 1926 Capper declared that the revolt in the Midwest was against the present Republican tariff. He stated with pride that "the farmers of the Middle West are Republicans. They have no desire to tear down the tariff structure, but only to make necessary changes to benefit the farmer. Western members of Congress will make a demand for revision of the tariff in the next Congress."[41] Capper specifically mentioned some of the problems the farmers had with the present tariff. He wanted a duty imposed on hides and the rates on wheat and cattle raised. He pointed out that there was something terribly wrong with the duty on canned beef when canned beef from Argentina was being sold in Kansas.[42]

Senator Capper had the support of both Secretary of Agriculture W. M. Jardine, appointed by Coolidge in 1925, and Louis J. Taber, master of the National Grange, which boasted a membership of 800,000. Both Jardine and Taber echoed Capper's position when they stated that the average farmer wanted more protection and not less, and they urged the president to place hides on the dutiable list and to raise the duties on both wheat and butter.[43] Coolidge had wanted to give the agricultural position to Herbert Hoover, but the secretary of commerce respectfully declined. The job was then offered to Jardine, who had a good working relationship with Hoover. After the secretary of commerce was elected to the presidency in 1928, Jardine and Taber, among others, convinced the new president of the importance of upward tariff revision. All of this eventually led to the passage of the Hawley-Smoot Tariff in 1930.[44]

In September 1926 Hull verbally attacked his colleague Will Wood for remarks the Indiana congressman had made concerning the tariff. Wood had stated that 96 percent of what the farmers had purchased was free from tariff duties. Hull called the statement a hoax and went on to blame the tariff for the high cost of both production and living in the United States.[45]   Hull's position on the tariff as a detriment to the farmer was supported by two of his fellow Democrats.   Both Congressman William Oldfield of Arkansas and Senator James Reed of Missouri claimed that protectionists failed to understand that farmers who bought in a highly competitive market and sold in a free world market could not benefit from higher rates.[46]

In September 1926 economic statistics were released by farmers' groups that proved that protection had failed to solve the agricultural depression. The figures showed that the Fordney-McCumber Tariff had already raised the rates on most farm machinery. For example, an average harness set that had sold for $46 in 1918 sold for $75 in 1926. During the same time frame the fourteen-inch plow doubled in cost from $14 to $28, mowing machines went from $45 to $95, and farm wagons increased in price from $85 to $150. The purchasing price of the farmer's dollar decreased from $1.12 in 1918 to 60.3 cents in 1926.[47]

THE FORDNEY-McCUMBER TARIFF AND THE DEBT PAYMENTS

The United States emerged from World War I as a creditor nation. In 1920 the foreign trade of the United States was larger than at any other time in its history. The value of exports stood at $8.25 billion, an increase of 4 percent over the year 1919 and 333 percent greater than in 1913. The value of imports stood at $5.75 billion, a 35 percent increase from 1919 and nearly 300 percent over 1913. More than half of this trade was now carried in ships flying the American flag, whereas prior to the war most of the trade had been carried on European vessels.[48]

During World War I the United States had loaned the European nations $10.3 billion. The United States expected these loans to be repaid as soon as possible. The Europeans could not understand the inflexibility of the American government on the debt question. In Europe's view the war had been fought for common objectives. The war had begun in August 1914, almost three years before the United States entered the conflict. The number of wounded and dead was much less for the United States, and there was really no destruction of property in America since the fighting took place abroad. How could the United States complain about debts when it had lost so little during the war and had become so wealthy afterwards?[49]

Though the United States claimed that it had loaned Europe $10.3 billion during World War I, the true figure stood at $7 billion, and nine-tenths of the $7 billion had been used to buy American goods. The other $3.3 billion was loaned after the war for relief and rehabilitation. However, the American government and people cared little if the money had been borrowed during or after the war; they wanted the debt repaid with the agreed-upon 5 percent interest. As Coolidge aptly put it, "They hired the money, didn't they?"[50]

The problem was that Europe could not meet its debt obligations. Europe suffered a gold drain from 1914 to 1917 when it shipped gold to the United States to pay for American goods. Any further depletion in the European gold supply would cause a severe depreciation in European currencies. Two other factors complicated the debt question. First, the British government had loaned its financially weaker allies billions of dollars during the war to keep them fighting, and then $33 billion in reparations had been imposed upon Germany. The German government was blamed for starting World War I and was forced to pay reparations for both civilian and military damages. According to America's allies, unless Germany paid them the reparations, the allies would be unable to pay their debts to the United States. In February 1920 Great Britain took the lead among the allies and asked the American government if it would cancel all war debts. The United States refused the request and further emphasized that the debts and reparations were unrelated issues.[51]

In January 1923 the reparations and the debt payments became a serious matter. The German government could not make its reparations payments. Both the French and Belgian governments responded by occupying the Ruhr, a German industrial area. This in turn led to a general strike in the area by German workers, a serious decline in production, and galloping inflation. The French government refused to scale down the reparations payments, and the House of Morgan, Germany's bankers, would not lend money to Germany until the reparations payments were reduced.[52]

In early 1924 an economic conference was called by the Coolidge administration to help Germany through its financial crisis. The House of Morgan had asked the American government to initiate the proceedings. Secretary of State Charles Evans Hughes appointed two people close to the House of Morgan, Owen Young, chairman of General Electric, and Charles Dawes, a prominent Chicago banker and later Coolidge's vice president, to attend the conference.[53] The conference led to the Dawes Plan that went into effect in September 1924. It called for an international loan of $200 million in gold, most of it coming from the United States, the reorganization of the Reichsbank under allied supervision, and the issuance of a new monetary unit, the reichsmark, with a gold value of 23.8 U.S. cents. No precise figure was set for reparations; however, based on a careful study of Germany's capacity to pay, the plan proposed a graduated schedule of annuities, beginning at $250 million in the first year and rising over a period of five years to $625 million.[54]

The U.S. government initiated the Dawes Plan hoping to both to revive the German economy and to get the European nations to make repayment of their World War I debts. Again, as stated earlier, unlike the European nations, the United States never admitted that reparations and war debts were related. Nevertheless, the Dawes Plan did connect the two. For example, the American loans to Germany through the Dawes Plan were partially used to pay reparations to the European governments, and then these governments used the reparations to make war-debt payments to the United States.[55]

The concern of the United States with helping Germany and demanding repayment of its war debts made no sense whatsoever in view of the Fordney-

McCumber Tariff. There was never a need for the bizarre Dawes Plan, and debt repayment would have been easier and more sensible if the tariff had been reduced. Sir Josiah Stamp, a British financial expert and a member of the commission that wrote the Dawes Plan, claimed that debt payments could not be made unless the Fordney-McCumber Tariff was reduced considerably to enable the European nations to sell their goods in the United States.[56]

Several days after Stamp's statement on the relationship of the debt payments to the tariff, Coolidge denounced the Briton's linkage of the two issues. The president declared that the tariff had nothing to do with debt payments because the latter were financial obligations of the European nations. The tariff, according to Coolidge, was a domestic issue that was necessary to protect American industry.[57]

The relationship of the Fordney-McCumber Tariff to the debt payments and reparations played an important role in American politics in the 1920s. Congressmen Green and Oldfield took opposing sides on the issue. Green supported his president and, like Coolidge, called the tariff a domestic issue that was totally separate from debt payments. The Iowa congressman was disappointed that the tariff failed to help the farmer, but he praised it as a great revenue-raising bill.[58] Oldfield, on the other hand, claimed that the tariff had cost American consumers more than $400 million yearly. Furthermore, it had built a wall around America causing the destruction of foreign trade and prohibiting debt repayment. Oldfield asked, "How can foreign peoples buy our surplus wheat, meat products, cotton, copper, automobiles, and shoes, if we do not take their goods in payment of our surplus."[59]

By 1924 many American bankers began criticizing the Fordney-McCumber Tariff. Obviously, the most vociferous critics of the tariff were those bankers who had made foreign loans during and after World War I. They saw the high tariff as a serious barrier to repayment. Dr. Benjamin Anderson, Jr., economist of Chase National Bank in New York, declared that the United States should reduce the tariff to attract more goods into the country to relieve the gold pressure in Europe. As mentioned earlier, Europe had suffered a gold drain that threatened the value of European currencies. Anderson believed that a lower tariff would allow the payment of debts in goods rather than gold. He warned that the high tariff had reduced imports and eventually this would cause a slump in American exports. He pointed out that the high tariff would eventually lead to a worldwide recession. What had kept the recession in check thus far had been the large volume of foreign loans that had been made. These loans by the bankers had been sustaining the U.S. export industry. For example, in 1924 foreign loans amounted to just over $1 billion, and in the first six months of 1925 the figure stood at $444 million. Anderson echoed the sentiment of other economists when he declared that the United States was a creditor nation in the 1920s, and that this alone justified lowering the tariff.[60]

Business affected negatively by the tariff did not remain silent. In 1926 Senator Joseph Robinson, Democrat from Arkansas, spoke before the National Council of Importers and Traders, a group opposed to the high tariff. Robinson called the Fordney-McCumber Tariff "a dismal failure and disappointment."[61] He claimed that the tariff made it impossible for most importers to make a living. He demanded that the Coolidge administration lower rates so that more European goods could reach American markets. He echoed the bankers by stating that the export of large amounts of capital was allowing foreigners to purchase American goods. Why not just lower the tariff?[62]

In 1928 Henry Ford, one of the most famous businessmen in the 1920s, a supporter of free trade, attacked the Fordney-McCumber Tariff. He claimed that free trade benefitted everybody by keeping prices low and consumption and production high. It held the key to high wages and general prosperity, while tariffs simply created unfair artificial advantages. It should be mentioned that the American automobile industry did not need protection since it already dominated the American market. Ford and his American competitors were interested in expanding foreign sales.[63]

Though 1929 brought a new president, Herbert Hoover, to the White House, the economic mentality regarding the tariff and the debt payments remained the same. Hoover, like Coolidge, regarded the tariff as a domestic issue and refused to consider lowering it to relieve the debt-payment problem. Instead, when economic conditions in Germany deteriorated in the summer of 1929 and a halt to reparations and debt payments was once again threatened, a new economic plan was proposed. The Young Plan, named after Owen D. Young, who had worked on the Dawes Plan in 1924, reduced reparations payments to $8 billion that were to be paid over fifty-nine years at an interest rate of 5.5 percent. A $300-million loan was made, of which $200 million went to European nations that owed the United States and $100 million to Germany. Once again, for the United States, loans became the preferred method of dealing with Europe's financial problems, while the high tariff remained untouchable.[64]

INTERNATIONAL RETALIATION TO THE FORDNEY-McCUMBER TARIFF

The 1920s saw an increase in tariffs throughout the world. Tariffs had been applied after World War I to protect new industries that had grown up during the war when trade was cut off. One of the arguments in favor of tariffs was that they protected the national security of a country. Obviously, a country could not depend on other countries to provide essential materials during wartime. As new countries were created from the defunct Austro-Hungarian Empire in the 1920s, tariffs were imposed to protect their domestic industries against dumping and the surge of exports from countries with depreciated currencies.[65] As countries moved to protect their industries, some examples being the United States, Great Britain, and Czechoslovakia, several international conferences were held, one in Brussels in 1920 and another in Genoa in 1922, to protest tariffs and to begin a movement toward free trade. Little was accomplished at the conferences primarily because of the uncooperative nature of the United States, which viewed the tariff as a domestic issue that benefitted the national interest only.[66]

    With the passage of the Fordney-McCumber Tariff in 1922, the United States, for a creditor country, had the highest tariff rates in the world. After failing to convince the United States to lower its tariff duties, many European and Latin American countries decided to retaliate and raise their duties. Between 1925 and 1929 there were 33 general revisions and substantial tariff changes in 26 European nations, and 17 revisions and changes in Latin America.[67] In August 1926 both Bulgaria and Czechoslovakia protested against the Fordney-McCumber Tariff; these countries threatened immediate retaliation unless the United States cut its rates.[68] In 1927 and 1928 Australia, Canada, and New Zealand all raised their tariff rates in response to the Fordney-McCumber Tariff.[69]

    Canada particularly suffered from the provisions of the U.S. tariff act. C. E. Burton, general manager of the Robert Simpson Company of Toronto, claimed that the tariff forced his company and other Canadian companies to close their New York offices. Burton stated that "we feel the tariff policy is antagonistic to Canada, and for that reason buy as little in the United States as possible. At that, Canada is the best customer of the United States, although it is treated the worst by the tariff laws."[70]

    Both the French and the Spanish governments responded to the Fordney-McCumber Tariff by raising their rates. In April 1927 the French raised import duties in general but specifically targeted the American automobile companies. They announced an increase on American automobile import duties from 45 percent of their value to 100 percent. At the same time, however, the French government announced that there was still a chance for compromise with the Americans. The French wanted to gain concessions for their exporters of silks, perfumes, and handmade lace.[71] In May 1927 the Spanish government announced a 40 percent increase in duties on American exports to Spain. The increase was blamed on the failure of the United States to renew a commercial agreement with Spain.[72]

    The League of Nations, concerned about the tariff wars, organized a World Economic Conference in Geneva, Switzerland, in 1927 to negotiate a tariff truce. The assembled body, including a representative from the United States, called for a convention to abolish prohibitions on imports. However, the convention failed due to the many reservations and loopholes demanded by countries and the lack of leadership shown by the United States. The delegate from the United States made speeches in favor of a reduction in the European trade barriers, even going so far as to denounce high tariffs as "stupid." However, the U.S. position was that the Geneva conference only applied to European tariffs and not the Fordney-McCumber Tariff.[73]

    Shortly after the failure of the World Economic Conference to lower tariff rates, Germany and Italy both imposed high import duties on wheat, escalating the tariff and trade wars. European nations, after 1925, began using the same fallacious argument as the United States to rationalize high tariff rates. The domestic producer had the right to protect his market and the worker the right to job protection and higher wages. The fallacy behind this reason either was not understood or was ignored by policy makers. Any shift from imports to domestic production would be offset by a contraction of production for exports. Simply put, a country can only export by continuing to import.[74]

THE PROTECTIONISTS

From the 1860s, the first Republican administration, protection in general and for industry in particular was regularly advocated by the Republican party. With the White House occupied by Republican presidents and the Senate in Republican hands in 1922 and 1930, there were few obstacles to revising upward existing tariff schedules. One of the leading advocates of protection in the 1920s was George Warren Barbour, president of the American Tariff League. Barbour, who considered himself the guardian of protectionism in the United States, worried about Congress yielding to the farmers and free traders and lowering tariff rates. Barbour, owner of the Linen Thread Company, warned the members of his American Tariff League in January 1927 that many American manufacturers were indifferent to the dangers of general tariff revision.[75]

At the 1928 meeting of the American Tariff League, Barbour was certain that Congress would revise the tariff rates downward for six reasons: (1) American producers had become indifferent on the tariff issue. They had forgotten that their continued prosperity was based on a protected market. (2) Farmer opposition to the high tariff had convinced many politicians to revise rates downward. (3) International bankers and industrialists had become disillusioned with protectionism. Bankers wanted repayment of debts owed by foreign nations and were convinced that lower rates would achieve this goal. Industrialists, on the other hand, were looking for new markets for their exports. The high tariff hindered exports because foreigners retaliated. (4) Women were convinced that the high tariff meant high prices. They failed to understand, according to Barbour, that many of the things bought in the domestic market remained unaffected by the tariff. (5) Foreign opposition to the tariff had grown as foreign nations put pressure on the American government to lower its rates, and if this failed to work, these nations retaliated by raising their rates. (6) There was a new political alignment in the Congress. The majority of members in 1928 had had no part in framing the Fordney-McCumber Tariff in 1922.[76]

The Home Market Club of Boston was another protectionist organization that reinforced the protectionist sentiment in the United States. At its forty-first annual meeting in November 1927, it referred to the Fordney-McCumber Tariff as the linchpin of U.S. national welfare. It attacked critics who blamed the high tariff for the depression in the textile industries of New England. It praised the tariff for protecting young industries and making those industries more competitive by protecting the United States against cheap foreign labor.[77]

Andrew Mellon, secretary of the Treasury from 1921 to 1932, the longest term of office for any cabinet member since Albert Gallatin, declared that the economy in 1927 was continuing to grow as a result of business investment and the tariff. The optimistic Mellon dismissed rumors that a depression was imminent.[78] Republican Senator Smoot of Utah opposed tinkering with the tariff in the next session of Congress. The Senate Finance Committee chairman criticized the findings of a committee appointed by the Chamber of Commerce that recommended tariff reduction. Smoot insisted that tariff reduction would cause unemployment in manufacturing and a general economic panic that would prove fatal to the home market. The senator believed in protecting the home market to save jobs and to guard the well-being of the nation. He was concerned about foreign nations dumping goods in American markets. The tariff would prevent any kind of dumping; it would equalize the cost of production between foreign and domestic producers and neutralize any advantage the foreigner had over the domestic producer in lower taxes and cheaper labor.[79]

The argument for equalizing the cost of production that Senator Smoot and other protectionists supported was based upon fallacious reasoning. For example, producers in any country have different and changing costs for the same product. Take the low-wage argument that the United States loses in trading with low-wage countries that can undersell in American markets. This might be true if high prices always resulted from high wages and low prices from low wages. However, in the United States in the 1920s, high wages, for the most part, were a consequence of the high productivity of American workers, which explained their high living standard. Perhaps Professor Frank Taussig, the tariff and trade economist of the early 1920s, presented the best argument against the equalization of costs when he declared that it was difficult enough to determine the costs of production in the United States and almost impossible to calculate them abroad.[80]

EVENTS LEADING TO THE HAWLEY-SMOOT TARIFF

In July 1926 Republican Senator Simeon Fess of Ohio, an ardent protectionist, declared that the Fordney-McCumber Tariff did not adequately protect the agricultural sector. He hoped that the administration would revise the tariff to give the farmer the same protection as manufacturers. Fess claimed that since 92 percent of the farmers' production was sold domestically, the farmer was dependent on a protective tariff. He told his constituents that the government had begun a scientific study of the farm problems and that relief was near.[81]

In January 1928 the farm bloc decided to support higher tariff rates on behalf of the farmer. It was a good time to begin the fight for tariff revision, as a presidential election was scheduled for November, and the farmers were demanding help from the government. The farm bloc's leadership in the House introduced a bill in the House Ways and Means Committee to increase import rates on more than a dozen farm commodities and to transfer a number of others from the free list to the protected list. For example, the bill would double tariff rates on cottonseed oil, peanut oil, live cattle, and fresh beef. It would take hides off the free list and protect them at five cents per pound. At the same time, Congressman Hamilton Fish, a Republican from New York, introduced a bill proposing an increase in tariff rates on dairy farming to help his upstate dairy-farming constituents.[82]

The Republican leadership in the House decided not to take any action on tariff revision until after the nomination of a presidential candidate. In August 1927 Coolidge had announced that he did "not choose to run for President in 1928."[83] On June 10, 1928, the Republican convention met in Kansas City, Missouri, and nominated Herbert Hoover. The tariff issue played an important role at the convention. William N. Butler, the chairman of the Republican National Committee, spoke out in favor of tariff revision for farmers. He was joined by Senator Fess, the temporary chairman of the convention. They claimed that since the present Fordney-McCumber Tariff of 1922 no longer took into consideration the present industrial state of Europe, it had to be revised upward. Both men supported increased duties on farm goods and promised to reduce the free list considerably. They believed that manufacturing groups would support an upward revision for the farmer as long as there was no tinkering with their interests.[84]

Congressman Willis C. Hawley, the new chairman of the House Ways and Means Committee, spoke at the Republican convention urging farmers to stand by the party of protection and not to chase "false gods." Though he contended that the farmer had reaped substantial benefits from the Fordney-McCumber Tariff, he would support the Republican platform calling for more protection for the farmer.[85] That platform called for the continuation of a high protective tariff and praised it for stimulating the development of U.S. natural resources. The platform declared that the tariff provided full employment at higher wages by promoting industrial activity and raising the standard of living, general comfort, and well-being of the American people. Finally, the platform promised that the tariff would provide the farmer with a major market for his goods.[86] The Republicans proudly pointed out that the Fordney-McCumber Tariff had justified itself in the expansion of U.S. foreign trade from 1922 to 1927. Domestic exports over that period had increased from $3.8 billion in 1922 to $4.8 billion in 1927 while imports had increased over that same period from $3.1 billion to $4.4 billion.[87]

The Democratic convention opened in Houston, Texas, on June 26, 1928, and nominated Al Smith for the presidency. The Democrats refused to denounce the tariff in general, as support for it was increasing among the destitute farmers who were looking for something to change their luck. Therefore, the Democratic party, in its platform, defined its kind of tariff: (1) A tariff should maintain high wages. (2) It should increase the purchasing power of wages and income by reducing the monopolistic and extortionate tariff rates bestowed on the nation in payment of political debts. (3) Tariff duties should be established to allow effective competition and produce revenue for the government. (4) The tariff should provide an equitable distribution of both benefits and burdens among all.[88]

Shortly after the election of Hoover and a Republican-controlled Congress in November 1928, Republican Wesley Jones of Washington, the assistant majority leader of the Senate, announced his support for a special session of Congress, as soon as possible after Hoover's inauguration on March 4, to deal with both farm relief and tariff reform. He claimed that both issues could be accomplished in two to three months' time.[89]

In early January 1929 the House Ways and Means Committee set in motion the machinery of a new tariff law in anticipation that Hoover would call a special session. Public hearings were to begin on January 7 and last until the end of February. The committee made public the reasons for tariff revision, stating that since the passage of the Fordney-McCumber Tariff in 1922, conditions of production and marketing both at home and abroad had changed. For example, in 1922 Europe was still in the process of recovery from the war, world conditions were in flux, and currencies were far from stabilized. Europe was now fully recovered, and the 1922 tariff no longer applied to current conditions.[90]

Another issue that the House Ways and Means Committee wanted to discuss was whether to maintain the flexible tariff provisions of the 1922 tariff discussed early in this chapter. Some senators wanted the flexible provisions repealed. In 1928 Senators Joseph Robinson of Arkansas and Robert M. La Follette of Wisconsin signed a report calling for the repeal of the flexible provisions.[91]

Agricultural rates would be the most important issue taken up by the House Ways and Means Committee. American farmers wanted protection under any new tariff. They suffered from the agricultural depression that had begun in 1920 and blamed everyone but themselves for their problems. The fact was that overproduction along with inelastic demand kept farm revenue low. However, the farmer saw how manufacturing benefitted from high tariffs by reducing competition. Farmers in the late 1920s wanted to eliminate many of the Danish dairy goods coming into the country that competed with their products.[92] Hoover, in his inaugural address, promised to raise tariffs to assist farmers struggling with falling prices. On March 7, 1929, shortly after his inauguration, Hoover called for a special session of Congress to meet on April 15 to make good on his promise to the farmers. When Congress met for its special session, it would pass the Hawley-Smoot Tariff Act, the most protective tariff in American history.[93]

NOTES

1. For a detailed account of the Fordney-McCumber Tariff see Edward S. Kaplan and Thomas W. Ryley, *Prelude to Trade Wars: American Tariff Policy, 1890-1922* (Westport, CT: Greenwood Press, 1994), pp. 95-130.

2. John D. Hicks, *Republican Ascendancy, 1921-1933* (New York: Harper and Row, 1960), pp. 18-19; Arthur M. Schlesinger, Jr., *The Crisis of the Old Order, 1919-1933* (Boston: Houghton Mifflin Company, 1957), p. 105; Barry Eichengreen, "The Political Economy of the Smoot-Hawley Tariff," *Research in Economic History* 12 (1989): 6-8.

3. Kaplan and Ryley, *Prelude to Trade Wars*, pp. 100-101, 112.

4. Ibid., p. 111.

5. Schlesinger, *Crisis of the Old Order*, pp. 105-106.

6. Ibid., p. 434.

7. Ibid., p. 84; *New York Times*, January 14, 1923, p. 8.

8. *New York Times*, August 1, 1923, p. 1.

9. Ibid., August 20, 1923, p. 20.

10. Ibid., March 18, 1923, p. 8.

11. Ibid.

12. Ibid., September 5, 1923, p. 19.

13. Ibid., January 11, 1924, p. 3; January 16, 1924, p. 2.

14. Kaplan and Ryley, *Prelude to Trade Wars*, pp. 1-4 and 124.

15. *New York Times*, January 16, 1924, p. 2; October 24, 1924, p. 1.

16. Ibid., January 16, 1924, p. 2.

17. Schlesinger, *Crisis of the Old Order*, pp. 106-109; John A. Garraty, *The Great Depression* (New York: Harcourt Brace Jovanovich, 1986), p. 56.

18. Garraty, *The Great Depression*, p. 56; Hicks, *Republican Ascendancy*, pp. 195-196.

19. Hicks, *Republican Ascendancy*, pp. 196-197.

20. Ibid.

21. Garraty, *The Great Depression*, p. 56.

22. *New York Times*, June 9, 1924, p. 16.

23. Ibid., May 15, 1924, p. 31; June 9, 1924, p. 29.

24. Hicks, *Republican Ascendancy*, pp. 57-58, 66.

25. *New York Times*, September 8, 1924, p. 6.

26. Ibid., p. 14.

27. Ibid., October 12, 1924, pp. 1-2.

28. Ibid.

29. Hicks, *Republican Ascendancy*, p. 101.

30. *New York Times*, February 11, 1925, p. 29; February 12, 1925, p. 18.

31. Ibid., June 11, 1925, p. 1.

32. Ibid.; *New York Times*, February 15, 1925, p. 5.

33. *New York Times*, October 17, 1925, p. 17.

34. Ibid.; *New York Times*, December 10, 1925, p. 3; January 25, 1926, p. 23.

35. *New York Times*, January 19, 1926, p. 8.

36. Ibid., January 31, 1926, p. 5; February 6, 1926, p. 7.

37. Ibid., February 14, 1926, p. 7.

38. Ibid., March 11, 1926, p. 20.

39. Ibid., August 27, 1926, p. 16.

40. Schlesinger, *Crisis of the Old Order*, pp. 105-106.

41. *New York Times*, August 21, 1926, p. 2.

42. Ibid.

43. Ibid., August 22, 1926, p. 2; August 24, 1926, p. 2.

44. Schlesinger, *Crisis of the Old Order*, pp. 107-108.

45. *New York Times*, September 6, 1926, p. 2.

46. Ibid., August 22, 1926, p. 3; November 6, 1927, p. 21.

47. Ibid., September 13, 1926, p. 4.

48. Hicks, *Republican Ascendancy*, pp. 9-10.

49. Ibid., p. 136.

50. Ibid.

51. Ibid., p. 137.

52. Charles P. Kindleberger, *The World in Depression, 1929-1939* (Berkeley: University of California Press, 1986), p. 20.

53. Ron Chernow, *The House of Morgan: An American Banking Dynasty and the Rise of Modern Finance* (New York: Simon and Schuster, 1990), p. 249.

54. Hicks, *Republican Ascendancy*, p. 141.

55. Kindleberger, *World in Depression*, pp. 25-26.

56. *New York Times*, June 24, 1925, p. 1.

57. Ibid., June 27, 1925, p. 1.

58. Ibid., June 29, 1925, p. 4.

59. Ibid., September 11, 1925, p. 25.

60. Ibid., August 24, 1925, p. 22; November 4, 1926, p. 26.

61. Ibid., April 8, 1926, p. 11.

62. Ibid.

63. Ibid., April 11, 1928, p. 5.

64. Hicks, *Republican Ascendancy*, p. 143; Kindleberger, *World in Depression*, pp. 67-68.

65. Kindleberger, *World in Depression*, p. 61.

66. Ibid., pp. 61-64.

67. Eichengreen, "Political Economy of the Smoot-Hawley Tariff," p. 32.

68. *New York Times*, August 25, 1926, p. 20.

69. Eichengreen, "Political Economy of the Smoot-Hawley Tariff," p. 32.

70. *New York Times*, February 9, 1928, p. 43.

71. Ibid., April 26, 1927, p. 37.

72. Ibid., May 20, 1927, p. 9; May 21, 1927, p. 29.

73. Ibid., June 29, 1927, pp. 10, 24; Kindleberger, *World in Depression*, p. 64.

74. Kindleberger, *World in Depression*, pp. 64-65; Franklin Root, *International Trade and Investment*, 7th ed. (Cincinnati, OH: South-Western Publishing Co., 1994), pp. 166-167.

75. *New York Times*, January 21, 1927, p. 24.

76. Ibid., January 20, 1928, p. 37.

77. Ibid., November 28, 1927, p. 20.

78. Ibid., November 15, 1927, pp. 1, 14.

79. Ibid.

80. Root, *International Trade and Investment*, pp. 165-168; F. W. Taussig, *The Tariff History of the United States*, 8th ed. (New York: G. P. Putnam Sons, 1931), p. 480.

81. *New York Times*, July 22, 1926, p. 3.

82. Ibid., January 21, 1928, p. 22; January 22, 1928, p. 5.

83. Ibid., January 22, 1928, p. 5; Hicks, *Republican Ascendancy*, p. 201.

84. *New York Times*, June 11, 1928, p. 3.

85. Ibid.

86. Ibid., June 15, 1928, p. 8.

87. Ibid.

88. Ibid., June 29, 1928, p. 5.

89. Ibid., January 6, 1929, p. 27.

90. Ibid., January 6, 1929, p. 4.

91. Ibid.

92. Ibid.

93. Kindleberger, *World in Depression*, p. 64; *New York Times*, March 8, 1929, p. 1.

2

The Hawley-Smoot Tariff

The Hawley-Smoot Tariff of 1930 was mostly the outcome of the post-World War I agricultural recession. In the political campaign of 1928, Hoover stressed the importance of the protective tariff as an aid to agriculture and promised, if elected, to revise the tariff to help the farmer. After Hoover's victory in November, 1928 farm groups throughout the Middle West demanded that the new president call a special session of Congress to revise agricultural duties upward.[1] Republican Senator Wesley Jones of Washington insisted upon a special session of Congress as soon as possible after the March 4 inauguration, and he predicted that tariff revision would take only two to three months time. Already in early January hearings on tariff revision were taking place in the House Ways and Means Committee under the astute leadership of Republican chairman Willis C. Hawley of Oregon.[2]

Both Republican Senator Reed Smoot of Utah, chairman of the Senate Finance Committee, and President-elect Hoover insisted that any tariff revision would be limited. There was no need for a general revision of the Fordney-McCumber Tariff rates of 1922. Smoot wanted the special session to revise the agricultural rates of the 1922 tariff only. Hoover said as much when he issued a proclamation calling Congress into special session for April 15 to consider agricultural relief and legislation for limited changes in the tariff.[3]

Limited revision never had a chance due to the political nature of tariff making and the failure of the new president to exercise leadership. Presidential leadership during the passage of the new tariff will be discussed later in the chapter. However, a brief discussion of the political nature of the tariff should precede examination of its actual passage through Congress.

In 1929 the House Ways and Means Committee consisted of twenty-five members, of whom fifteen were Republicans, the majority party. The majority party in Congress was responsible for the framing of the Hawley-Smoot Tariff of 1930. The subcommittee chairmen, all Republicans, were assigned to specific tariff schedules like textiles, metals, and chemicals. Generally, each subcommittee chair was given a schedule that represented the interests of his constituents. For example, the Massachusetts member was likely to chair the subcommittee on textiles, and the member from Pennsylvania was given charge of iron and steel. When the fifteen members met as a whole, each subcommittee had finished its work on the tariff pertaining to its area of interest. There was generally no interference with what the other subcommittees accomplished. In other words, "You allow me to help my constituents and I will do the same for you." The members of the minority party, the Democrats in 1929, had absolutely no say in the tariff-making process in the House Ways and Means Committee. They were not a part of the subcommittees, and when the fifteen Republican members met as a whole, the Democrats could not attend. Only after the tariff bill was written was it presented to the Democrats for their inspection.[4]

In the Senate, while the procedure differed, the result was the same, the complete domination of the Republican majority party in the Senate Finance Committee. The committee consisted of nineteen members, of whom eleven were Republicans. Like the House Ways and Means Committee, the Senate Finance Committee divided its work among the subcommittees chaired by members of the Republican party. Unlike the House, each subcommittee in the Senate consisted of members of both parties. All hearings were formal and open; however, after the hearings finished, the Republicans met alone to prepare the tariff bill that was presented to the Democrats to study. Democratic amendments to the bill could be made only after the Senate Finance Committee passed on it and it came to the floor of the Senate for a full vote.[5]

THE TARIFF IN THE HOUSE

On March 16 Chairman Hawley informed President Hoover that the House Ways and Means Committee should finish its work on tariff reform by April 20. He indicated that the committee would propose a limited revision to the full House raising agricultural rates to new highs. He warned the president that the new tariff would most certainly anger Canada, a large exporter of farm goods to the United States. The Canadian government had already retaliated against the Fordney-McCumber Tariff in 1927 by raising its rates against U.S. exports. Hawley expected further retaliation when the new tariff bill eventually passed.[6]

Willis Chatman Hawley was more an economist than a politician. He was educated in country schools before taking a science degree at Willamette University, the oldest Protestant college west of the Mississippi. In 1884 he became principal of the Umqua Academy for two years. A few years later he returned to Willamette University to receive both an academic and a law degree. From 1893 to 1902 he was president of his alma mater while finding the time to be admitted to the bar. Before he came to Congress in 1907, he was already an ardent protectionist and an expert on tariff and tax laws.[7]

By the first week in April limited tariff revision favored by Hoover, Hawley, and Nicholas Longworth, Republican Speaker of the House of Representatives, faced its first formidable opposition by a congressional delegation from

Pennsylvania. The Pennsylvania congressmen favored higher rates on textiles, cement, and chemicals. Longworth claimed that to raise the duties on these articles would cause inflation and a possible recession.[8] This was the first attempt to make limited tariff revision to help the farmer into general tariff revision to aid the industrial East. As we will see, by the time the Hawley bill passed the House, general tariff reform was an accomplished fact.

The Republicans on the House Ways and Means Committee finished their version of the tariff bill by the end of the first week in May and submitted it to the Democrats for their inspection. The bill would now be presented to the full House of Representatives for action, where the Democrats hoped to make numerous amendments. However, Speaker Longworth, who wanted quick action on the bill and considered the Democrats obstructionists, favored prohibiting all amendments to the bill on the House floor except those proposed by the Republican members of the House Ways and Means Committee.[9]

Congressman Hawley praised the bill that his committee presented to the House as fulfilling the campaign promises made by the Republican party to the farmer. There was no question that it contained concessions to the farmer element in the form of higher duties on agricultural products, but what Hawley did not mention was that it also raised duties on many other articles such as sugar, silk, razors, carpets, textiles, and dressed fur.[10] This was certainly not a limited tariff revision, as almost all of the hundreds of rate changes were upward. The *New York Times* in an editorial claimed that the farmer had been fooled into thinking that the high tariff rates on his goods would benefit him. For example, the duty on corn was increased from 15 to 25 cents, but imports on corn amounted to only .05 percent of the total production in the United States.[11]

When the Hawley bill was made public in the House, opposition to its inclusions and exclusions became more vocal, as expected. For example, nine Republicans from California served notice that unless figs, dates, hides, and long-staple cotton were taken off the free list and made dutiable, they would vote with the Democrats to recommit the bill to the House Ways and Means Committee for further study.[12] Massachusetts and New York Republicans by unanimous vote opposed the increase in sugar rates. Cuban sugar was admitted under the Fordney-McCumber Tariff of 1922 at a rate of 1.76 cents per pound, but under the Hawley bill the rate increased to 2.4 cents per pound. Raw sugar went from 2.21 cents per pound in the 1922 tariff to 3 cents per pound. Since sugar was a main ingredient in many food products, eastern Republicans expected food prices to rise, angering housewives throughout their districts. On the other hand, western Republicans favored higher sugar duties to protect the sugar growers in their districts.[13]

Congressmen from Massachusetts were concerned about food prices rising but not about boot and shoe prices. These congressmen demanded higher duties on boots and shoes to protect their shoe industry against imports, claiming that higher rates were not meant to raise prices, but to provide job protection in their districts.[14]

Originally this bill was designed to provide the farmer relief from low agricultural prices by raising the tariffs on farm goods. Though the Hawley bill did increase the tariff rates on farm goods, many farmers criticized it as being insufficient. For example, farmers wanted higher rates on oil, fats, oil-bearing raw materials, dairy products, hides, live cattle, and long-staple cotton, none of which were increased in the Hawley bill that emerged from the House Ways and Means Committee.[15] Senator Arthur Capper, Republican from Kansas and a leader of the farm bloc, denounced the Hawley bill in the House as inadequate to meet the needs of agricultural interests. Capper wanted to see a tariff that would create economic equality with industry. He claimed that it made little sense to raise rates on agricultural goods and then raise them on goods farmers had to purchase. For example, Capper asked how the farmer benefitted from taking cement, maple and birch lumber, and cedar lumber and shingles off the free list and making them all dutiable. Capper was especially incensed by the 15 percent ad valorem rate placed on maple and birch lumber and the 25 percent rate on cedar lumber and shingles.[16]

The Democrats wasted little time in criticizing the Hawley bill. Both Cordell Hull of Tennessee and John Nance Garner of Texas, leaders in the House of Representatives, pointed out that the Hawley bill favored industry over agriculture. Garner declared that the bill did not provide parity with manufacturing and that the farmers were being misled into believing that this bill would prove their salvation.[17]

The Democrats also assailed the Republicans for attempting to change the bipartisan nature of the Tariff Commission. The members of the commission had been chosen in a bipartisan manner ever since the inception of the commission during the Wilson Administration in 1916. President Hoover and many Republicans believed that the Commission should not be divided up equally among Republicans and Democrats, but that the president should choose the best available candidates.[18]

Democratic Senator Joseph Robinson of Arkansas and Garner were dissatisfied with the flexible provision of the Fordney-McCumber Tariff Act of 1922 that allowed the president to raise or lower rates up to 50 percent on the recommendation of the Tariff Commission. Robinson, Garner, and others believed that this power belonged to the Congress and not the president.[19] Less than a week after Robinson and Garner recommended taking away the president's power to raise or lower rates, Hoover, on the recommendation of the majority of the Tariff Commission, increased duties on flaxseed, milk, cream, and window glass. The new rates on these articles were exactly those written in the Hawley bill.[20]

For the first time in a tariff bill labor was mentioned in its title. Hawley wanted the support of labor in getting the bill through Congress. He realized that the bill, by stressing how much it would do for the farmer in raising his prices, would cause the workingman to worry about inflation. Hawley claimed that the average rate of wages abroad was 40 percent less than in the United States, and it was the objective of the Hawley bill to maintain wages consistent with the American standard of living.[21]

Hoover took no leadership role during the drafting of the bill in the House Ways and Means Committee even though he was kept informed by Hawley, with whom he had been good friends for many years. However, during the debate on the House floor the president claimed that the Hawley bill's rates were too high and that they would cause inflation. He declared that the higher farm duties were acceptable, but that the House went beyond its mandate by imposing duties on building materials such as lumber and shingles. He also criticized the 3-cent duty on raw sugar as too high. Hoover would leave it to the Senate to make the necessary changes.[22]

On May 24 the House adopted what the Democrats called a "gag" rule by a vote of 234 to 138—a Republican device to limit debate on the Hawley bill. The House decided that the only amendments accepted would come from the Republican members of the House Ways and Means Committee. The objective was to rush the bill through the House as quickly as possible.[23] Four days later the House passed the Hawley bill by a vote of 264 to 147. Only 12 Republicans joined the Democrats to vote against the bill, while 20 Democrats voted with the Republicans to pass it.[24]

The Hawley bill passed by the House increased duties on every article of food and necessities such as clothing, boots, and shoes. Boots and shoes that had been on the free list since 1913 now were dutiable at 20 percent ad valorem, and hides admitted free under the Fordney-McCumber Tariff carried a duty of 10 percent ad valorem.[25] Duties on dairy products increased under the Hawley bill. For example, the duty on butter went from 12 cents per pound in the 1922 tariff to 14 cents, that on cream from 20 cents per gallon to 42 cents, and that on milk from 2.5 cents per gallon to 6.5 cents.[26] According to the Tariff Commission, the average equivalent ad valorem rates on farm goods went from 40.81 percent in the Fordney-McCumber Tariff to 54.17 percent in the House-passed Hawley bill. Rates on manufacturing goods increased from 34.78 percent to 38.62 percent.[27]

Of the 12 Republicans who voted against the Hawley bill, 9 came from the corn belt. They were, for the most part, pleased about the higher agricultural rates, but berated their colleagues for supporting higher rates on manufacturing goods such as clothes, boots, and shoes. These dissident House members wanted parity with industry by raising rates on agricultural goods and lowering them on other goods.[28] But the House, when it voted on the Hawley bill, played politics with the tariff by allowing members of the House Ways and Means Committee to liberally amend the bill. A coalition was formed allowing limited protection to everyone involved. These Republican dissidents were joined by President Hoover in asking the Senate to restore the original objective of the bill—limited tariff revision.[29]

THE HAWLEY BILL IN THE SENATE

On June 3 Hoover made public his dissatisfaction with the Hawley bill. He criticized specifically the high rates on sugar and shoes and hinted at a veto unless the rates were reduced on these and other articles. He declared that the bill did not conform to the tariff statement in the Republican platform in 1928.[30]

Republican Senator Reed Smoot of Utah, chairman of the Senate Finance Committee, announced on June 3 that instead of holding hearings by the full committee, he would form subcommittees to handle the various tariff schedules in open hearings. When the senator was asked by a reporter how long the process would take, he declared that he expected to have a Senate version of the Hawley bill by November 1, 1929.[31]

Senator Smoot was as much a protectionist as Congressman Hawley in the House. He was a spokesman for his state of Utah and its main product, beet sugar. He had been on the Senate Finance Committee during the passage of the Fordney-McCumber Tariff and, in fact, had been appointed to the Conference Committee that finalized the 1922 tariff. Smoot was both respected by the majority of his colleagues and experienced to lead the tariff fight in the Senate.[32] When asked about his sentiments on tariff revision, the senator replied, "I favor not only tariff revision for farm relief, but whatever really is necessary."[33] Obviously the senator from Utah had no intention of limiting tariff revision in the Senate version of the Hawley bill. Senator Robinson, the Democratic leader in the Senate, when asked how he thought Smoot would revise the tariff, was quick to respond, "I have not the slightest doubt that the Senator from Utah, if given free rein, would bring back to the Senate a bill even worse for the farmers than the House bill, and God knows, that is bad enough."[34]

By the end of June it appeared that the Hawley bill had little chance of survival in the Senate, as it was attacked by major farm organizations, Democrats, and Republicans. Chester H. Gray of the American Farm Bureau Federation declared that rates in the House bill would hurt agriculture more than the present Fordney-McCumber Tariff. He claimed that farm products did not receive adequate protection and that manufacturing tariff rates were too high. Congressman Hull, who had voted against the Hawley bill, stated that the House proceedings had been dominated by "sinister and selfish" forces. Republican Senator Smith Brookhart of Iowa made the best argument of all against the Hawley bill when he declared that no matter how high the tariff was, it would not help the farmer unless there was first a reduction in farm surplus. Brookhart used wheat as the classical example. With a 42-cent duty and a surplus of wheat, the total benefit to the farmer was about $17 million a year. With no surplus, the benefit of the tariff increased to $380 million a year.[35]

On July 7 Senator Furnifold Simmons of North Carolina, the ranking Democrat on the Senate Finance Committee and author of the Underwood-Simmons Tariff in 1913, declared the Democratic strategy in dealing with the Hawley bill. The Democrats would try to lower the duties on all goods the farmers had to purchase. Then they would attempt to amend the flexible provision of the Hawley bill to give Congress rather than the president the power to raise and lower tariff duties.[36] Simmons had the support of Senator William Borah, a progressive Republican from Idaho, whose major objective was to reduce the power of the president by changing the flexible provision.[37]

As the Senate Finance Committee began its work on the Hawley bill in late July, Democratic Senator T. H. Caraway of Arkansas challenged Hoover to take a firm stand against the Hawley bill. In May, when the Hawley bill had passed the House, Hoover had criticized its high rates on nonfarm goods. Ever since the president had remained silent on the tariff.[38] There was a rumor circulating in Washington that the president had asked Senator Smoot to support lower rates on many manufacturing goods in the Hawley bill. Smoot had denied that Hoover had spoken to him about lower rates or had interfered in any way with the work of the Senate Finance Committee.[39]

As August approached, the Senate Finance Committee began working at night in order to finish its revision of the Hawley bill. The farmers applauded when the committee finally placed logs, shingles, and lumber on the free list.[40] Due to consumer protest, sugar duties were reduced. The Hawley duty on raw sugar of $3 per hundred pounds was lowered to $2.75 and the Cuban sugar duty of $2.40 per hundred pounds to $2.20. This did not satisfy the Democrats, who continued to insist that sugar duties were still too high.[41]

The automobile industry failed to get the committee to reduce the 25 percent ad valorem rate on imported autos to 10 percent. Ford, General Motors, and the rest of the American auto industry depended on the European market to increase their sales. The high tariff had angered the French press and government and had brought retaliation against the American automobile industry.[42]

On August 20 the Senate Finance Committee had finished revising the Hawley bill. Senator Smoot had indicated that 431 changes were made in the House bill's rates. Of the 431 changes, 177 were increases in the tariff rates, while 254 were decreases.[43] On the following day Smoot announced an entirely new system of valuation under which the Tariff Commission would translate the ad valorem rates in the pending tariff bill. Instead of the president proclaiming the translated rates as received from the Tariff Commission, now Congress would be the sole judge on whether rates were adopted.[44]

On September 2, Smoot sent the Senate Finance Committee's report to the floor of the Senate after a partisan vote of 11 to 8. Though the Democrats did not write a minority report, they and the progressive Republicans, led by Borah, threatened to defeat the bill. Borah and Democratic Senator Kenneth McKellar of Tennessee stated that the revised Hawley bill was not improved by the Senate Finance Committee, and that it differed little from the House version. The farmer still did not have parity with industry, and the Republican party did not keep its election pledge to the farmer. Representatives of the farmer in the northwestern and mountain states rebelled, complaining that manufacturing states in the East received more protection and tariff favors.[45]

Senator Smoot, in a visit with President Hoover in early September, told the president that quick passage of the tariff was uncertain. Hoover told Smoot that he was unhappy with the flexible clause imposed by the Senate Finance Committee that gave Congress the power to alter tariff rates. Hoover insisted that it was in the national interest for the president to retain the power to alter rates. Senator Simmons, on the other hand, claimed that tariff making was a form of taxation, and that taxation was always levied by Congress and never the president.[46]

While the Senate worked on the tariff bill, Frederick E. Murphy, publisher of the *Minneapolis Tribune* and a leading spokesman for the farm bloc, reminded the president of his pledge to help the farmer gain parity with industry. According to Murphy, the Hawley bill made little sense when the duty on hides increased 10 percent to help the farmer, and then Congress raised duties on shoes and boots between 15 and 35 percent. Murphy contended that the farmer would fight against this duplicity by the politicians.[47]

In October women began organizing against the high food prices that the new tariff bill would bring. Dr. Gertrude Duncan and Mrs. William H. Good, prominent civic workers, formed the Women's Non-Partisan Fair Tariff Committee, made up of business and professional women. This group hoped to merge the interests of housewives to protect the economic foundations of the American home. It began as a local organization in New York but expected within the year to expand nationally.[48]

On October 4 the Senate made a very important decision on the tariff bill. The Hawley bill, that had emerged from the House called for a change in the structure of the Tariff Commission. It called for a seven-member nonpartisan Tariff Commission instead of the present six-member bipartisan commission. The president in each case would appoint the commission. Hoover favored the House version. However, the Democrats and the progressive Republicans on the Senate Finance Committee wanted to keep the bipartisan six-member commission and made the change back to the original version. Hoover hoped that the full Senate would accept the House version and keep politics out of tariff making. However, the Senate voted to retain its Finance Committee's version, notwithstanding the president's wishes.[49]

As the days of October began to wane, Borah and Smoot started blaming each other for the delay in the tariff bill. Borah insisted that the tariff be rewritten to conform to Hoover and the Republican party's pledge in 1928. He stated emphatically that the tariff in its present form would not pass. Smoot called Borah, Brookhart, who wanted to add one hundred amendments to the bill requested by farmers, the progressive Republicans, and the Democrats obstructionists. According to Smoot, these groups were taking 75 percent of the debate time to delay Senate passage.[50]

On November 20 the Senate voted 49 to 33 for adjournment of the special session that had begun the previous April. The tariff bill had passed the House during this session but had become stalled in the Senate. President Hoover denounced the inaction of the Senate but could do nothing until the Senate reconvened in early January 1930.[51] Jouett Shouse, chairman of the Democratic National Executive Committee, blamed the failure to enact the tariff bill in special session on Hoover's lack of decisive leadership. He declared that the president did not once intervene on behalf of the farmer. According to Shouse, Hoover would accept any tariff bill as long as it maintained the flexible provision allowing him and not the Congress to change tariff rates.[52]

After the Christmas holiday Senator Smoot met with the president and predicted that the Senate would pass the tariff bill by February 15. However, when the Senate began deliberations on January 6, 1930, action on the tariff moved slowly. Many senators wanted to make amendments to the bill. For example, progressive Republican Senator Robert M. La Follette of Wisconsin, an opponent of the Hawley bill, offered over two hundred amendments.[53]

By the middle of February 1930 the Senate farm-schedule rates were made public and were quickly denounced by the major farm organizations throughout the country. Representatives of the American Farm Bureau Federation, the Farmers' Union, the Central Cooperative Association, the National Cooperative Milk Producers Federation, the American Cotton Growers Exchange, the National Livestock Producers Association, and the American National Livestock Association all assailed the bill as inadequate to the needs of the American farmer. They criticized the low rates on sugar, blackstrap molasses, casein, hides, fats, and oils. The general consensus was that the farmers'interests were better served by the present Fordney-McCumber Tariff than this new Hawley-Smoot bill. They attacked Hoover for failing to keep his pledge in 1928 to help the farmer.[54]

The Hawley-Smoot Tariff bill finally passed the Senate on March 24, 1930, by a vote of 53 to 31. Of the 53 affirmative votes, 46 were Republicans and 7 were Democrats, while 26 Democrats and 5 Republicans voted against the measure.[55] Senator Smoot declared that the debate on the tariff had covered 2,638 pages of the *Congressional Record* and over 4 million words. The total cost of printing, paid for by the American people, was $132,000. The Senate amended the bill 1,253 times.[56]

In American tariff history since 1890, the Hawley-Smoot Tariff was before the Senate longer than any other tariff bill. The McKinley bill in 1890 took 3 months and 2 days; the Wilson-Gorman bill in 1894, 1 month and 18 days; the Dingley bill in 1897, 2 months and 3 days; the Payne-Aldrich bill in 1909, only 28 days; the Underwood-Simmons bill in 1913, 1 month and 29 days; the Fordney-McCumber bill in 1922, 4 months and 8 days. The Hawley-Smoot bill spent 6 months and 18 days in the Senate.[57]

The Senate reduced most of the tariff rates in the House bill, raising only those on agricultural goods. The rates were the highest in American history for farm products. The average Senate rates were 4.16 percent lower than the House rates. However, the average ad valorem rates of both the House and Senate versions of the Hawley-Smoot Tariff were higher than those of the Fordney-McCumber Tariff. The average rate in the House version was 8.54 percent higher than the 1922 tariff, while that in the Senate version was only 4.38 percent higher.[58]

An "export debenture" plan was added to the Senate version of the 1930 tariff. This plan was originally part of legislation creating the Federal Farm Board in 1929 but was deleted from the measure due to Hoover's hostility. The Senate now attached it to the Hawley-Smoot Tariff before sending it to the Conference Committee. The idea behind the export debenture plan came from Professor Charles L. Stewart of the University of Illinois, who found a way to help the farmer financially using the tariff. The plan called for a bounty on agricultural exports using debenture certificates. These certificates would be given to exporters of farm products as a sort of export bounty or subsidy. For example, if a farmer should ship 1,000 bushels of wheat, he would be entitled to receive from the government a certificate valued at one-half the duty that would be levied on a similar amount of wheat if it were imported from a foreign country. As the duty on wheat was 42 cents a bushel in 1929, one-half the import duty on 1,000 bushels would amount to $210. This debenture of $210 would be redeemable in payment of customs duties. The farmer would dispose of it by selling it to a customs broker or an importer who had large dealings with customs. In order to get the broker to accept it, the farmer had to sell it at a discount of approximately 5 percent, $10.50 less than its face value.[59]

THE HAWLEY-SMOOT TARIFF IN THE CONFERENCE COMMITTEE

On April 2 the Hawley-Smoot Tariff was sent to the ten-member Conference Committee to reconcile the House and Senate versions of the bill. The five senators chosen to the Conference Committee were Smoot, Republican James Watson of Indiana, Republican Samuel Shortridge of California, Simmons, and Democrat Pat Harrison of Mississippi. They were all members of the Senate Finance Committee. The House conferees, all members of the House Ways and Means Committee, were Hawley, Republican Isaac Bacharach of New Jersey, Republican Allen Treadway of Massachusetts, Garner, and Democrat James Collier of Mississippi. The rule in the Conference Committee was to keep the proceedings secret. However, Garner refused to abide by it, and he leaked information to his colleagues and the press.[60]

On April 17 the Conference Committee restored the duties on hides, leather, and shoes. Senator David Walsh and Congressman Treadway were spokesmen for the shoe and boot industry in Massachusetts. In their opinion, the tariffs on leather and shoes were needed to deter the large shipments of shoes from Czechoslovakia.[61] On the other hand, the farm bloc opposed the duties on shoes and leather, as mentioned earlier. However, in order to get duties on hides, they had to agree to duties on shoes and leather. Farmers in the western states had fought for duties on hides for more than seventeen years. In the tariffs of 1913 and 1922 hides were placed on the free list. The Hawley bill in the House imposed a 15 percent duty on hides that was raised by the Senate Finance Committee to 17.5 percent. The Senate restored hides to the free list, but the Conference Committee imposed a 10 percent duty to placate the farmers.[62]

On April 19 Garner complained that the Conference Committee appeared to be following the House version of tariff reform by restoring industrial rates. The farm bloc was working with Garner and others to keep agricultural rates high and industrial ones low. The farm bloc worried also about its export debenture plan. Hoover believed that the plan was unconstitutional and threatened to veto any tariff that contained it. The president also assailed the legislative flexible tariff provision that gave Congress and not the executive the right to change tariff rates. He urged the Conference Committee to restore that power to the executive.[63]

From April 20 to May 15 the tariff bill went from the Conference Committee to the House to the Senate and back to the Conference Committee with many important issues left unresolved. For example, both the export debenture plan and the legislative flexible tariff provisions threatened the entire tariff bill. Hoover, supported by party leaders, had the conference report sent first to the House, where the provisions were turned down. Hopefully, this would put pressure on the Senate to do the same.[64] But the Senate Democrats and progressive Republicans insisted upon the export debenture plan and the legislative tariff. Smoot, who worked so diligently on the tariff bill, was irritated at his fellow senators. He predicted a defeat for the tariff bill unless the Senate agreed to compromise on these issues.[65]

On May 23 the Conference Committee voted to reject the export debenture plan and keep the flexible provisions of the Fordney-McCumber Tariff with minor changes. For example, the Tariff Commission, after making an investigation with respect to a proposed change in the rates, could raise or lower rates by 50 percent and then present the change to the president. The president could accept or reject the recommendations of his Tariff Commission. Neither the Tariff Commission nor the president could transfer goods from the dutiable to the free list or vice versa. The basic change came in regard to the Tariff Commission personnel. The terms of the office of the existing commissioners were ended and the president was empowered to set up an entirely new body. He could reappoint the same commissioners, but the number of commissioners (six) remained the same, and no more than three could belong to the same party. Hoover had agreed to the compromise, ending a major impediment to passage of the Hawley-Smoot Tariff Act.[66]

The Conference Committee's report was passed by the Senate on June 13, 1930, by a vote of 44 to 42. Five Democrats voted with the Republicans in favor of the tariff, while 14 Republicans voted with the Democrats against it.[67] A geographical breakdown of the vote in the Senate showed that the vote in favor of the bill came from the industrial New England, middle Atlantic, and Great Lakes states while the vote against it came from the southern and middle western farm states. For example, 11 of the 12 New England senators voted for it. Only David Walsh of Massachusetts voted against it. All the middle Atlantic states' senators voted for it except 3. On the other hand, all but 5 of 26 senators from the South voted against it, and only 3 of 8 senators from the Middle West favored it.[68]

On the following day the House passed the report by a vote of 222 to 153, with 208 Republicans and 14 Democrats in favor while 133 Democrats and 20 Republicans opposed it.[69] On June 17 Hoover signed the Hawley-Smoot Tariff into law using six gold pens.[70]

According to tariff historian F. W. Taussig, the bill that went to Hoover for his signature was not at all in accord with his recommendations. Taussig criticized Hoover's leadership in the year and a half it took Congress to frame the bill. He had numerous opportunities to intervene to assure limited tariff revision, yet the only time the president threatened a veto was when the Senate attached the export debenture plan and tried to impose the legislative flexible tariff. The threatened veto was enough to make Congress back down. Perhaps Hoover did not want to challenge Congress on the tariff in 1930 because at that time the country was in the middle of the Great Depression. He believed that the tariff would help the country during the depression. When he signed the bill, he declared that "nothing would so retard business recovery as continued agitation over the tariff."[71]

THE MAJOR PROVISIONS OF THE HAWLEY-SMOOT TARIFF

The Hawley-Smoot Tariff Act of 1930 continued the high rates of the Fordney-McCumber Tariff Act of 1922. In many cases the rates were higher in 1930 than in 1922, especially in Schedule 7, the agricultural schedule. The rates on products from mines and quarries were increased from 50 to 100 percent from 1922 to 1930. In a few cases the rates were lower, a good example being the reduced rate on automobiles. Autos were reduced from 25 percent ad valorem in 1922 to 10 percent ad valorem in 1930.[72] The following table compares the rates of the 1922 and 1930 tariffs on some of the major products.[73]

Article	1922	1930
Raw sugar	2.21 cents per lb.	2.50 cents per lb.
Cuban sugar	1.76 cents per lb.	2.00 cents per lb.
Milk	2.50 cents per gal.	6.5 cents per gal.
Butter	8 cents per lb.	14 cents per lb.
Olive oil	7.5 cents per lb.	9.5 cents per lb.
Bricks	Free	$1.25 per M.
Hides	Free	10 percent
Sole leather	Free	12.5 percent
Shoes and boots	Free	20 percent

Another way of comparing the 1922 and 1930 tariff acts is to check the average rates by schedules. The following table shows average rates, by schedules, of the two tariff acts.[74]

Schedule	1922	1930
Chemicals, oils, and paints	29.22	31.40
Earths, earthenwares, and glassware	45.62	53.62
Metals	33.71	35.01
Wood	7.97	10.49
Sugar and molasses	67.85	77.21
Tobacco	63.09	64.78
Agricultural products	19.86	33.62
Spirits, wines, and other beverages	36.48	47.44
Manufactures of cotton	40.27	46.42
Flax, hemp, and jute	18.16	19.14
Manufactures of wool	49.54	59.83
Manufactures of silk	56.56	59.13
Manufactures of rayon	52.68	53.62
Paper and books	24.72	26.06
Sundries	21.97	27.39

The Hawley-Smoot Tariff Act raised American import duties to their highest levels in American history, with the rates on raw materials from 50 to 100 percent above those of the Fordney-McCumber Tariff Act.[75]

FOREIGN RETALIATION AGAINST THE HAWLEY-SMOOT TARIFF

During the year and a half in which the tariff was debated in the Congress and the two years following its passage in June 1930, the governments of foreign countries, their businesses, and their presses vented their anger toward U.S. tariff policy by direct protest to the U.S. government, articles criticizing the new tariff, and tariff retaliation. These foreign countries resented the United States, which had become a creditor nation after World War I. The debtor countries of the world needed both markets for revenue and a favorable trade balance. Therefore, if the United States would not listen to reason by maintaining a low tariff, world nations, mostly in Europe, would retaliate by negotiating reciprocal trade agreements and most-favored-nation clauses with each other, leaving the United States to fend for itself. Each time a foreign country retaliated against the United States, the supporters of low-tariff and free-trade policy felt vindicated.[76]

In 1929 French Foreign Minister Aristide Briand of France proposed the idea of an economic European Federation, aimed at the United States. He declared that Europe could be as prosperous as the United States by developing its own market, and he called for a United States of Europe. The idea of a European market was discussed at the economic conferences in Geneva in the late 1920s and early 1930s but failed to gain enough support. It would take another war before the European Common Market would be born.[77]

When the tariff hearings began in the United States in January 1929, the French government, fearful of economic domination by the United States, called attention to the one-sided application of the Franco-American tariff compromise of 1927, under which the United States, had received most-favored-nation treatment (a nation treats a second nation as favorably as it treats any third nation) for 471 chief items of import shipped to France each year. In return, the United States was to make changes in the handling of French pharmaceutical and agricultural imports and lower the high tariff on French silk imports. The United States denied that these promises had ever been made.[78]

In June 1929 both the French Chamber of Commerce and former Premier and Finance Minister Francois Marsal criticized the United States' high-tariff policy. Marsal said, "These increases in the tariff are in no way justified by necessity arising from an adverse commercial balance. We, therefore, are led to believe that the United States wishes to become a closed state."[79]

As a result of the Hawley-Smoot Tariff that contributed to an unfavorable balance of trade, in 1931 the French government resorted to a quota system specifically aimed at the United States. Quotas, limitations on the number of goods imported into a country, were placed on coal, flax, wines, woods, meats, eggs, and poultry.[80]

On May 10, 1929, the Argentine government assailed the Hawley bill in Congress as endangering trade between the United States and Argentina. On the following day the League of Nations Consultative Committee expressed concern about the American tariff, fearing that it would lead to a new round of tariff increases worldwide. On May 15 K. Uchiyama, acting consul general of Japan, declared that Japan ranked fourth among nations that bought American products, and he hoped that the new tariff would not interfere with Japanese silk imports to the United States or U.S. cotton exports to Japan.[81]

In early July thirty-eight nations sent protests to the Senate Finance Committee, urging that the bill be defeated. Some of these countries were Great Britain, France, Belgium, Italy, Austria, Spain, Denmark, Switzerland, Norway, Sweden, Australia, and all the Latin American countries. Briefly, Australia complained about wool duties, Denmark feared the duties on hides and skins, and Belgium assailed the duties on glass. Senator Harrison claimed that foreign resentment to this tariff was very great. He asserted that foreign countries felt that the United States had initiated an imperialistic policy in trade and commerce much like general imperialism in 1900. Harrison warned his colleagues that foreign nations would retaliate by developing cartels to divide the markets among themselves, impose high tariffs against the United States, or make commercial treaties with each other while boycotting American goods.[82]

Smoot criticized Harrison for his speech warning of retaliation against the tariff bill. The Senate Finance Committee chairman had minimized the protests filed with his committee. He declared that the complaints were of interested parties and not so much of foreign governments. According to Smoot, Harrison was trying to make it seem that foreign governments were protesting a policy. Harrison replied that Smoot was resorting to "sham and pretense" in an effort to belittle the importance of the exchanges, practically all of which were diplomatic documents filed with the State Department by accredited representatives of the governments concerned.[83]

On September 1, 1929, Dr. Nicholas Murray Butler, the president of Columbia University and the Carnegie Endowment for International Peace, in an address at the Parrish Art Museum, proclaimed that the new American tariff was a menace to peace. According to Butler, economics had replaced politics as the center of gravity in the world arena. The controlling motive of life and thought in the world was no longer liberty but wealth. He denounced tariff legislation as nationally minded while U.S. economic interests were becoming more and more international. Therefore, Americans should no longer listen to the selfish pleas of paid lobbyists in tariff making.[84]

The Swiss watch and clock industry exported between 90 and 95 percent of its product. The United States absorbed about 18.5 percent of all Swiss watch exports in 1929. The Hawley bill passed in the House increased the duties on both watches and clocks, and the Swiss government protested vehemently. The Senate restored the rates to their 1922 levels only to have the Conference Committee impose the higher House duty once again. The Swiss press called for a boycott of American products as protest meetings were held throughout the country. Nonetheless, the higher duty on Swiss watches and clocks in the 1930 tariff caused a 48 percent decline from their 1929 import levels. This hurt the Swiss economy, as income dropped from 56,807,000 francs in 1929 to 29,579,000 francs in 1930.[85]

The Italian government condemned the high agricultural rates of the Hawley-

Smoot Tariff. The Italian press began a campaign to keep American cars from entering Italy. In December 1929 Italian government, supported by the people and led by the press, sharply increased duties on imported automobile parts from the United States. On June 30, 1930, only sixteen days after the passage of the Hawley-Smoot Tariff, the Italian government increased duties on all U.S. auto imports. In 1930 Benito Mussolini, the Italian dictator, claimed that Italy would make purchases only in countries that bought Italian agricultural products.[86]

Spain and the United States had signed a treaty in August 1908 giving each other most-favored-nation treatment.[87] When, after World War I, prohibition in the United States cut off all Spanish wine exports to America and caused an alarming deficit in the Spanish trade balance with the United States, the Spanish government still maintained its commercial treaty and friendly relations with the United States. However, with the passage of the Hawley-Smoot Tariff, relations with Spain quickly deteriorated. The Spanish government declared that its commercial treaty with the United States would end once the American tariff went into effect. Once again, as in Switzerland and Italy, the Spanish press led the attack against the American tariff, calling it a declaration of war against Spain.[88]

Spanish retaliation against the United States came in the form of the Wais Tariff, passed on July 22, 1930. This Spanish tariff reduced imports from the United States by raising duties on almost all American goods, including automobiles, tires, tubes, and motion- picture films. Duties on sewing and embroidering machines doubled, and safety-razor duties increased 700 percent.[89] Though the Wais Tariff affected other European countries, especially France and Italy, Spain was willing to negotiate special commercial treaties with these countries to negate the effects of its tariff. The Wais Tariff was passed as a response to the Hawley-Smoot Tariff, and the effect was to enter the trade war against the United States.[90]

In May 1929 the *Economist*, a British publication and an ardent supporter of free trade, condemned the high-tariff policy of the United States. It contended that if the world followed the same policy on trade as the U.S. government, trade would not exist. It claimed that the United States was setting the wrong example for the world.[91] One month later, the *London Times* declared that the new American tariff was a menace to British industries. The British paper blamed the American people, who failed to understand that higher duties would hurt them financially.[92]

Of all the countries in Western Europe, Great Britain and its dominions were the last bulwark of free trade. Prior to 1931 Great Britain had only limited protection. Stanley Baldwin, a British statesman in May 1930, believed that tariffs were bad for business, and he supported free trade. However, just before the signing of the Hawley-Smoot Tariff, Baldwin declared that Britain would not become the dumping ground of Europe. Already, leading industrialists were calling for an imperial British conference to consider the wisdom of retaliatory measures. On February 4, 1932, Great Britain passed the Import Duties Act, which provided British industry with the first measure of general protection in nearly a century.[93] In July 1932 Great Britain and its dominions, India, and the colonies met in Ottawa, Canada, to sign the Ottawa Agreements. These accords consolidated empire unity and prosperity by allowing free trade between Great Britain and its dominions, but imposed high duties on all imports from the United States. In 1930, 70.5 percent of all U.S. exports entered Great Britain duty free. By 1932, as a result of British retaliation to the Hawley-Smoot Tariff, only 20.5 percent of these same goods entered British ports duty free.[94]

Canada, the United States' neighbor and most important trading partner, was outraged by the Hawley-Smoot Tariff. Canada purchased U.S. products in 1929 to the value of almost $950 million, while the United States purchased Canadian products the same year valued at $504 million. The United States sold to Canada mostly manufactured products such as iron, steel, autos, auto parts, industrial machinery, and agricultural machinery, while the United States bought many raw products from Canada, including newsprint, lumber, wood pulp, copper, nickel, cattle, furs, and dairy products.[95]

The Hawley-Smoot Tariff antagonized every element of the Canadian population. The tariff on halibut was doubled, offending the eastern provinces; tariff duties on potatoes, milk, cream, and butter were radically increased, angering the populations of Quebec and Ontario; the prairie and western provinces were provoked by increasing duties on cattle and fresh meats; British Columbia and Alberta criticized the high duties on apples, logs, and lumber.[96] Only three months after Hoover signed the Hawley-Smoot Tariff in June 1930, the Canadian government passed the Canadian Emergency Tariff, which imposed high duties on American imports such as textiles, agricultural implements, electrical apparatus, meats, gasoline, shoes, jewelry, and fertilizers.[97]

Senator Alben Barkley, Democrat of Kentucky, described the folly of tariffs and how they affected world trade in a speech at the annual dinner at the National Council of American Importers and Traders. He declared that foreign trade must flow both ways. It was impossible to build tariff walls without foreign reaction.[98]

THE HAWLEY-SMOOT TARIFF AND THE AMERICAN ECONOMY

The Hawley-Smoot Tariff Act was passed after the Great Depression had begun. Though it was not a cause of the depression, it contributed to the economic misery that existed throughout the nation. On May 9, 1929, Senator David Walsh of Massachusetts warned his colleagues that the new tariff would raise the living costs of the American people. In August Henry Wallace, editor of *Wallace's Farmer*, declared that the new tariff bill would do more harm than good for agriculture.[99]

On September 3, about a month before the Wall Street stock-market crash, Senator Caraway ridiculed both Hawley and Smoot on the economic effects of the new tariff bill. Hawley claimed that the new tariff would help the economy by encouraging both industrial and agricultural growth. The Oregon congressman believed that labor would greatly benefit from the tariff; it would provide employment to 27 million wage earners. Smoot assured the American people that the tariff would not raise the cost of living. Caraway, on the other hand, saw the tariff as inflationary. He claimed that the main purpose of a protective tariff was to provide a barrier against the importation of foreign goods. This allowed American manufacturers to raise the prices of their goods above world market prices. Cost increases generally followed inflation, causing a contraction and not an expansion in economic growth.[100]

Congresswoman Mary Norton of New Jersey called Senator Smoot naive for declaring that the tariff would not raise the price of women's clothing. She asked who would pay the 20 percent tariff on shoes. Norton claimed that Smoot must consider the women of the country "devoid of Intelligence."[101]

After the stock-market crash in October 1929, the economy became progressively worse. Overspeculation in the market, caused by a low discount rate, contributed directly to the crash. On February 14, 1929, the New York Federal Reserve proposed that the discount rate, the interest rate charged by the Federal Reserve to banks that borrow from it, be raised from 5 to 6 percent to check speculation in the market. However, the Federal Reserve Board in Washington refused to raise the rate. Hoover agreed with this decision, and by the time the rate went up in the summer, it was too late to halt the rampant speculation in the market. By the fall of 1929 the economy was entering the depression. In June 1929 indexes of industrial and factory production reached their peak and began to turn down. By October the Federal Reserve Index of Industrial Production stood at 117, compared to 126 four months earlier.[102]

Some bankers and businessmen blamed the stock-market crash on the delay by Congress in passing the Hawley-Smoot Tariff. F. I. Kent, director of the Bankers Trust Company, declared that the opposition in Congress to the tariff caused a panic among business, and this led to the crash. Senator Borah ridiculed Kent's statement, claiming that it was an "insult to the intelligence of mankind."[103]

In February 1930 Republican Congressman Frank Murphy of Ohio blamed the rising unemployment in the country on the delay in passing the tariff. When Democratic Congressman William Connery of Massachusetts complained about the unemployment and hungry people in his district, Murphy told him that he should rally the people of his state to support the tariff that would protect them from hunger and joblessness.[104]

The opponents of the tariff bill became more vocal as it neared passage in Congress. On March 29 Dr. Henry R. Seager, professor of economics at Columbia University, stated that the Hawley-Smoot Tariff would destroy America's export industry and hurt both farming and manufacturing.[105] On May 17 a petition consisting of 1,028 signatures from teachers and professors in economics from 179 colleges and universities was sent to the Congress and President Hoover protesting the Hawley-Smoot Tariff bill. The signers urged Congress to vote against the bill, and if Congress would not listen to reason, they wanted Hoover to veto it. The petition warned that the new tariff would raise prices and the cost of living, limit exports of both farm and manufactured products, negatively affect American investment abroad, and promote tariff and trade wars. Senator Shortridge replied to the petition by declaring that he was "not overawed or at all disturbed by the proclamation of the college professors who never earned a dollar by the sweat of their brow by honest labor."[106]

The Hawley-Smoot Tariff did more damage to the economy than good. It dealt a crushing blow to world industry by preventing other countries from earning dollars and destroyed the last possibility that the United States would ever collect the money it had lent the allies during World War I. In fact, Hoover declared a one-year moratorium on all intergovernmental debts in June 1931.[107] The world needed international cooperation in ending the worldwide depression, but instead the Hawley-Smoot Tariff led to trade wars. The farmer, laborer, manufacturer, and consumer all suffered during the Great Depression. The tariff did raise prices in the country, which proved disastrous during the depression. Retaliation reduced the exports of farmers and manufacturers, while high prices reduced domestic consumer demand. Prices should have fallen with demand, but in many non-competitive industries, auto, steel, and household appliances, they remained high for too long, resulting in massive unemployment. In 1933 the unemployment rate in the United States was about 25 percent, and the gross national product, the total market value of all goods and services produced in the United States, was one-third less than in 1929. The GNP did not reach its 1929 level again until 1937.[108]

The stock market is considered today by economists as one of the leading economic indicators. That means, for example, that over a period of time, if it continues to fall, the economy could be headed for trouble. It was prophetic that on June 16, 1930, the day Hoover announced that he would sign the Hawley-Smoot Tariff Act, a wave of selling swept through the stock market as prices of stocks sank to their lowest levels in years. Declines in the New York Stock Exchange ranged from three to twenty-two points in active issues. The tariff also affected the commodities market, as both cotton and grain prices fell to their lowest levels in three years. Perhaps the Wall Street investors were trying to tell people that the tariff could only make the Great Depression worse.[109]

NOTES

1. Abraham Berglund, "The Tariff Act of 1930," *American Economic Review* 20 (September 1930): 467-469.

2. *New York Times*, January 6, 1929, p. 27; January 11, 1929, p. 1.

3. Ibid., February 10, 1929, p. 3; March 8, 1929, p. 1.

4. F. W. Taussig, *The Tariff History of the United States*, 8th ed. (New York: G. P. Putnam's Sons, 1931), pp. 491-492.

5. Ibid., p. 493.

6. *New York Times*, March 17, 1929, p. 14; April 3, 1929, p. 11; John D. Hicks, *Republican Ascendancy, 1921-1933* (New York: Harper and Row, 1960), pp. 164-165.

7. *New York Times*, May 19, 1929, p. 9.

8. Ibid., April 8, 1929, p. 16.

9. Ibid., May 5, 1929, p. 9; May 7, 1929, p. 3.

10. Ibid., May 8, 1929, pp. 1, 3; Taussig, *Tariff History of the United States*, p. 494.

11. *New York Times*, May 8, 1929, p. 30.

12. Ibid., May 9, 1929, p. 1.

13. Ibid., May 8, 1929, p. 1; May 10, 1929, p. 1; May 12, 1929, p. 1.

14. Ibid., May 12, 1929, p. 2.

15. Ibid., May 11, 1929, p. 2.

16. Ibid., May 20, 1929, p. 12.

17. Ibid., May 10, 1929, p. 2; May 12, 1929, p. 2.

18. Ibid., May 9, 1929, p. 1.

19. Ibid.

20. Ibid., May 15, 1929, p. 1.

21. Ibid., May 11, 1929, p. 2.

22. Ibid., May 13, 1929, p. 1.

23. Ibid., May 25, 1929, p. 1.

24. Ibid., May 29, 1929, p. 1.

25. Ibid., p. 24.

26. Ibid.; Berglund, "Tariff Act of 1930," p. 472.

27. *New York Times*, May 29, 1929, p. 24.

28. Ibid.

29. Taussig, *Tariff History of the United States*, pp. 494-495; Barry Eichengreen, "The Political Economy of the Smoot-Hawley Tariff," *Research in Economic History* 12 (1989): 3.

30. *New York Times*, June 4, 1929, p. 1.

31. Ibid.

32. Taussig, *Tariff History of the United States*, p. 496.

33. *New York Times*, June 15, 1929, p. 2.

34. Ibid.

35. Ibid., June 23, 1929, p. 2; June 24, 1929, p. 10.

36. Ibid., July 8, 1929, p. 1.

37. Ibid., July 10, 1929, p. 19.

38. Ibid., July 16, 1929, p. 14.

39. Ibid., July 26, 1929, p. 2.

40. Ibid., July 31, 1929, p. 19.

41. Ibid., August 17, 1929, p. 1.

42. Ibid., July 31, 1929, p. 19.

43. Ibid., August 21, 1929, p. 1.

44. Ibid., August 22, 1929, p. 1.

45. Ibid., August 23, 1929, p. 5; September 3, 1929, p. 1; September 5, 1929, pp. 1, 14; Taussig, *Tariff History of the United States*, p. 496.

46. *New York Times*, September 6, 1929, p. 8; September 25, 1929, p. 1; September 30, 1929, p. 1.

47. Ibid., October 3, 1929, p. 2.

48. Ibid., October 30, 1929, p. 2.

49. Ibid., October 5, 1929, p. 1.

50. Ibid., October 14, 1929, p. 1; October 15, 1929, pp. 1, 20; October 17, 1929, p. 15.

51. Ibid., November 21, 1929, p. 1.

52. Ibid., November 25, 1929, p. 12.

53. Ibid., December 28, 1929, p. 7; February 2, 1930, p. 1.

54. Ibid., February 10, 1930, p. 1.

55. Ibid., March 25, 1930, p. 1.

56. Ibid., p. 2; *New York Times*, March 4, 1930, p. 21.

57. *New York Times*, March 23, 1930, p. 1.

58. Ibid., March 30, 1930, p. 19.

59. Ibid., May 16, 1929, p. 22; Hicks, *Republican Ascendancy*, pp. 217-218.

60. *New York Times*, April 3, 1930, p. 3; April 5, 1930, p. 1.

61. Ibid., April 18, 1930, p. 24.

62. Taussig, *Tariff History of the United States*, p. 508.

63. *New York Times*, April 20, 1930, pp. 1, 24.

64. Ibid., April 25, 1930, p. 1.

65. Ibid., May 15, 1930, p. 5.

66. Ibid., May 24, 1930, p. 1; Berglund, "Tariff Act of 1930," p. 475; Taussig, *Tariff History of the United States*, p. 526.

67. *New York Times*, June 14, 1930, p. 1.

68. Ibid., p. 2; Hicks, *Republican Ascendancy*, p. 221; *Congressional Record*, June 13, 1930 (71st Congress), p. 10635.

69. *Congressional Record*, June 13, 1930 (71st Congress), p. 10635; *New York Times*, June 15, 1930, p. 1.

70. *New York Times*, June 18, 1930, p. 1; Arthur Schlesinger, Jr., *The Crisis of the Old Order, 1919-1933* (Boston: Houghton Mifflin Company, 1957), p. 164; Hicks, *Republican Ascendancy*, p. 221.

71. Schlesinger, *Crisis of the Old Order*, p. 164; Taussig, *Tariff History of the United States*, pp. 499-500.

72. Berglund, "Tariff Act of 1930," pp. 470-471.

73. Ibid., p. 472.

74. Taussig, *Tariff History of the United States*, pp. 518-519; *Congressional Record*, June 11, 1930 (71st Congress), pp. 10465-10466.

75. Hicks, *Republican Ascendancy*, p. 221.

76. Joseph M. Jones, *Tariff Retaliation: Repercussions of the Hawley-Smoot Bill* (Philadelphia: University of Pennsylvania Press, 1934), pp. 5, 258-259.

77. Ibid., pp. 261, 274.

78. *New York Times*, January 10, 1929, p. 6.

79. Ibid., June 14, 1929, p. 2.

80. Jones, *Tariff Retaliation*, pp. 140-141, 168-172.

81. *New York Times*, May 11, 1929, p. 2; May 12, 1929, p. 3; May 16, 1929, p. 22.

82. Ibid., July 10, 1929, p. 1.

83. Ibid., July 11, 1929, p. 1.

84. Ibid., September 2, 1929, p. 1; Berglund, "Tariff Act of 1930," p. 467.

85. Jones, *Tariff Retaliation*, pp. 106-131.

86. Ibid., pp. 75-83.

87. Ibid., p. 34.

88. Ibid., p. 50.

89. Ibid., p. 54.

90. Ibid.

91. *New York Times*, May 19, 1929, p. 3.

92. *London Times*, June 29, 1929, p. 13.

93. Jones, *Tariff Retaliation*, p. 223.

94. Ibid., pp. 237-238.

95. Ibid., pp. 176-177.

96. Ibid., pp. 177-178.

97. Ibid., pp. 193-195.

98. *New York Times*, April 9, 1930, p. 8.

99. Ibid., May 10, 1929, p. 2; August 16, 1929, p. 8.

100. Ibid., September 4, 1929, p. 22.

101. Ibid., September 5, 1929, p. 1.

102. John Kenneth Galbraith, *The Great Crash, 1929* (Boston: Houghton Mifflin Company, 1979), pp. 31, 88.

103. *New York Times*, November 12, 1929, p. 3; November 13, 1929, p. 2.

104. Ibid., February 19, 1930, p. 17.

105. Ibid., March 30, 1930, p. 22.

106. Ibid., May 18, 1930, p. 4; Berglund, "Tariff Act of 1930," p. 478.

107. John A. Garraty, *The Great Depression* (New York: Harcourt Brace Jovanovich, 1986), p. 15; Hicks, *Republican Ascendancy*, p. 245.

108. Galbraith, *Great Crash*, p. 168.

109. *New York Times*, June 17, 1930, p. 1.

3

The Building
of a Liberal Trade Policy

BACKGROUND TO THE RECIPROCAL TRADE AGREEMENTS

The Great Depression brought an end to the Republican domination of the presidency in 1932 with the election of Franklin D. Roosevelt. Throughout the 1920s the Republican administrations of Warren Harding, Calvin Coolidge, and Herbert Hoover believed in low taxes and high tariffs. Now with a Democratic president and Congress, changes in trade policy were expected as part of the Roosevelt "New Deal" program.

Cordell Hull, Tennessee congressman and member of the House Ways and Means Committee, was chosen by the new president to become secretary of state in 1933. Hull would lead the fight against high tariffs in the 1930s until his resignation in 1944. More than anyone else, Hull became the chief architect of America's new liberal trade policy.[1]

Cordell Hull made his first political speech in favor of low tariffs when he supported Grover Cleveland for the presidency in 1888. Not yet seventeen in 1888, he continued to oppose high tariffs in the next century. In 1916, during the Woodrow Wilson administration, Hull viewed the tariff from an internationalist rather than a nationalist perspective. Before 1916 he saw the high tariff as only affecting the domestic economy by raising the cost of living and causing the growth of monopolies. After 1916 Hull saw low tariffs and the movement toward free trade as a means of preventing wars. He declared that if the world could have free trade, free of discrimination and obstruction, so that one country would not be jealous of others, and the living standards of all countries could rise, it could eliminate the economic dissatisfaction that breeds war, and it might have a chance for a lasting peace.[2]

The Democratic National Convention in 1932 adopted Hull's version of low tariffs in its platform. Al Smith, the Democratic presidential candidate in 1928, and John J. Raskob, his friend and campaign manager that year, remained economic nationalists in favor of high tariffs. They attempted, unsuccessfully, to derail Hull's efforts in the 1932 Convention in Chicago by lining up delegates to vote against the low-tariff platform.[3]

Hull realized that the United States had changed to a major exporting country in the late 1920s and could no longer ignore the importance of international trade. For example, by 1929 the United States exported more than half of its cotton, one-third of its copper and tobacco, one-fifth of its wheat and flour, and one-fourth of its agricultural machinery. By 1932 Hull was able to convince others, including Roosevelt, that the country was no longer a self-contained unit, and that foreign markets were crucial to America's economic growth and prosperity.[4]

Secretary of State Hull believed that the United States should take the lead in the international arena to stop the tariff and trade wars. He wanted Congress to empower the president to negotiate commercial treaties with important trading nations of the world in order to lower existing tariff rates by as much as 50 percent in return for equivalent concessions for American exports in foreign markets. Hull had favored multilateral rather than bilateral pacts (agreements between many nations at one time rather than between two nations); however, as we shall see later, he settled for bilateral trade agreements that were easier to complete and then extended them to other countries through the unconditional most-favored-nation policy—a program that would generalize to all most favored nations the concessions made by treaty to any one of them. [5]

On May 31, 1933, Hull led a large American delegation to the London Economic Conference. When he sailed from New York, he firmly believed that Roosevelt had agreed both to stabilization of the currency at its current level in gold and, most important, to a program of tariff reduction. In fact, the secretary of state had in his pocket a copy of a Reciprocal Trade Agreements Act (RTA) that would allow the president to lower tariffs as previously explained. Hull had hoped that the president would push the bill through the special session of Congress while he sold it to the delegates in London.[6] However, while en route, Hull learned that Roosevelt had other matters on his mind and refused to submit the RTA bill, as the special session of Congress was about to recess. The disappointed Hull quickly cabled Roosevelt from the ship declaring that his hopes for tariff reductions in London depended on the immediate passage of this bill. He explained to Roosevelt that the passage of the RTA Act would be "the most outstanding achievement of your Administration."[7]

When the conference opened on June 12, with delegates from sixty-six countries, in attendance, Hull's hope of lower tariffs and currency stabilization was shattered. The president failed to support the RTA Act in 1933 and refused to agree to currency stabilization, taking the United States off the gold standard. Hull, the internationalist, could accomplish little at the London conference. He hoped for world cooperation in trade and money matters, but his president, by becoming, temporarily, an economic nationalist, had undermined his own secretary of state. Hull was reported to be on the verge of resigning his position, but he soon realized that Roosevelt was under the influence of Raymond Moley, an ardent economic nationalist. The secretary of state had already blamed Moley for making a radio speech on May 20, 1933, proclaiming that foreign trade was of little importance to the United States. After Moley's speech was broadcast nationally, Hull worried that foreign countries would not believe that the United States was interested in tariff reduction.[8]

THE RECIPROCAL TRADE AGREEMENTS

Throughout 1933 Cordell Hull, the "Galahad of internationalism," labored in the nationalist administration. However, by 1934 the secretary of state had secured the backing of Henry Wallace, the secretary of agriculture. Wallace was the author of the influential pamphlet entitled "America Must Choose" that charted a middle course between total self-sufficiency and internationalism. He convinced Roosevelt that a RTA Act would help the farmer. Henry Stimson, a Republican internationalist, former secretary of state in the Hoover administration, and a good friend of Roosevelt, also supported the RTA and lower tariffs.[9]

On March 2, 1934, Roosevelt asked Congress to pass the RTA Act. The RTA Act would be an amendment to the Hawley-Smoot Tariff Act of 1930. Under the provisions of the RTA the president was given authority to negotiate bilateral concessions raising or lowering existing tariff rates up to 50 percent, providing reciprocal arrangements were made by the other party for American products. Each agreement contained an unconditional most-favored-nation clause so that all concessions made by either party to third countries would freely and automatically apply to the trade of the other party. Thus the United States would always receive most-favored-nation treatment of its exports from every agreement country. The United States would grant the concessions it gave to all countries, whether parties to the agreement or not. The RTA Act was to run for three years, at which time it would be subject to renewal by Congress.[10]

Under the RTA Act the president did not have to submit any of the agreements made to Congress for approval. This eliminated the congressional practice of logrolling where Congressmen agree in advance to support each other's bills. This technique pertains especially to the trading of votes among legislators in order to gain support for appropriations beneficial to each legislator's home district. The RTA Act would significantly reduce the power of Congress in the tariff-making process.[11]

Another provision of the RTA Act prevented the president from transferring to the free list any imports now paying duty or taking any imports on the free list and making them pay duty. He could not cancel the war debts owed the United States, and he had to give public notice before negotiations. Before concluding an agreement, the president had to seek information and advice from the Tariff Commission and the Departments of State, Agriculture, and Commerce.[12]

Senators Arthur Vandenberg, Republican of Michigan, L. J. Dickinson, Republican of Iowa, and Borah led the fight against the RTA bill. Borah and Vandenberg both claimed that the bill was clearly unconstitutional because it delegated power that belonged to Congress to the president. Vandenberg pointed out that the power to tax belongs to Congress and not the president. He denounced the bill as being "Fascist in its philosophy," while Dickinson claimed that the bill would make the president a "domestic trade dictator."[13]

On March 8 both Hull and Wallace appeared before the House Ways and Means Committee to urge speedy passage of the RTA Act. Hull told the members of the committee that the chief executives of other countries already had the power to raise and lower tariff rates and that Roosevelt needed that same power in order to make tariff agreements. Hull said that the primary purpose of the bill was to restore U.S. foreign trade. He pointed out that in 1929 U.S. trade had amounted to $24 billion, but by 1933 it had declined to a paltry $3.5 billion. He claimed that there was an inconsistency in being a large exporter and maintaining the status of a creditor nation while at the same time erecting high tariff barriers against imports.[14] Wallace assured the committee that the RTA bill would not create any more unemployment. He stated that "It is important for Congress to realize that high tariffs cause unemployment just as surely as low tariffs—it is just a question of where the unemployment will be."[15]

Roosevelt threw his full support behind the RTA bill in the House. During the debate in the House in March, the president sent a message to Congress extolling the virtues of the RTA bill. He declared that it would create employment, increase wages, and raise the standard of living in the United States. He claimed that "a full and permanent domestic recovery depends in part upon a revived and strengthened international trade and American exports cannot be permanently increased without a corresponding increase in imports."[16] Roosevelt attempted to assure protectionists in Congress that the RTA bill's goal was the expansion of foreign commerce and that reasonable protection would not be abandoned.[17]

Congressman Robert Doughton of North Carolina, chairman of the House Ways and Means Committee, guided the bill through the House. On March 20, 1934, the House passed the RTA bill by a vote of 274 to 111, with only 11 Democrats voting against it.[18] The bill went to the Senate Finance Committee, where Chairman Harrison speeded discussion, and on June 4 the Senate voted 57 to 33 in favor of the measure, with only 5 Democrats opposing it.[19] On June 12 Hull watched the president sign the RTA bill in the White House. He stated, "Each stroke of the pen seemed to write a message of gladness on my heart. My fight of many long years for the reciprocal trade policy and the lowering of trade barriers was won."[20]

On June 27 Roosevelt formed the Interdepartmental Committee for Reciprocity Information to hear the opinions of interested persons concerning any trade agreement. One day later the Committee on Trade Agreements was created, under Hull's supervision, to administer the act. It was a nonpartisan body composed of representatives from the Departments of State, the Treasury, Agriculture, and Commerce and the Tariff Commission. Hull chose Assistant Secretary of State Francis B. Sayre, the son-in-law of former President Woodrow Wilson, to head the new committee. Sayre was in charge of economic and commercial policy in the State Department.[21]

The Committee on Trade Agreements took the responsibility of surveying the field to find countries who wanted to negotiate tariff reductions. Usually the country's ambassador in the United States or the American ambassador abroad was approached by the committee. If the country agreed to negotiate, Hull would approach the president for his approval to initiate negotiations.[22]

The Committee for Reciprocity Information allowed U.S. manufacturers of imported goods to give their views on how the RTA Act would affect them at a public hearing. Usually, interested American producers presented their briefs and made statements that were then passed on to the Committee on Trade Agreements. According to Hull, each complaint was given serious consideration before the RTA was put into operation. Among the loudest protesters were the very small industries that employed two hundred to three hundred people and that could supply only a small fraction of the country's needs. However, a few large industries also complained. For example, the American iron and steel industry protested the importation of iron and steel from Sweden and Belgium, even though the quantity of imports amounted to less than 1 percent of the exports of such goods. Hull claimed that most of the protesters did not need protection, but insisted on higher tariffs in order to take advantage of the American consumer, who had to pay higher prices.[23]

The passage of the RTA Act did not immediately settle the question of New Deal trade philosophy. There were two possible approaches within the framework of the bill. Hull's bilateral approach, with a system of unconditional most-favored-nation treaties, has already been discussed. George Peek's conditional most-favored-nation bilateral philosophy represented the other approach.[24]

In December 1933 Peek was appointed by Roosevelt as special assistant on trade policy, and in March 1934 he became foreign trade adviser. Hull believed that the president had supported him on trade matters and was shocked by Peek's appointment as foreign trade adviser. The secretary of state declared, "If Mr. Roosevelt had hit me between the eyes with a sledge hammer he could not have stunned me more than by this appointment."[25]

Hull, Peek, and Sayre worked together to push the RTA Act through Congress. Hull praised Peek's cooperation and said that he worked well with people, but the secretary of state found his economic ideas unsound.[26] Peek, on the other hand, saw Hull as a visionary for wanting a freely trading world. Peek believed that tariffs, exchange controls, and quotas were an integral part of American trade policy. Peek condemned Hull's unconditional most-favored-nation clause philosophy, where reductions in trade applied to all countries that did not discriminate against the United States, even if they did not make an agreement with the American government. Peek referred to Hull's program as "unilateral economic dis-armament." Peek favored bilateral pacts, but with a conditional principle by which concessions would be extended only to nations that themselves granted concessions equivalent to those made by the first nation. For Peek, the problem was finding ways of making mutually advantageous exchanges between countries through government-managed trading.[27]

Peek and Hull continued to argue their trade policies into 1935. While Moley supported Peek, Wallace, Henry Grady, later to manage the Committee on Trade Agreements, and other New Dealers supported Hull. In 1935 the president resolved the issue of policy when he backed Hull. Peek, with Roosevelt's approval, had negotiated a deal with Germany to dispose of American surplus cotton. Hull had claimed that the deal was incompatible with the RTA program. Roosevelt, who was known for supporting different positions and changing his mind frequently, now supported Hull. Peek offered Roosevelt his resignation in July 1935, but the president refused it. However, Peek continued his assault on Hull's RTA program. On Armistice Day (now Veterans Day), November 11, 1935, Peek spoke to the War Industries Board Association in New York, claiming that the administration must choose between a trade policy of Americanism or Hull's internationalism. Roosevelt criticized the speech, and when Peek, once again, offered his resignation, the president accepted it gladly.[28]

Along with the new RTA Act in 1934, Congress established the new Export-Import Bank to stimulate trade. This independent agency of the U.S. government finances exports of U.S. goods and services and offers direct credit to foreign borrowers. It also guarantees loans made by commercial lenders.[29]

With Hull in charge of the RTA program, trade agreements were quickly made with foreign countries. The United States signed its first agreement with Cuba on August 24, 1934, only two and one-half months after Roosevelt signed the RTA Act into law. The agreement lowered the tariff on Cuban sugar from 2 cents per pound to 0.9 cents per pound. The supporters of the agreement estimated that Cuban-American trade would double in only one year. Hull hoped that Cuba's exports to the United States would rise from $50 million in 1933 to over $100 million between 1934 and 1935. On the other side, Cuba reduced the tariffs on textiles, rayon-yarns fabrics, wool articles, and automobiles. The agreement with Cuba was expected to help the American farmer, who would now benefit from lower Cuban duties on corn, wheat, flour, and pork products.[30]

Within three weeks after signing the agreement with Cuba, the United States announced its intention to negotiate agreements with Brazil, Belgium, Haiti, Sweden, Colombia, Honduras, Spain, Guatemala, and Nicaragua. American exports to these countries increased 14 percent, in contrast to the 4 percent rate of increase with nations outside the agreement.[31]

The Brazilian and Belgian agreements were made in February 1935. Brazilian coffee was admitted into the United States free, and American tariffs on manganese ore, Brazil nuts, and castor beans were reduced substantially. On the other hand, Brazil reduced duties of U.S. products over a broad range from 20 to 67 percent of the present rates.[32] The Belgian agreement was the first with a European country. The Belgian government reduced tariffs on American products from 13 to 80 percent. Belgian imports to the United States showed a reduction in duties for 47 products from 16 to 50 percent.[33]

By the end of 1936 France, Switzerland, Finland, and Costa Rica had all signed agreements with the United States to reduce their tariffs. In 1937, with sixteen agreements in effect, exports to these countries were 60 percent greater than in 1935, compared to an increase of 39 percent in exports to all other countries. There was no question that the RTA Act of 1934 had stimulated American trade. From 1934 to 1937 exports had risen by $1 billion, while imports had climbed by less than $700 million. However, the RTA Act would expire on June 12, 1937, and its renewal was not automatic.[34]

On February 2, 1937, Chairman Doughton and the majority of the House Ways and Means Committee urged extension of the RTA Act based on the increase in American exports in 1936. Roosevelt told Hull that he wanted no term limit on this version of the RTA. He did not want to submit it to the Congress every three years for renewal. Hull told the president that he did not believe that it would pass that way. Nonetheless, the president sent it to the House Ways and Means Committee without a term limit, only to have it added later.[35]

Hull testified before the committee and warned it that any abandonment of the RTA would result in economic warfare. He told the members of the committee that a return to trade wars could lead to general warfare. When Hull made the statement that economic warfare could lead to general warfare, war clouds were already hovering over Europe and the Far East as Germany, Italy, and Japan were rattling their sabers.[36]

On February 9 the House of Representatives passed the RTA extension by a vote of 284 to 100.[37] One day later Hull again used the threat of warfare when he sent the Senate Finance Committee a letter urging quick passage of the RTA. Unlike the House Ways and Means Committee, Hull's Republican opponents on the Senate Finance Committee were much more vocal in their denunciation of the RTA. Senator Capper complained that the United States had granted concessions to seventy nations, of which only fifteen had reciprocated. Senator Vandenberg declared that "this particular kind of reciprocity is unfortunate, ill-advised, unwarranted, and in direct violation of the Constitution of the United States."[38]

On February 12 spokesmen for both the Chemical Foundation and the National Association of Manufacturers told the Senate Finance Committee that it should defeat the renewal of the RTA. They contended that the RTA allowed a flood of imports to enter the country and endangered the jobs of the American people. They specifically criticized the unconditional most-favored-nation clause in the agreements as being against the best interests of the United States. Republicans for the most part opposed the bill, but Democrats from the cattle, wool, and copper states also criticized it. The watch manufacturers howled at the agreement with Switzerland that decreased U.S. tariffs on certain kinds of watches. Lumber interests resented the deal with Canada that allowed Canadian lumber to enter the United States more cheaply.[39]

On February 19 the Senate Finance Committee defeated seven amendments proposed by Vandenberg and Capper and then voted to send the RTA bill to the Senate floor. Six days later the Senate voted 58 to 24 in favor of renewing the RTA for another three years. Prior to the final vote Senator Capper attempted unsuccessfully to amend the bill to make all trade agreements treaties that required Senate ratification.[40]

By the time the RTA Act was about to expire on June 12, 1940, the United States had negotiated trade agreements with twenty-one nations that accounted for 60 percent of its foreign commerce. Great Britain and France, both signatories to trade agreements with the United States, had attached numerous restrictions to the agreements to enable them to import only the materials needed for the war effort.[41]

The fight to renew the RTA Act began on December 5, 1939, when Hull made a speech in Chicago to the American Farm Bureau. He extolled the RTA program and proclaimed that it must be continued through the war years in order to pave the way for post-war cooperation among the nations of the world.[42] Roosevelt echoed these very sentiments in a message to Congress on January 3, 1940, when he said that the RTA Act "should be extended as an indispensable part of the foundation of any stable and durable peace."[43]

Doughton invited Hull to defend the RTA program before the House Ways and Means Committee on January 11. The secretary of state assured the committee that the continuation of the plan would develop closer economic relationships among countries while increasing income and employment in the United States.[44] On February 26 Hull defended his trade program before the Senate Finance Committee, where the opponents of the RTA used the same arguments they had in 1937. They continued to insist that the whole program was unconstitutional because it gave the president the authority that belonged to Congress. They also declared that reductions in tariff duties were harmful to agriculture, labor, and industry and that U.S. tariff concessions to one country were granted to other countries without any return benefits. Dr. John Lee Coulter, an economist for the National Manufacturers Association, wanted the Congress to suspend the pacts until the end of the war. Hull's opponents even went so far as to claim that the secretary of state wanted to run for president in 1940 and would use the trade agreements to his political advantage—a point Hull vigorously denied.[45]

On February 23 the House passed the extension of the RTA by a vote of 216 to 168 after defeating all twenty-four amendments to the bill. On April 5 the Senate voted in favor of Hull's bill by a vote of 42 to 37. Democratic Senator David Walsh of Massachusetts attempted unsuccessfully at the last moment to attach an amendment to the bill that would limit its extension to one year rather than three. Fifteen Democrats joined the Republicans to vote against the bill. Most of the negative votes came from the western protectionists. The Democrats in favor of the bill came from the low-tariff South and the industrial sections of the nation.[46]

Though World War II had reduced the proportion of the trade affected by the RTA program, the United States, by 1943, had made trade agreements with twenty-seven countries. Of these countries, only Finland was at war with the Soviet Union, an ally of the United States. Sixteen countries were fighting with the United States, six had broken relations with the Axis, and 4 were neutral.[47]

In April 1943 Senate Republicans attempted to reduce the RTA renewal term from three years to two years. Republican Senator John A. Danaher of Connecticut also wanted to amend the RTA Act to make trade agreements revocable. His amendment would subject all of the existing agreements with the twenty-seven countries, and any new ones negotiated, to termination six months after the war, either by joint resolution of Congress or by presidential proclamation.[48] On May 19 the Senate Finance Committee approved the Danaher amendment by a vote of 11 to 10, despite Hull's warning to Congress that it would usher in a return to economic nationalism and trade wars.[49]

On April 18, 1,200 economists of the American Economic Association, in a letter to Congress, declared that the RTA program would lead to economic cooperation in the post-war years. On the other hand, the weakening of the program or its quick termination would wreck post-war reconstruction and sow the seeds for the next conflict.[50]

On May 13 the House passed the RTA extension, for a two-year period, by a vote of 342 to 65. The Senate voted 59 to 23 in favor of the House version on June 2. However, it rejected the Danaher amendment, giving Roosevelt and Hull a major victory. Both Roosevelt and Hull wanted the usual three-year term, but both houses of Congress demanded two years, claiming that the war would end by that time and that new agreements should be made then.[51]

On March 26, 1945, less than one month prior to his death, Roosevelt asked Congress, once again, to renew the expiring RTA program. The president declared that the war would soon end, and it was crucial that the United States continue to reduce trade barriers for greater prosperity throughout the world. Unlike previous requests to renew RTA in past years, Roosevelt proposed a major change in the program. Previously, the tariff could be reduced up to 50 percent of the 1934 rates with each country. This meant that by 1945 the United States had already used up its authority to cut tariff rates with Great Britain, Canada, France, the Netherlands, Belgium, and Turkey. The president recommended to Congress that the 50 percent limit be brought up to date so that he could reduce the tariff with each country up to 50 percent of the 1945 rates.[52]

On May 26 the House passed the RTA extension 239 to 153, allowing President Harry Truman (Roosevelt had died on April 12) to cut the tariff up to 50 percent of the 1945 rates. Democratic Speaker Sam Rayburn of Texas was able to garner enough votes to defeat every Republican amendment and get the administration's bill through the House.[53] On June 20 the Senate followed the House and passed the bill 54 to 21, with only 5 Democrats voting against it, while 15 Republicans supported it.[54]

After World War II Congress held mixed views toward the RTA program. It continued to allow the president to reduce tariff rates, but it added measures to protect domestic industries. For example, the peril-point provision required the Tariff Commission to set minimum rates for contemplated concessions below which domestic industries might be harmed by imports. The escape-clause provision permitted the withdrawal of a tariff concession previously made. The defense-essentiality amendment called for the restriction of imports if these imports threatened to harm the nation's national security.[55]

With the Republicans back in the White House in the 1950s, the RTA program came under closer scrutiny. The Republicans launched attacks against the RTA program by opposing specific rate reductions and using the peril-point and escape-clause provisions more frequently. President Eisenhower's administration continued to use the item-by-item approach to bargaining, and this resulted in a proliferation of tariff subclassifications for numerous products in order to confine the benefits of the lower duties to the negotiating parties. Otherwise, these benefits would have been given to third countries producing similar but not identical products without reciprocal concessions because of the unconditional most-favored-nation principle.[56]

In evaluating the RTA program, we can say that it had limited success. It failed to redress the imbalance caused by the position of the United States as a creditor nation. Since exports are such a small part of America's gross domestic product, the RTA Act had a limited effect on the level of domestic economic activity. In looking at the quantity of tariff reduction from 1934 to 1962, we see that over 400 U.S. industrial products remained unaffected by negotiations and therefore still subject to the high rates of the Hawley-Smoot Tariff of 1930.[57] Nonetheless, under the RTA program U.S. tariff rates fell from an average of 51.4 percent for dutiable imports in 1934 to 11.1 percent in 1962 just prior to the Trade Expansion Act. Moreover, the percentage of dutiable imports to total imports rose from 37.6 percent to 61.6 percent over the same period.[58] The RTA Act did not end the Great Depression and brought no economic miracle, but it did mitigate the harshness of the Hawley-Smoot Tariff. It won the political goodwill of Europe and Latin America and paved the way for America's leadership in the post-World War II era.

THE GENERAL AGREEMENT ON TARIFFS AND TRADE

The RTA program set the pattern for the General Agreement on Tariffs and Trade (GATT). It was the intellectual and for the United States, the legislative progenitor of the GATT. While the RTA program ended congressional domination in tariff making, giving the President the power to make bilateral pacts raising or lowering tariff rates with foreign countries up to 50 percent, the GATT went further by allowing multilateral pacts (agreements between many countries).[59] The GATT was designed and promoted by the United States in the 1940s. During World War II the U.S. government began working on ways to continue the close economic cooperation with foreign nations after the war. The war demonstrated that nations, in a crisis, could cooperate to overcome their mutual problems. The question was whether the United States, in the post-war period, could prevent the economic chaos and trade wars that had prevailed in the early 1930s. The RTA program had worked well between 1934 and 1945, but now something more was needed to help Europe recover from the ravages of war.[60]

In 1946 the United States, Great Britain, and other countries called for a United Nations Conference on Trade and Employment. The conference established a preparatory committee, consisting of eighteen governments, that created the charter for the International Trade Organization (ITO). The drafting of the charter took about eighteen months, with meetings in London, New York, Geneva, and Havana, Cuba. On March 23, 1948, the Havana Charter, which created the ITO, was signed by the United States and fifty-two other countries.[61]

At the meeting of the preparatory committee in Geneva in 1947, the United States pushed for a GATT agreement as quickly as possible. The Truman administration had to finish its multilateral negotiations in Geneva before the president's authority to negotiate under the RTA program expired in June 1948.

Truman and his advisers recognized that the growing hostility to the liberal trade policies in the Congress could threaten the passage of an ITO Charter bill. Therefore, in 1946 the United States had suggested that multilateral tariff negotiations be undertaken at the same time, but independently of the ITO negotiations. The United States hurried representatives to Geneva and together with the representatives of twenty-two other governments participated in the tariff reduction talks, whose results were embodied into the GATT and would eventually be incorporated into the trade chapter of the ITO. GATT negotiations were completed in August 1947, and GATT became operative on January 1, 1948.[62]

The general provisions of the GATT were originally intended to be a temporary device for safeguarding the tariff concessions made by the contracting parties. Therefore, some trade provisions intended for the ITO Charter were also written into the GATT in order to protect the value of the tariff commitments. This was done because the United States was allowed to enter into trade agreements, but could not join organizations without the approval of Congress. Therefore, when it became apparent that the GATT would enter into force before the ITO negotiations were completed, the GATT text was modified to remove any suggestion that it was an organization. This was why the "contracting parties acting jointly" became the highest GATT authority. This maneuver to avoid the need for congressional approval of the multilateral negotiations under the GATT angered many members of Congress. They declared that the GATT was an organization that came under Congress's auspices, and that the president had exceeded his constitutional authority.[63]

After the ITO Charter was completed in March 1948, the signatories had to present it to their legislative bodies for ratification. To become operative, the charter was required to be approved by the majority of the signatory nations. However, most of the signatories decided to wait for the U.S. Congress to ratify the charter before sending it to their legislative bodies for approval. In April 1949 the charter was sent to the House Committee on Foreign Affairs, where numerous hearings were held. Truman's request for a joint resolution permitting U.S. participation in the ITO died in the committee; it never had the opportunity to be voted on by the entire House.[64] At the end of 1950 the State Department announced that the ITO Charter would not be resubmitted to Congress. When the United States failed to ratify it, most of the other signatories did not bother to try for ratification. It was obvious that the ITO could not survive without American participation. With the demise of the ITO, the GATT became the founding document for an international institution and assumed the commercial policy role that had been assigned to the ITO.[65]

The American Congress believed that the ITO issue had neither relevance nor urgency at the time of ratification. The beginnings of the Cold War dominated foreign policy in the early 1950s. Many in Congress were also unhappy with what they saw as executive infringement on the congressional domain—the authority given to the president over tariff policy under the RTA program. When the ITO Charter came up for ratification, Congress refused to approve an international organization that enhanced the president's power and over which it had no control.

In 1955 the same fate awaited the Organization for Trade Cooperation (OTC), another international organization. The Eisenhower administration supported the OTC, which was designed as a substitute for the ITO. The OTC would have had an assembly, an executive committee, and a secretariat and would have been empowered to carry out many of the functions of the GATT. However, once again, Congress refused to ratify it.[66]

The GATT as a "contracting party" and technically not an organization needed no congressional approval. The president's authority to negotiate the GATT accord was given under the RTA program. From 1945 until 1962 seven more Trade Agreement Extension Acts were passed. Inserted in many of these acts was the following statement: "The enactment of this Act shall not be construed to determine or indicate the approval or disapproval by the Congress of the Executive Agreement known as the General Agreement on Tariffs and Trade."[67] The Trade Expansion Act of 1962 was the first legislation to authorize U.S. participation in multilateral trade negotiations under GATT.[68]

The GATT began in 1948 with only 23 countries, but by 1994, 125 countries subscribed to GATT's trading rules. This accounts for over 90 percent of world trade. Through a number of negotiating rounds that will be discussed in subsequent chapters, world tariff levels have declined from an average of 40 percent in 1948 to 4 percent in 1994. [69]

The GATT consists of two parts: (1) the so-called general provisions, which are the numbered articles that set forth rules for the conduct of trade between the contracting parties, and (2) the schedules of tariff concessions resulting from the multilateral negotiations from the Geneva Round in 1947 to the Uruguay Round in 1993. Article I of the GATT sets forth the broad objectives of the agreement. It declares that all countries should enjoy a high standard of living, full employment, and growing real income and effective demand by fostering production and an exchange of goods and services.[70]

Despite its complexity, the GATT deals with four basic principles: (1) There should be no discrimination in trade relations among the participating countries. (2) Everyone is committed to observe the negotiated tariff concessions. (3) No nation can use quantitative restrictions (quotas) on exports and imports. (4) The GATT supports the promotion of trade in developing countries. The remaining provisions of the GATT deal with the exceptions to these general principles, trade measures other than tariffs and quotas, and various procedural matters. Let us briefly discuss the four basic principles and their exceptions.[71]

The GATT states that the "contracting parties" of the GATT are obligated to accord nondiscriminatory, most-favored-nation (MFN) treatment to all other members with respect to import and export duties. Under the MFN principle any tariff concession granted by one country to any other country is automatically extended to all other countries. GATT members must apply the MFN principle to other GATT members, but they are free to apply it to nonmember countries as well. An exception to the rule of nondiscrimination can be made in cases of well-known tariff preferences. For example, countries of the British Commonwealth can give tariff preferences to its members. However, no new preference can be created, and existing preferences cannot be increased.[72]

Article XIX of the general provisions contains an escape clause that allows any member to withdraw or modify a tariff concession if the concession leads to an increase in imports that causes or threatens serious injury to domestic producers. When a member country uses the escape clause, it must consult with other nations as to remedies. If an agreement is not reached, those countries affected by the escape clause may withdraw equivalent concessions. The escape clause is now referred to as the safeguard provision. Though there is no clear statement on the matter, it is accepted that Article XIX should be applied on a nondiscriminatory basis. Most countries would rather not be subject to the discipline of the safeguard provision. Thus, when a country is challenged by another with exporting excessive quantities of goods, it will voluntarily reduce its exports by implementing voluntary export restraints (VERs).[73]

The GATT prohibits the use of quantitative import and export restrictions. There are, however, exceptions to this rule. The four most important exceptions pertain to agriculture, the balance of payments, economic development, and national security.

The United States and other GATT countries have been allowed to place import restrictions on agricultural goods when surpluses exist in these countries. When a serious decline occurs in a country's monetary reserves that threatens its balance of payments, that country can restrict its imports. The GATT recognizes the special position of developing countries and allows them to use nondiscriminatory import quotas to encourage the development of infant industries. In order to do this, a country must get prior approval from the collective GATT membership. A GATT country can use trade controls for the purpose of national security. The strategic controls on U.S. exports fall under this category.[74]

The GATT membership engages in numerous activities. For example, the members of the GATT meet in regular annual sessions and special tariff conferences. There is a council that works between sessions and prepares the agenda for the next session. The GATT membership behaves like an international organization in several ways. For instance, it has obtained a secretariat from the United Nations that publishes the annual report, and the member governments maintain close contact by consulting with each other between sessions. The "contracting parties" to the GATT have participated in eight tariff conferences, beginning with the Geneva Round in 1947 where 45,000 tariff concessions were completed that represented half of world trade. Subsequently, major tariff conferences were held in Annecy, France, in 1949 and in Torquay, England, in 1951, primarily to give countries that had not participated in the Geneva Round an opportunity to do so. Only modest tariff reductions were made at Annecy, and at Torquay tariffs were reduced 25 percent of their 1948 level. Another Geneva Round occurred from 1955 to 1956 and then came the Dillon Round, named after Kennedy's secretary of the Treasury, C. Douglas Dillon. Neither of these rounds produced much tariff cutting. However, in the next three rounds, the Kennedy Round (1963-1967), the Tokyo Round (1973-1979), and the Uruguay Round (1986-1993), major tariff reductions were made that will be discussed in subsequent chapters.[75]

The settlement of trade disputes between members is one of the least publicized but most important contributions of GATT. Before GATT trade disputes were usually settled between the disputants without a third party, and usually the weaker country gave way to the stronger. GATT has adopted complaint procedures where an aggrieved nation can voice its complaint. For example, in recent years the European Economic Community has filed a complaint in GATT against Japanese trade practices, and the United States has filed petitions against European subsidies on agricultural exports.[76]

In 1989 GATT implemented a trade-policy review mechanism to ensure that its members lived up to their multilateral commitments. Under this policy the council regularly reviews the international trade regime of member countries. The four largest trading entities, the European Community, the United States, Japan, and Canada, are reviewed every two years; the next sixteen biggest trading countries every four years; and the remaining GATT members every six years.[77]

On April 15, 1994, a GATT conference was held in Marrakesh, Morocco, where the delegates from 125 nations created the World Trade Organization (WTO) to replace GATT. The name change took place in January, 1995, shortly after the Uruguay agreement was ratified by its signatories. The formation of the WTO will be discussed later.[78]

THE BIRTH OF THE EUROPEAN ECONOMIC COMMUNITY

The European Economic Community, later called the European Community and now called the European Union, was created in March 1957. However, its roots can be traced to the end of World War II when Western Europe's economy, weakened by the exertions of the war (the 1936 production levels of many countries were not reached again until 1949), faced the dire threat of Soviet communism. The United States, emerging from the war as the major economic power in the world, was determined to both protect and help Europe through these difficult times. Jean Monnet, a French civil servant and a EU founding father, told Walt Rostow, an American economist, in 1947 that European unity was in the best interests of all concerned. He said, "First we must modernize France. Without a vital France there can be no Europe. Then we must unite Western Europe. When Western Europe unites and gathers its strength, it will draw in Eastern Europe. And this great East-West Europe will be of consequence and a force for peace in the world."[79]

In March 1947 President Harry Truman asked Congress for $400 million to aid both Greece and Turkey in their fight against communism. Congress not only approved what became known as the Truman Doctrine, but in the following year it approved a $12-billion European Recovery Act, better known as the Marshall Plan. It was named after Secretary of State George Marshall, who gave some details of the plan in his June 1947 Harvard commencement speech. The Marshall Plan, unlike the Truman Doctrine, put the European nations in charge of the recovery. The aid was conditional on effective cooperation among European governments; they were responsible for planning how the money would be used. The European nations established the Organization for European Economic Cooperation (OEEC) in 1948 to allocate the Marshall Plan aid and to accelerate the recovery of Europe.[80]

Along with the OEEC, the European Payments Union (EPU) was also created in 1948. The EPU was a powerful instrument for expansion of trade between countries whose currencies were not convertible into dollars. It served as a clearance agency to settle trade imbalances of the member nations whose trade was expanded in preference to dollar trade. Both the OEEC and the EPU contributed to the rapid expansion of intra-European trade and economic recovery. The United States both encouraged and financially supported the early stages of European unity and trade expansion while retaining a powerful influence on its policy for three reasons: (1) The United States saw trade expansion as an instrument for promoting economic growth and political stability and thwarting Soviet expansion. (2) Though the United States encouraged European unity, it never believed that it would be achieved by dividing Europe from the rest of the world. The United States was willing to condone temporary discrimination against the dollar until Europe recovered from the trauma of the war. (3) The United States believed that a healthy united European economy would be to everyone's advantage, and that the reduction of trade barriers was still the ultimate economic goal.[81]

The Schuman Plan, named after Foreign Minister Robert Schuman of France, led to formation of the European Coal and Steel Community (ECSC) in 1952. Six nations, France, West Germany, Italy, Belgium, the Netherlands, and Luxembourg, joined together to form a common market in coal, steel, and iron ore. Five years later, on March 25, 1957, these same countries signed the Treaty of Rome to create what was then called the European Economic Community which was renamed the European Union (EU) after the signing of the Maastricht agreement on December 11, 1991, the name by which we will continue to refer to it. Aside from the original six, Great Britain, Denmark, and Ireland became members in 1973, Greece in 1981, and Portugal and Spain in 1986. On March 29, 1994, the EU approved the membership of Austria, Finland, Norway, and Sweden.[82]

The main feature of the EU was the creation of a full customs union in July 1968 for both industrial and agricultural goods. The result has been the abolition of all restrictions on trade among member countries and the creation of a common external tariff. Great Britain and other countries did not favor a common external tariff and refused to join the EU in 1957. In 1959, two years after the birth of the EU, the European Free Trade Association (EFTA) was formed at Stockholm. Great Britain, Sweden, Norway, Denmark, Switzerland, Austria, and Portugal joined together to form a free-trade area. Unlike the EU, the EFTA allowed each member to retain control of its own tariffs on nonmember trade. The EU and the EFTA were not rivals, but cooperated fully with each other. For example, in 1991 they created a European Economic Area with free movement of capital, services, workers, and goods representing nineteen European countries and 40 percent of the world trade. Many members of the EFTA in 1959 have since joined the EU.[83]

In 1987 the twelve members of the EU signed the Single European Act (SEA) creating one international market by eliminating all frontiers by 1992. The passage of this act formed the largest single market in the world, consisting of 345 million people. It abolished internal frontiers and ensured the free movement of goods, services, persons, and capital throughout the area. In December 1991 the Maastricht Treaty calling for a single currency and a single European Central Bank was signed by the leaders of the EU nations. The treaty went into effect and the European Union began on November 1, 1993, after Germany, the last of the twelve countries, ratified it.[84]

The United States and the EU have maintained a cooperative partnership since the beginning of the EU in 1957. Just prior to the signing of the Treaty of Rome, President Dwight Eisenhower praised the formation of the EU, claiming that it could only strengthen U.S.-European relations.[85] One year after the formation of the EU, American companies were opening offices in Europe, prepared to take advantage of the new market. For example, Ford International opened an office in Brussels to guide its operations in the common market, and H. J. Heinz bought a Dutch plant to produce its goods. American firms that were unsure in which country to set up offices could now establish an office in only one country and gain access to the entire market.[86]

The internal market program of the EU is a potential opportunity for the United States as long as the market remains open and the EU abides by the GATT. The EU realizes that it cannot compete with the United States and Japan without dismantling trade barriers. Some American economists and politicians feel that European integration may lead to the protectionism of the food-products, pharmaceutical, and service industries. Certain trends are apparent in the EU regarding the open market. France and Italy are much more nationalistic than Great Britain and Germany. Both the French and Italians have limited their trade with non-EU countries. For example, France and Italy have restricted auto imports from the United States. However, Great Britain and Germany reject this protectionism and support an open EU market to the rest of the world. It is interesting to note that both Great Britain and Germany, within the EU, have the largest volume of trade with the United States.[87]

Though the United States has supported European unity and the birth of the EU, problems between the two trading partners have always existed, especially in the agricultural sector. The common market has a Common Agricultural Policy (CAP) that was established along with the customs union and relies on three main principles: market unity and common prices, EU preference, and financial solidarity. The United States has complained that the CAP discriminates against the American farmer. For example, the objective of the EU in the early 1960s was to create a common market for farm products by equalizing support prices. The EU's aim was to raise farm income by increasing productivity. The disposal of farm surpluses created by overproduction became the responsibility of the EU, and it was permitted to assist farmers by interfering in their national markets. While all agricultural imports from outside countries were controlled by variable tariffs, EU preference determined internal trade. This meant that French wheat growers were to have first chance at German and Dutch markets that were supplied by American farmers.[88]

Today the EU is the largest importer of farm products in the world, whereas the United States is the world's largest exporter. American agricultural policy continues to be aimed at opening up foreign markets to American farm products, while the EU wants to restrict imports because it wants to avoid production controls and surpluses by placing the burden of adjustments on third country suppliers, notably the United States. The entry of Great Britain, Ireland, and Denmark into the EU has caused a sharp decline in American agricultural exports to those countries. Though the United States remains irritated by the trade-diversion effects of the EU's CAP, it is working to avoid trade wars by eliminating trade-distorting subsidies. The American government wants to stop all subsidies by the year 2000, while the EU wants only gradual reductions.[89]

Steel production is another issue that divides the United States and the EU. In the 1950s the United States produced 50 percent of the world's steel, while today that figure has declined to 10 percent. On the other hand, steel production in the EU tripled from 1950 to 1970. Today the United States has a quota program that keeps steel imports below 20 percent of the quantity sold in the country. The EU complains about this quota and contends that American sectors in textiles, sugar, dairy products, machine tools, automobiles, and semiconductors remain protected as well.[90]

Many nontariff barriers still exist between the EU and the United States, such as differences in classification, varying taxation systems, border restrictions (for security, health, and technical reasons), and state monopolies. The EU and the United States also have different approaches to trade. For example, the EU is more likely than the United States to prefer interventionist or regulatory solutions to trade problems. The EU's customs union is not really compatible with the goals of the GATT. For instance, though the customs union involves free trade among its member countries, it imposes tariffs on imports from nonmember or third countries, while the GATT wants to reduce and someday eliminate all tariff and nontariff trade barriers.[91]

Today the EU and the United States are economically interdependent. The American government made the right decision in supporting the EU in the early years. It realized that in the long run a common market would increase trade opportunities. The free movement of goods and services, without national regulations and border restrictions, a uniform business code, and a more homogeneous consumer population would only facilitate transactions between the EU and the United States. Critics of the EU point to the large trade deficits and blame them on both the EU and Japan. With regard to American and EU trade from 1968, the year the customs union became fully effective, the United States ran surpluses in its balance of trade every year until 1983, except for 1972. From 1983 until the present it has run deficits with the EU, and most of these deficits can be blamed not on unfair trade practices by the EU, but on high interest rates in the United States that cause the value of the American dollar to appreciate.[92]

The EU is an important market for the United States not only for commodity exports, but also in such services as television programming. For example, American cable television such as Turner Network Television has offices in England and sells programming to the EU. American producers increased revenues from television sales by six times in the 1980s. In 1993, 40 percent of U.S. investment abroad and 25 percent of all American exports went to EU nations. American imports from the EU are about 20 percent of its total imports. Half the world's trade is conducted in the EU. The combined GDP of all its members makes it the second-largest economic bloc in the world, behind North America. The EU in 1993 had a population of 345 million people, the second-largest market in population next to India. It has 228 of the top 1,000 companies in the world, behind Japan with 310 and the United States with 345.[93]

In 1960 the EU shocked the United States by abandoning the item-by-item bargaining approach. Item-by-item bargaining refers to tariff negotiations centered on specific products as opposed to across-the-board negotiations centered on linear percentage reductions in entire tariff schedules for all parties. The United States had followed the principal-supplier concept by offering concessions in negotiations with another country only on products for which that country was the major supplier to the United States. When the EU proposed in the Dillon Round in 1961-1962 to reduce its common external tariff by a uniform 20 percent, American negotiators were unprepared to take action. They believed that across-the-board negotiations were inconsistent with the congressional mandate of item-by-item bargaining. When the Kennedy administration proposed a further round of tariff negotiations in 1962, it first sent the draft Trade Expansion Act to Congress both authorizing a 50 percent reduction in most tariffs and implicitly sanctioning across-the board-negotiations. The administration believed that with the passage of this act, the United States would abandon the item-by-item method and implement the linear method of tariff negotiations. The Trade Expansion Act and the Kennedy Round will be discussed in detail in the next chapter.[94]

NOTES

1. See Cordell Hull, *The Memoirs of Cordell Hull*, 2 vols. (New York: Macmillan Company, 1948), vol. 1, pp. 352-365.

2. Ibid. 1:81.

3. Ibid. 1:152.

4. Joseph M. Jones, *Tariff Retaliation: Repercussions of the Hawley-Smoot Bill* (Philadelphia: University of Pennsylvania Press, 1934), p. 301.

5. Ibid., p. 303; Hull, *Memoirs* 1:356.

6. Arthur M. Schlesinger, Jr., *The Coming of the New Deal* (Boston: Houghton Mifflin Company, 1958), p. 210.

7. Ibid; Hull, *Memoirs* 1:251.

8. Hull, *Memoirs* 1:248; Schlesinger, *Coming of the New Deal*, p. 210.

9. William E. Leuchtenburg, *Franklin D. Roosevelt and the New Deal* (New York: Harper and Row, 1963), pp. 203-204.

10. Hull, *Memoirs* 1:359.

11. Schlesinger, *Coming of the New Deal*, p. 254.

12. Hull, *Memoirs* 1:359; Abraham Berglund, "The Reciprocal Trade Agreements Act of 1934," *American Economic Review* 25 (September 1935): 416.

13. Schlesinger, *Coming of the New Deal*, p. 25; *New York Times*, January 3, 1934, p. 8; March 5, 1934, p. 3.

14. Berglund, "Reciprocal Trade Agreements Act of 1934," p. 411.

15. *New York Times*, March 9, 1934, p. 1.

16. Hull, *Memoirs* 1:356-357.

17. Berglund, "Reciprocal Trade Agreements Act of 1934," p. 417.

18. Hull, *Memoirs* 1:357.

19. Ibid.; *New York Times*, June 5, 1934, p. 1.

20. Hull, *Memoirs* 1:357.

21. Ibid. 1:356, 366.

22. Ibid. 1:366-367.

23. Ibid. 1:366-367, 370, 376.

24. Schlesinger, *Coming of the New Deal*, p. 255.

25. Hull, *Memoirs* 1:370.

26. Ibid.; Schlesinger, *Coming of the New Deal*, p. 255.

27. Schlesinger, *Coming of the New Deal*, pp. 255-257.

28. Ibid., p. 258.

29. Ibid.

30. Berglund, "Reciprocal Trade Agreements Act of 1934," p. 420; Oswald Garrison Villard, "The New Cuban Reciprocity Pact," *Nation*, September 12, 1934, p. 287.

31. Hull, *Memoirs* 1:368.

32. Berglund, "Reciprocal Trade Agreements Act of 1934," p. 421.

33. Ibid., pp. 421-422.

34. Hull, *Memoirs* 1:375; Schlesinger, *Coming of the New Deal*, p. 259.

35. Hull, *Memoirs* 1:518-519.

36. Ibid.

37. *New York Times*, February 10, 1937, p. 42.

38. "Congress Gives the President More Time," *Newsweek*, March 6, 1937, p. 11.

39. *New York Times*, February 13, 1937, p. 6; Hull, *Memoirs* 1:518-519; "Background to Peace: Cordell Hull and the Trade Agreement Policy," *Fortune* 16 (September 1937): 90.

40. *New York Times*, February 26, 1937, p. 1.

41. Hull, *Memoirs* 1:746.

42. Ibid. 1:747.

43. Ibid.; *New York Times*, January 4, 1940, p. 1.

44. Hull, *Memoirs* 1:748.

45. Ibid. 1:748-750; *New York Times*, February 4, 1940, p. 18.

46. *New York Times*, February 24, 1940, p. 1; April 6, 1940, p. 1; Hull, *Memoirs* 1:748-750.

47. Hull, *Memoirs* 2:1212.

48. *New York Times*, April 16, 1943, p. 10.

49. Ibid., May 20, 1943, p. 16; May 22, 1943, p. 9.

50. Ibid., April 19, 1943, p. 5.

51. Ibid., May 14, 1943, p. 1; June 3, 1943, pp. 1, 6.

52. Ibid., March 27, 1945, p. 1.

53. Ibid., May 27, 1945, p. 1.

54. Ibid., June 21, 1945, p. 1.

55. Franklin Root, *International Trade and Investment*, 7th ed. (Cincinnati, OH: South-Western Publishing Company, 1994), pp. 216-217.

56. Ibid., p. 217.

57. Schlesinger, *Coming of the New Deal*, p. 259; Root, *International Trade and Investment*, pp. 217-218.

58. Root, *International Trade and Investment*, p. 217.

59. Patrick Low, *Trading Free: The GATT and U.S. Trade Policy* (New York: Twentieth Century Fund Press, 1993), p. 37.

60. Ibid., p. 38.

61. Kenneth Dam, *The GATT: Law and International Economic Organization* (Chicago: University of Chicago Press, 1970), p. 10; "The GATT and Its Origin," *Congressional Digest* 33 (January 1954): 6.

62. Low, *Trading Free*, p. 39.

63. Ibid., pp. 39-40.

64. Ibid., p. 41; "GATT and Its Origin," p. 6.

65. Dam, *GATT*, p. 11; Low, *Trading Free*, p. 41.

66. Low, *Trading Free*, pp. 41-42; Dam, *GATT*, pp. 337-338.

67. Low, *Trading Free*, p. 55; "The 1947 Multilateral Agreement-GATT," *Congressional Digest* 37 (April 1958): 104.

68. Low, *Trading Free*, p. 55.

69. Joseph G. Carson, "Why GATT Is Important to the United States," *Measuring Success*, August 1994, p. 1.

70. Dam, *GATT*, pp. 391-393.

71. Ibid., pp. 391-447.

72. Ibid., pp. 391-393.

73. Low, *Trading Free*, pp. 152-153.

74. Root, *International Trade and Investment*, pp. 189-190.

75. Ibid., p. 192; Dam, *GATT*, pp. 56-57.

76. Root, *International Trade and Investment*, p. 194.

77. Ibid., pp. 194-195.

78. *New York Times*, April 15, 1994, p. 1; April 16, 1994, p. 35.

79. "The European Union," *Economist*, October 22, 1994, p. 22; Loukas Tsoukalis, *The New European Economy: The Politics and Economics of Integration* (New York: Oxford University Press, 1993), p. 14.

80. Tsoukalis, *New European Economy*, p. 14.

81. Don D. Humphrey, *The United States and the Common Market: A Background Study* (New York: Frederick A. Praeger, 1963), pp. 24-25; Nicholas V. Gianaris, *The European Community and the United States: Economic Relations* (New York: Praeger, 1991), p. 40.

82. Gianaris, *European Community and the United States*, pp. 19-23.

83. Humphrey, *United States and the Common Market*, p. 4; Gianaris, *European Community and the United States*, pp. 25-26.

84. Root, *International Trade and Investment*, pp. 270-273.

85. *New York Times*, March 1, 1957, p. 3.

86. "Opportunity Knocks for U.S. Business," *Time*, August 11, 1958, p. 64.

87. Gianaris, *European Community and the United States*, pp. 9-10, 115.

88. Ibid., pp. 125, 132; Humphrey, *United States and the Common Market*, pp. 171-172; Root, *International Trade and Investment*, p. 277.

89. Root, *International Trade and Investment*, p. 277.

90. Gianaris, *European Community and the United States*, p. 139.

91. Low, *Trading Free*, pp. 27, 101.

92. Gianaris, *European Community and the United States*, pp. 115, 125.

93. Ibid., p. 114; James Dudley, *1992: Understanding the New European Market* (Chicago: Dearborn Financial Publishing, 1991), p. 26.

94. Dam, *GATT*, p. 67.

4

The Trade Expansion Act and the Kennedy Round

THE TRADE EXPANSION ACT

The Trade Expansion Act was a direct response to the growing power and influence of the European Economic Community, now called the European Union. President Kennedy wanted the power to negotiate with the EU to reduce trade barriers in a way that would allow the United States to sell in the European market on equitable terms. In order to accomplish his goal, Kennedy had to persuade the Congress to give him the power to abolish the item-by-item negotiations method established in the Reciprocal Trade Agreements Act in 1934 and to utilize the EU method of across-the-board negotiations, better known as the linear method, that was explained in the previous chapter. The president stressed that the United States had to take the lead in world trade. He declared that "the United States did not rise to greatness by waiting for others to lead."[1]

The groundwork for the Trade Expansion Act began on November 1, 1961, when two strong appeals were made for a new trade program. Former Secretary of State Christian Herter of the Eisenhower administration and William Clayton, an early administrator of the RTA program, spoke before the Foreign Economic Policy Subcommittee of the Joint Economic Committee of Congress. They described how current U.S. trade policy was outdated and of the inadequacy of the RTA program. They suggested that the United States open negotiations for a trade partnership with the EU. On the same day George Ball, soon to be under secretary of state for economic affairs, spoke before the National Foreign Trade Convention in New York warning of the polarization of the American and European industrial markets. According to Ball, it was in the best interests of the United States to negotiate tariff reductions with the EU, and a new trade law was needed to accomplish this goal. The Ball speech tested public reaction to a new trade initiative with positive results. On November 29 the president indicated that he was working on a new trade law to give him the power to make major reductions in tariff rates.[2]

On January 1, 1962, Kennedy spoke in Palm Beach, Florida, but said little about his liberal trade program. He briefly talked about the rapid growth of the EU and how it necessitated a new approach to trade in the United States. He hoped for bipartisan support in Congress and favorable public opinion. However, after his speech, the details concerning the new trade law remained a mystery. People knew only that the Kennedy administration supported a liberal trade program.[3]   Though the trade bill was drawn up in 1961 by Ball and Howard Petersen, the special assistant for international trade matters, the president believed that the protectionist sentiment in Congress that year was too powerful to overcome.   Therefore, Kennedy decided to wait until 1962 to make the Trade Expansion Act the cornerstone of his domestic policy.[4]

Five days after the president's vague speech on trade in Palm Beach, Republican Senator Prescott Bush of Connecticut, a member of the Congressional Economic Committee, an ardent protectionist, and the father of former President George Bush, condemned liberal trade and warned the president that he would oppose the trade program whose details were still a mystery. It is interesting to note that almost thirty years later George Bush would denounce protectionism and support the passage of the North American Free Trade Agreement.[5]

On January 6, the day after Bush spoke against liberal trade, Kennedy countered the Connecticut senator's talk by revealing the rationale behind the new trade program. He asserted that the trade act was necessary for three reasons: (1) Great Britain was seeking admission into the EU in 1962. If the British were successful, they would support the United States in working for lower tariffs within the EU. Unfortunately for Great Britain and the United States, President Charles de Gaulle of France vetoed British admission in 1962, making Britain wait until 1973 to join the EU. (2) Kennedy claimed that the trade act would help the U.S. balance of payments, which had had a deficit in 1961. It would increase U.S. exports and enable businessmen to sell more on equal terms to the EU. (3) The Reciprocal Trade Agreements Act was due for its twelfth renewal in June 1962. The president decided to dump the antiquated RTA and to replace it with his Trade Expansion Act. He declared that his new trade program would prevent economic disintegration in the Western world by keeping the United States and the EU from moving into separate trading blocs that competed with each other.[6]

Kennedy's decision to dump the RTA program came after much discussion with his economic advisers. Throughout 1961 Ball had urged the president to support a bold new trade program that would challenge the Common Market, as the EU was sometimes called. However, Petersen pressed for revising the RTA in 1962, claiming that it would be a sure victory for the president during an election year. Petersen was doubtful that Kennedy could get the Trade Expansion Act passed by a protectionist Congress. However, Ball convinced Petersen that RTA was useless in dealing with the EU and was able to enlist his support for the new bill. The only difference between Ball and Petersen was the timing of the bill. Ball wanted to wait until 1963 after the midterm election—he did not want the new bill to become a political issue. The delay would also give the United States time to see if Great Britain would be successful in its bid to join the EU. On the other hand, Petersen wanted to send the bill to Congress in early 1962 to allow time to get the bill passed so preliminary hearings could take place for the next major international conference. Kennedy supported Petersen's position and decided to sell his trade bill to Congress in January 1962.   He felt confident that he would secure the support of the public and successfully guide the bill through Congress before the November election.[7]

Though the full Trade Expansion Act was not unveiled until January 25, when Kennedy finally sent his tariff message to Congress, parts of the trade act were purposely revealed in early January by members of the administration and Kennedy himself to assess public reaction. For example, on January 7 the American Farm Bureau Federation, representing numerous farm organizations, came out in support of the president's program. The federation declared that farmers favored tariff concessions to prevent barriers against their exports to the EU. This piecemeal revelation of the trade-expansion bill, prior to its being sent to Congress in late January 1962, would help the Kennedy administration garner the public support necessary for its passage in Congress.[8]

When it came to the Trade Expansion Act, the president left nothing to chance. He established a country-wide campaign in 1962, and with the help of the Committee for National Trade Policy, he was able to enlist the support of numerous business and labor leaders. Kennedy in an early message to Congress declared that "the two great Atlantic markets will either grow together or they will grow apart."[9]

On January 8 additional parts of the trade proposals were outlined by Petersen. The special assistant for international trade matters discussed the necessity of revising the peril-point provisions in the existing trade regulations. The peril-point provisions, as they stood in the old trade law, were the levels determined by the Tariff Commission below which tariffs could not be reduced because domestic industry would be harmed. Under the new Kennedy proposal, the Tariff Commission would now be given a list of goods on which negotiations were proposed. After hearings and investigations, it would present to the president a mass of information on the extent to which imports would make productive facilities idle and cause loss of profits and employment. From this information the president would determine what to place on the reserve list for which tariff reductions could not be negotiated. This revision in the peril-point clause shifted power from the Tariff Commission to the president.[10]

The Kennedy administration lobbied congressmen for support of the president's liberal trade bill to be announced on January 25.   On January 15 Kennedy told a group of congressmen invited to a White House coffee that he was confident that they would support his trade program once they had studied the facts. Republican Senator Kenneth Keating of New York, impressed by Petersen's speech a week before and Kennedy's enthusiasm on liberal trade, agreed to support the Kennedy trade proposal on one condition—Congress must have the right to veto any presidential change. According to Keating, any trade proposal would become effective sixty days after being submitted to Congress unless it was vetoed by two-thirds of both houses. Keating insisted that Congress had the constitutional authority to regulate commerce, and if the president wanted broad support for his bill, it would be helpful for him to agree to the congressional veto.[11]

Henry Ford II, chairman of the Ford Motor Company, in a speech before the

Advertising Council on January 17, gave Kennedy the help he needed in the business community when he declared that Congress should support liberal trade on a reciprocal basis. Ford, like his father in the 1920s, opposed tariffs or any restrictions on trade. The automobile industry had become a major exporter, and it was concerned that trade restrictions would lead to retaliation and financial losses.[12]

Two days later, on January 19, Kennedy was joined by both Secretary of State Dean Rusk and Secretary of the Treasury C. Douglas Dillon at a Washington conference of business and labor leaders. They declared that the passage of the new trade bill would reduce the balance-of-payments deficit. Kennedy claimed that if exports could be increased by 5 percent while prices were kept constant, the balance-of-payments deficit could be cut by $1 billion. A 10 percent rise in exports would eliminate the balance-of-payments problem.[13]

The day after his speech to business and labor leaders, the president revealed how his new trade program differed from the Reciprocal Trade Agreements. He told the press that he would ask Congress to allow him to reduce tariffs by broad categories over the next five years. He explained to the press that across-the-board reductions would replace the item-by-item approach of the RTA program. He criticized the item-by-item approach as focusing too much on the special-interest items of all parties, while cutting by broad category tended to obscure the special interest of all sides. Kennedy emphasized that since the EU no longer used the slow, old-fashioned, and cumbersome item-by-item approach, the Congress should give the president the authority to cut across the board.[14]

The president's speech on January 20 was praised by former President Harry Truman. Truman, who had supported the RTA program as senator, vice president, and president, declared that it was time to revise the old trade program. Dillon, in a television interview, said that the new program would have the support of the American people. However, the sentiment toward the trade program in Congress remained uncertain. New York Senator Jacob Javits, like his Republican colleague Keating, would support a new trade bill only if Congress was given veto power over presidential trade agreements. Wilbur Mills from Arkansas, the Democratic chairman of the House Ways and Means Committee, the committee that becomes the first stop of all trade bills, told the AFL-CIO legislative conference that a broader trade bill was necessary, but he had many questions regarding the Kennedy bill. For example, would the president need all the power he would ask for? Would Congress have the right to veto trade bills? Should negotiations be based on the new across-the-board method or the current item-by-item approach?[15]

The text of the Trade Expansion Act was submitted to Congress on January 25. Kennedy asked Congress for new tariff-bargaining powers. He wanted to reduce tariffs by 50 percent over the next five years. In addition, he asked for special authority to negotiate the reduction or elimination of all tariffs on those groups of products such as tractors, autos, heavy machinery, machine tools, washing machines, aircraft, and perfumes where the United States and the EU together accounted for 80 percent or more of world trade. The president insisted that the trade bill would benefit all sectors of the American economy. For example,

Kennedy pointed out that since one of seven farm workers produced for export, the increase in exports provided by new markets would prove a bonanza for agriculture. The one of three American workers employed in export industries would be made more secure in their jobs, and American consumers would benefit from more choices and lower prices.[16]

The escape clause provision under the RTA that permitted the Tariff Commission, after finding that a tariff reduction had injured or threatened to injure a domestic industry, to recommend to the president that all or part of a tariff cut be restored was modified under the Trade Expansion Act. Under the proposal injury would now be defined as a prolonged shutdown of production facilities or the existence of unemployment caused by import competition. Only if such an injury were found in the case of the entire industry, and not just in the case of one product of a multi-product industry, could tariff relief be recommended to the president. If the injury applied to only part of the industry or to some products in the multi-product industries, only federal aid under the new adjustment assistance program could be recommended.[17]

Title III of the Trade Expansion Act defined adjustment assistance as assistance to firms, workers, and industries. For instance, technical and financial assistance and tax relief in the form of a special carry-back of operating losses could be given to firms. Workers might be given readjustment allowances in the form of compensation for partial or complete unemployment. Both retraining and relocation assistance also could be given to workers. Assistance to industries could take the form of the president increasing tariff duties. Under this authority the president could increase the duty for any article to a rate not more than 50 percent above that existing on July 1, 1934, or could impose a duty not to exceed 50 percent ad valorem on a free-list item. This authority to help industries would expire at the end of four years unless the president determined that the national interest mandated its continuation for a longer period.[18]

The Trade Expansion Act modified the manner in which trade negotiations were conducted. Under the RTA program the State Department had the primary responsibility for negotiating trade agreements, which could be influenced by foreign policy considerations. However, as part of the new act, the House Ways and Means Committee created the position of special representative for trade negotiations, responsible directly to the president. The special representative was to gather information and seek advice from representatives of industry, agriculture, labor, and appropriate government agencies and would supervise the preparation of negotiating positions. For the first time, members of the U.S. trade delegation included members of the legislative body. Two members from both the House Ways and Means Committee and the Senate Finance Committee, from different political parties, would be chosen to the trade delegation.[19]

Shortly after the President informed the country and the Congress about the new liberal trade bill, James Reston wrote an articulate column in the *New York Times* praising Kennedy's trade program. Reston urged the president to educate the American people on the importance of the Trade Expansion Act to the economic health of the whole nation. Reston pointed out that everybody in Congress supported more trade until it hurt somebody in his own district. The columnist asserted that all Americans must rise above their parochial interests. He declared that the American people and their congressmen should understand "that there is no future in saving the town and losing the nation."[20]

Luther Hodges, secretary of commerce, and Petersen became Kennedy's chief spokesmen for the Trade Expansion Act. Though Ball knew more about trade than anyone else in the Kennedy administration and was the chief architect of Kennedy's trade policy, he lacked the skills to deal with Congress. Ball could become impatient with the myopia of politicians and was not well received by them. On the other hand, Hodges, a former governor of North Carolina, was a politician.[21]

On January 31 Hodges, in a speech made before the Associated Business Publications, warned that U.S. exports had been only holding steady at about 18 to 20 percent in the last few years while the exports of the EU had been rising rapidly. Hodges urged businessmen to support the new trade bill, which would make the United States more competitive in world markets.[22]

The campaign to pass the Trade Expansion Act was run from the White House. Kennedy articulated the fact that foreign economic policy was a major element of American free-world leadership. The president clarified that the major goal of his trade act was to create more jobs and business in the United States. He assured the American people on a number of occasions that more jobs would be created than lost by the new bill. He also stressed that the United States needed the tools to bargain with the EU. He warned that if the Congress failed to pass the bill, exports would suffer badly because the members of the EU would turn inward and trade more with each other. The president received strong support from the AFL-CIO, which liked the adjustment assistance plan, the U.S. Chamber of Commerce, the American Farm Bureau Federation, and the Independent Committee for a National Trade Policy, headed by Carl J. Gilbert.[23]

The opposition to the Trade Expansion Act had no central organized leadership. However, Oscar Strackbein, chairman of the Nationwide Committee on Import-Export Policy, became its chief spokesman. He was a tireless lobbyist for protection, assailing every aspect of the Kennedy bill. When he testified before the House Ways and Means Committee in March, he warned that the bill would create massive unemployment in the United States. He claimed that no industry would be immune from import competition and listed specifically the danger to the steel, auto, and glass industries in the United States. He emphasized that the bill would strip Congress of its constitutional powers to regulate trade and commerce.[24]

Another argument used by the protectionists was that foreign nations enjoying lower standards could produce using cheaper labor. Though economic historians will agree that American wage rates were higher than those in the EU, the wage rate itself is not used to compare costs between nations. Instead, economists and statisticians rely on unit wage costs, an index that takes into account productive capabilities and the capacity to produce more or less for a given unit of labor. America's higher wages, technology, and capital investment allow it to export goods in which unit wage costs are low. For example, coal-industry wages in the United States were from three to seven times higher than in the EU. However, advanced technology allowed American mines to outcompete coal mines elsewhere. Even if the protectionists used wage rates rather than unit wage costs, the fact was that wages in Europe increased more rapidly from 1950 to 1958 than wages in the United States. For instance, during that period market wages in America rose 5 percent, while they increased by 8 percent in the EU.[25]

The House Ways and Means Committee began hearings on the Kennedy bill in early March. The president, anticipating a tough fight in the committee, had called Wilbur Mills, its chairman, to the White House in late January. The Arkansas Democrat did not commit himself to the bill then, but promised the president to keep an open mind.[26]

On March 12 Secretary of Commerce Hodges spent the whole day testifying before the House Ways and Means Committee. He read a fifty-nine-page statement and illustrated it with fifteen charts. Hodges emphasized that this legislation was of paramount importance as an instrument of foreign policy and national security. He asserted that the Kennedy bill would also strengthen the national economy. Republican Congressman John Byrnes of Wisconsin remained unimpressed with Hodges's presentation. Byrnes predicted major revisions in the bill and accused Hodges of statistical manipulation. The Wisconsin Republican wanted to know why the EU maintained a 22 percent tariff on U.S. autos while the U.S. tariff on autos was only 6.5 percent. Byrnes asserted that before a new trade bill was passed, these inequities should be remedied.[27]

The day after Hodges's testimony, Arthur Goldberg the secretary of labor, told the committee that the tariff cuts would spur a net gain in jobs. The secretary of labor admitted that 90,000 workers would lose their jobs in five years. However, he pointed out that 4 million jobs were already dependent on exports and imports and that 150,000 new jobs would be created with every billion dollars of new exports. Ball spoke after Goldberg, but he was immediately attacked by Republican Steven Derounian of New York for being a member of a law firm that represented foreign clients, including the European Coal and Steel Community.[28]

On March 15 it was the turn of Secretary of the Treasury Dillon to testify before the House Ways and Means Committee. He declared that since incomes in Europe had risen, tariff reductions would increase American exports and the American trade surplus would increase. He declared that "conditions now evident, and likely to persist for a number of years, make it more likely, however, that American exports to Western Europe would rise by a greater percentage than the exports of Western European countries to the United States."[29]

Industry generally supported the Trade Expansion Act except for textiles and glass. While the hearings were being conducted in the House committee, Kennedy invoked the escape-clause provision of the existing RTA and ordered tariff increases for carpets and glass recommended by the Tariff Commission. However, he rejected the Tariff Commission's recommendation to increase tariffs on ceramic mosaic tile and baseball gloves. This was the first time the president used the escape clause, and he could not have done so at a better time. Though he rationalized his actions on the basis that Belgian glass and textiles were harmful to American industry, he clearly softened the opposition of both the textile and the glass industry to his trade plan, especially after a White House spokesperson said that this showed that the president was serious about using the escape clause and would continue to do the same in the new bill.[30]

Though the action on carpet and glass eased domestic opposition to the trade act, the Belgian trade minister called it "a political blunder that risked compromising past and future trade agreements." The EU retaliated by raising tariffs on comparable amounts of U.S. exports of five other products.[31]

Kennedy realized that the Europeans probably would retaliate for his implementation of the escape-clause provision, but it was more important for him at the time to show both the textile and the glass industry that safeguards remained in place to protect them. About ten days after the president's action, the American Cotton Manufacturers Institute unanimously approved a resolution endorsing the Trade Expansion Act.[32]

As the House Ways and Means Committee prepared to vote on the Trade Expansion Act, Byrnes, the second-ranking Republican on the committee and the party's expert on taxes, tariffs, and trade, asserted that the trade bill needed revision before it could get the bipartisan support essential for passage. Specifically, Byrnes opposed the trade-adjustment provision, claiming that it should be used as a last resort only after increased tariffs failed to relieve the stress of producers. Byrnes suggested that the Tariff Commission should be given continued authority to hold hearings and recommend to the president tariff increases to help domestic industry. Under the new bill the Tariff Commission had fact-finding authority only.[33]

The Trade Expansion Act's most controversial provision dealt with giving the president special authority to eliminate tariffs when the United States and the EU accounted for 80 percent of world exports. This provision was incorporated into the bill to give the United States maximum flexibility in responding to developments in Europe, and few trade experts believed that it would ever be implemented. However, the provision was criticized by EU members, who viewed it as a threat to their common external tariff. Hodges had testified that U.S. exports that qualified under the 80 percent provision totaled $8.8 billion, as compared with $1.8 billion in imports. This strong net export position of the United States made Europeans wary of American motives in supporting the provision. Given these facts by the secretary of commerce, one would believe that there would be no objections to this provision in the Congress. However, Byrnes made it clear that he wanted this provision revised also. He declared that the authority to reduce tariffs to zero should be limited in such a way as to protect U.S. products that accounted for less than 30 percent of world exports.[34]

The debate on the 80 percent authority also centered on its geographical composition. Ball, supporting the administration's position, wanted it to include only the United States and the EU. Since Great Britain was not a member of the EU at the time, margarine and aircraft would be the only products the 80 percent authority covered. However, Representative Henry Reuss of Wisconsin and Senator Paul Douglas of Illinois offered an amendment to expand the area of the 80 percent authority to include the seven additional countries of the European Free Trade Association. Despite administration opposition, the amendment would eventually be passed in the Senate, only to be eliminated in the Conference Committee.[35]

On May 10 the House Ways and Means Committee, pressured by the American Farm Bureau Federation, approved an amendment to the Trade Expansion Act that prohibited tariff-reduction concessions to countries maintaining nontariff barriers against entry of American goods. This amendment was aimed mainly at a system of variable import fees being established by the EU. The fees were to equalize prices of imported and homegrown farm commodities. The administration accepted the amendment reluctantly, hoping that it would eventually break down agricultural export barriers.[36]

Kennedy was becoming concerned about the amendments to the Trade Expansion Act that were being offered in the House Ways and Means Committee. On May 17, in a speech made to the National Conference on United States Trade Policy, the president warned that crippling revisions in his trade bill could undo all the achievements of the United States in building the great Atlantic community. On that same day the committee upheld a key part of the bill when it passed the adjustment assistance provision, but at the same time it denied most-favored-nation treatment to Communist Poland and Yugoslavia. The president and his advisers were opposed to this amendment and would successfully work to have it rescinded in the Senate.[37]

On June 4 the House Ways and Means Committee finally approved the Trade Expansion Act by a vote of 20 to 5. All 15 Democrats and 5 Republicans decided to give the president all the powers he requested, including the adjustment assistance provision. However, before the bill reached the House Rules Committee, several amendments were offered. Byrnes wanted a substitute bill without the provision for adjustment assistance, but it was defeated handily. Republican Howard Baker of Tennessee proposed an amendment, at the last minute that would authorize Congress to override the president by a majority vote of both houses in escape-clause cases. If the president failed to implement the escape-clause provision and raise tariffs to protect vulnerable American industries, the Congress could impose the escape clause. Congress had the same power under the old RTA, but needed a two-thirds vote of both houses. The Baker amendment was approved, and the bill was sent to the House Rules Committee.[38]

On June 26 the House Rules Committee by a vote of 8 to 7 agreed to send the bill to the House floor under closed rules. This procedure prohibited filibusters or adding any additional amendments to the bill on the House floor. The protectionists now would have to wait until the bill reached the Senate before additional amendments could be added.[39]

Finally, on June 28, after a Republican substitute bill calling for a one-year extension of the RTA was voted down 253 to 171, the House passed the Trade Expansion Act by a vote of 298 to 125. The Democrats provided 218 of the affirmative votes, and they were joined by 80 Republicans. Only 35 Democrats and 90 Republicans voted against it.[40]

The Senate Finance Committee opened hearings on the trade bill on July 31. A group of independent oil operators led by Harold Decker of Houston, Texas, criticized the Trade Expansion Act, declaring that oil imports were hurting their industry. Decker wanted oil imports limited to 14 percent of domestic crude production. He claimed that the health of the petroleum industry had been steadily declining since 1956. Senator Prescott Bush offered an amendment calling for thirty-seven changes in the Kennedy trade bill. He wanted to eliminate the section of the bill permitting the president to cut to zero any tariff of 5 percent or less. He also called for restoring the original peril-point procedure under which the Tariff Commission had determined the extent to which a duty could be cut without causing injury before trade negotiations began.[41]

Kennedy received bipartisan support for his liberal trade bill. On August 13 Herter, a Republican who had succeeded John Foster Dulles as secretary of state in 1959, testified before the Senate Finance Committee that the Trade Expansion Act was the bare minimum necessary for the United States to compete in the world economic arena. He warned the committee that if the act failed to pass, many European governments would no longer take the U.S. commitment to lower tariffs seriously. He echoed the president in emphasizing that the United States must exercise economic leadership or the world would revert to the foolish restrictive trade policies of the past.[42]

From the time the bill left the House Ways and Means Committee until it reached the Senate Finance Committee, Kennedy and his advisers worked to have the most-favored-nation treatment restored to Poland and Yugoslavia. Ball, the last person to be queried by the Finance Committee, spent seven hours answering questions. He argued successfully that both Yugoslavia and Poland traded extensively with the West, and any attempt to deny them most-favored-nation treatment would drive both countries into the arms of Russia. On August 23, a week after Ball's testimony, the Senate Finance Committee rescinded the House provision and restored most-favored-nation status to both Poland and Yugoslavia.[43]

On September 14 the Senate Finance Committee voted 17 to 0 to pass the Trade Expansion Act. Five days later the full Senate voted 78 to 8 in favor of the bill. Kennedy had the support of 56 Democrats and 22 Republicans, while only 1 Democrat and 7 Republicans voted against the bill. The president had his biggest victory of the 87th Congress, as all his recommendations were carried out. As under the RTA, he could reduce any tariff by as much as 50 percent, but the new act now empowered the president to cut tariffs by as much as 100 percent on goods exported mainly by the United States and the EU. Such goods would have to constitute 80 percent or more of world trade in the goods. He could also repeal existing duties on all commodities if the present rate was 5 percent or less of value. His revision of both the peril-point and the escape clauses and his entire adjustment assistance program remained intact.[44]

On September 26 the Conference Committee met to reconcile minor differences between the House and Senate versions. The House conferees, led by Mills, insisted on restoring the House provision denying both Poland and Yugoslavia most-favored-nation status. The Senate members and the president, not wishing to jeopardize the rest of the bill, allowed the House to have its way.[45]

When the president signed the bill on October 11, 1962, he said, "By means of agreements authorized by the act, we can move forward to partnership with the nations of the Atlantic Community." In addition, he promised the leaders of both Poland and Yugoslavia that he would ask Congress, in the following year, to grant them most-favored-nation status.[46]

Members of the Congress did not want the bill administered by the secretary of state. Many believed that the conduct of foreign and trade policy should be carried out by separate entities to eliminate mutual influence. The House Ways and Means Committee created a new position called the special representative for trade negotiations. This special representative would replace the secretary of state in administering the Trade Expansion Act. On November 15 Kennedy made Herter the first special representative for trade negotiations. The Republican former secretary of state was instrumental in helping the Democratic president in getting his trade bill through Congress, and he was both liked and respected in international circles.[47]

European reaction to the Trade Expansion Act was generally positive, especially since it included the linear tariff-cutting authority and the adjustment assistance alternative to the unpopular escape clause. Only two days after Senate passage, the EU announced that it was ready to negotiate tariff cuts with the United States now that Kennedy had been given new authority to reduce tariffs across the board. However, some in the European press remained skeptical about the U.S. commitment to liberal trade. For example, Pierre Drouin, writing in *Le Monde* in September 1962, described the RTA program of the Roosevelt administration as a major success. He claimed that the Trade Expansion Act would certainly help the United States, but questioned whether the EU would benefit from it. The *Economist*, the British weekly, called the Kennedy trade bill the best trade legislation passed by Congress since 1934. However, it also questioned Kennedy's support of liberal trade. The British paper declared that Europeans were not blind to the protectionist actions taken by the American president outside the bill in order to assure its passage, for example, the American promotion of the international agreement limiting exports of cotton textiles and then the tariff increases on Belgian carpets and glass.[48]

In November 1962 the United States recommended to GATT that a ministerial meeting be convened for early 1963 to discuss the rules for tariff reductions. In December 1962 a GATT working party was established to prepare the way for the meeting that began the initial phase of what became known as the Kennedy Round. The groundwork for the Kennedy Round began in May 1963 at a ministerial meeting in Geneva, but the actual Kennedy Round negotiations started in May 1964 and lasted until the signing of the final agreement on June 30, 1967.[49]

THE KENNEDY ROUND

A GATT ministerial meeting consisting of six hundred delegates from fifty countries convened on May 16, 1963, in Geneva to determine the agenda for the upcoming Kennedy Round. These GATT negotiations were named after President

Kennedy because it was he who pushed through Congress the Trade Expansion Act that enabled the United States to participate. A negotiating committee was established to determine the rules and conduct of the negotiations. The committee placed three items on the agenda to be discussed and hopefully resolved at this preliminary meeting. They included expanding trade with developing nations, reducing agricultural rates, and rules for tariff cutting.[50]

The developed nations, led by the United States, passed a resolution reducing export barriers for less developed nations and promising that the less developed countries were not obligated to reciprocate. The resolution, agreed to in the May 1963 ministerial meeting, was criticized by Raul Prebisch, the secretary-general of the United Nations Conference on Trade and Development. He declared that lower trade barriers should be only the beginning, and that a complete economic overhaul to reduce the inequities between the rich and poor countries should be the goal of GATT. Eric Wyndham White, director-general of GATT and head of its Secretariat since GATT's beginning in 1948, echoed Prebisch when he said that if the developed nations were unable to go beyond lower trade barriers, less developed nations would see no need to join the GATT.[51]

The U.S. delegation, led by Herter and consisting of his deputy William Gossett, seven assistants and deputy assistants, and ten other senior advisers, arrived in Geneva on May 14. Herter demanded that the EU agree to equitable tariff and trade arrangements for agricultural goods. The new special representative for trade negotiations hoped to include agricultural products to the maximum extent possible in the automatic linear reduction formula adopted. However, Eugene Schaus, chairman of the EU's Council of Ministers and Luxembourg's foreign minister, refused to accept the idea of equal linear cuts for agriculture. He insisted on leaving the details of agricultural reductions for the start of the Kennedy Round in 1964.[52]

Though Herter was willing to leave the discussion of agricultural reductions for a later date, he wanted to negotiate a general rule for tariff cuts before the ministerial meetings ended on May 21. Herter was insisting on the linear formula in the Trade Expansion Act that all tariffs be reduced by 50 percent across the board. The EU opposed the American plan and suggested an alternative plan calling for tariff harmonization. All tariffs would be lowered halfway from their present levels to target levels, tentatively set at 10 percent for manufacturing, 5 percent for semimanufacturing, and 0 percent for raw materials. According to EU representatives, most EU tariffs were in the medium range of 10 to 20 percent, while U.S. tariffs were more widely dispersed. For example, some American tariff rates were at a low 10 to 20 percent, but many others ranged from 30 to 50 percent, and some were even 100 percent. If the EU adopted the American plan, a EU tariff, after a 50 percent cut, would be uniformly low, while the same 50 percent reduction for many American goods would still afford the United States a good deal of protection. The Council of Ministers of the EU endorsed its tariff-harmonization plan in Brussels on May 9, 1963, only one week prior to the Geneva ministerial meeting.[53]

Herter refused to accept to the EU plan, claiming that the average cuts would amount to a 10 to 12 percent reduction at most. Moderate tariffs would be subject to little or no reduction and high tariffs to large cuts. Thus the EU would end up doing less tariff cutting than the United States. The American trade representative blamed the French for pushing the tariff-harmonization plan. There was little question that President Charles de Gaulle of France was cool to the idea of a freer Atlantic economy that included Great Britain and the United States. The French president wanted to restrict the EU to continental Europe, which was politically, militarily, and economically dominated by France. He did not trust the United States to defend Europe and believed that Great Britain was too closely allied to the United States. The French president preferred to concentrate on expanding trade within the EU, while Great Britain, the United States, and West Germany sought global reduction of tariffs to further their overseas trading interests.[54]

The tariff-cutting dispute between the United States and the EU threatened to wreck the Kennedy Round before it even began. On Monday, May 20, Ludwig Erhard, the German economics minister, proposed a compromise to Herter that became known as the "Erhard compromise." It accepted the linear approach as the general rule for tariff cuts, but superimposed an automatic formula for reducing tariff disparities. Erhard wanted to leave the formula concerning the disparity rule for later discussion; he wanted the Americans to agree to the disparity principle that would allow the conference to end on a positive note. Herter rejected the compromise, emphasizing that all tariff negotiations should be based on a plan of substantial and equal linear reductions, and he criticized the EU's proposal of accepting equal linear cuts only where disparities did not exist. The United States was unwilling to accept any compromise that would require it to make deeper reductions when disparities existed.[55]

A compromise on a tariff-reduction formula was finally agreed to on May 21. It concluded that tariff negotiations should be based on a plan of substantial equal linear reductions "with a bare minimum of exceptions." In cases where "significant disparities" existed in tariff levels, the tariff cuts would be based on special rules of "general and automatic application." Herter agreed to accept the compromise only if the word "significant" was placed before "disparities." In other words, the disparities had to be meaningful in order to apply the rules of "general and automatic application." Exactly how "significant" was defined was left for later discussion.[56]

The GATT ministerial conference that established the foundation for the Kennedy Round ended on May 22, 1963. The participants agreed to the following: (1) The Kennedy Round on trade liberalization should begin on May 4, 1964, and should be based on the most-favored-nation principle. (2) The Kennedy Round trade negotiations should cover all classes of products, agriculture and nonagriculture. (3) The Kennedy Round talks should deal with both tariff and nontariff barriers. Some of the nontariff barriers included border taxes, antidumping regulations, and the American Selling Price, which will be discussed later in this chapter. (4) The Kennedy Round tariff negotiations should be based on equal linear-style reductions with a bare minimum of exceptions.[57]

During July 1963 Herter traveled around Europe to discuss the importance of the upcoming Kennedy Round. On July 16 the French government demanded that the United States reduce its high tariffs by more than the general average of EU cuts.[58] On July 18 Herter conferred in Bonn with Chancellor Konrad Adenauer, thanking the West German leader for his support of liberal trade. After stops in Italy and London, Herter returned to the United States on July 24 confident that he had been successful in selling the American position on trade liberalization.[59]

On September 17 Herter announced that the entire U.S. tariff list, consisting of 6,000 items, with fewer than 10 exceptions, would be subject to tariff cuts of up to 50 percent. American industry would be given four months to persuade the government to make further exemptions in hearings that would begin on December 2, 1963. Concerned American businesses had until November 20 to file requests to testify on the tariff list before the Trade Information Committee or the Tariff Commission. From December 1963 to March 1964, 1,500 witnesses appeared before or submitted statements to the Tariff Commission, and another 1,000 gave information to the Trade Information Committee. The next step was for the Tariff Commission to advise the president on the impact of the tariff cuts. Whatever the Tariff Commission told the president remained secret, except on 15 escape-clause cases where the commission found injury caused by imports. However, the president did not increase tariffs or take other remedial action on these cases. However, in cases where no recent improvement was found, such as umbrella frames, baseball gloves, briar pipes, and straight pins, the Trade Expansion Act mandatorily excluded any tariff cut in the Kennedy Round.[60]

On November 20, 1963, Herter assured American agricultural interests that the United States would not make concessions on industrial products unless the EU agreed to negotiate in good faith on agricultural items. Two days later President Kennedy was assassinated in Dallas and Vice President Johnson became president. The new president supported the Kennedy Round enthusiastically; he immediately denied rumors that the talks would be delayed until after the 1964 presidential election.[61]

The disparity issue was finally settled on December 19 when it was agreed that a tariff difference would get disparity identification if it qualified after being tested against four criteria: (1) There would be a disparity if a high tariff was twice as much as the low tariff and the difference between the two was at least ten percentage points. (2) There would be no disparity if a country with a low tariff rate did not import a product from a country with a high tariff rate. (3) A disparity would not apply if a EU country supplied a substantial portion of imports to high tariff countries. (4) A disparity would not apply if a low-tariff country did not produce a good that had a high tariff in a country that produced it.[62]

The Kennedy Round officially opened on May 4, 1964, in Geneva. Herter, who would travel back and forth to Geneva now had two deputies to help him. When Gossett had resigned in June 1963, Herter had appointed William Roth, a liberal Democratic businessman from California who would back up Herter in Washington, and W. Michael Blumenthal, who would handle the day-to-day negotiations in Geneva. Blumenthal had served as a U.S. negotiator in the International Coffee Agreement.[63]

On the first day of business in Geneva, Herter made an appeal to the delegates to concentrate on their work. He read a brief statement from President Johnson that said, "Your meetings exemplify the hope and commitment of our late President to bring together the nations of the world in peaceful pursuits. I believe, as he did, in the necessity of success in your work."[64] Shortly after his speech, the delegates voted unanimously to adopt two issues: (1) They confirmed the 50 percent rate as the working hypothesis for the linear cut. (2) They would submit an exceptions list of negotiable products by September 10. This list would include all items not offered for the 50 percent reduction, and it would apply to nonagricultural goods only. The lists were delayed purposefully until November 16, after governments in both the United States and the United Kingdom had held their national elections.[65]

During the 1964 presidential campaign William E. Miller, the Republican vice-presidential candidate, running with Barry Goldwater against the Democratic candidates Lyndon Johnson and Hubert Humphrey, attacked the Johnson administration's support of 50 percent tariff cuts while speaking to an Indiana audience. He said:

Of course Senator Goldwater and I have sympathy for the oppressed abroad, but we also have sympathy for you. We want to see you working and now the Administration wants a 50 percent reduction in tariffs so more foreign made goods can flood our markets. This makes less than little sense. This reduction is wrong in theory and in practice. We have seen how many industries have been affected adversely; how many jobs have been lost; how many plants have been closed from foreign competition.[66]

One week later Secretary of State Rusk denounced the Miller statement, declaring that if the Kennedy Round succeeded, it would provide more jobs both abroad and in the United States.[67]

On November 16 the countries presented in sealed envelopes their exceptions lists containing items not subjected to the 50 percent tariff reductions. The size of the lists were not comparable. Most EFTA countries claimed no exceptions. The U.S. list was quite short—less than 10 percent of dutiable nonagricultural imports, and petroleum represented 25 percent of these imports. Though the U.S. duty on petroleum was only 4 percent, a quota kept most foreign petroleum from entering the United States for national security reasons. The exceptions list for Japan and the EU made up 25 percent of their trade list. Of items not on the exceptions lists, 75 percent were industrial goods. The EU refused to subject agricultural goods to the 50 percent tariff cuts. In May 1965 Herter, speaking before the Metropolitan Washington Board of Trade, criticized the EU's large exceptions list. He said, "It is a fact that some of its negotiating partners, including the U.S., consider this list to be overly large."[68]

On November 18, about two weeks after Johnson's landslide victory over Goldwater, Johnson spoke to the National Foreign Trade Council, affirming his strong stand in favor of the Kennedy Round negotiations. The president was facing a decision on whether to endanger the talks by insisting on major agricultural concessions from the EU that it was not willing to grant, or to compromise on the agricultural sector in order to gain industrial tariff reductions.[69]

The United States, with the broadest geographic trade interests, established the largest delegation of almost forty members under Blumenthal and his deputy James Lewis, a foreign service officer from the Cordell Hull era. The American delegation was divided into five country negotiating teams responsible for the EU, the EFTA, Canada and Commonwealth countries, Japan, and developing countries. Each team had a chairman, technical secretary, and several commodity or country specialists from other executive agencies and the Tariff Commission. On occasion, several congressional members made visits to Geneva to observe and comment, the most active being Congressman Thomas B. Curtis of Missouri.[70]

On July 1, 1965, a EU internal crisis began involving the French that threatened the Kennedy Round negotiations. Briefly, the cause of the crisis was an invitation by the EU's Council of Ministers in December 1964, to the EU Commission to submit proposals by March 31, 1965, on financing a Common Agricultural Policy (CAP) and increasing the power of the European Parliament in the budget-making process for the period 1965-1970. The commission's proposal antagonized the French, who opposed giving the European Parliament more budget-making power. From July 5 until the end of the year, the French refused to participate in the Geneva discussions, which were recessed for the summer holidays. Though the United States was not overly concerned at the moment, it reminded its European and world allies that its negotiating authority granted in the Trade Expansion Act would expire on June 30, 1967.[71]

The French crisis was resolved at the end of January, 1966, and the French delegates once again participated in the Kennedy Round. Briefly, France claimed the right to veto a majority decision when critical French interests were at stake. The other five EU countries, not necessarily agreeing, but wanting to concentrate on more important political and economic issues, refused to challenge the French government on the matter.[72]

By the spring of 1966 the Kennedy Round negotiations had almost come to a halt. No progress had yet been made on the agricultural front, nor were there any firm agreements in some of the major nonagricultural areas such as chemicals. Both Blumenthal and Herter warned that at the current pace no agreement would be reached by June 30, 1967. Blumenthal spoke before the Institute for International Relations in Rome on March 12 and declared that "failure to make decisions will be a decision to fail."[73] In April Herter, speaking before a Senate subcommittee, believed that the talks had accomplished nothing of substance and said that he remained uncertain about whether the Kennedy Round could be completed by the June, 1967 deadline.[74]

The Trade Expansion Act deadline became an issue in the summer of 1966. Some supporters in the Congress like Representative Wayne Hays of Ohio urged Johnson to seek an extension of the Trade Expansion Act deadline. The Kennedy Round, in his opinion, could not be completed in a year's time at the current pace. However, when Herter testified before a congressional committee in August, he refused to ask for an extension. He detected a growing surge of protectionism in the country due to the failure of the current talks. In his opinion, Congress was in no mood to vote favorably on the issue. Herter believed that enough time remained for an agreement, and a firm deadline would hasten rather than retard the negotiations. In any event, the other nations at Geneva never pressed the Americans to extend the June 30, 1967 deadline.[75]

A major disagreement between the United States and the EU dealt with the American Selling Price (ASP). The United States wanted tariff reductions for chemicals, but the EU refused unless the United States first agreed to abolish its ASP. The United States used the ASP to assess duties on certain benzenoid chemicals and a few other products. When a good was imported into the United States, the ASP of a similar American good was used to determine the duty charged. Since the ASP was considerably higher than the price of the imported good, the import duties were much higher than they would have been if the foreign price had been used. In March 1966, when Blumenthal declared that the United States was prepared to negotiate on the ASP, he caused an uproar in both the chemical industry, which insisted on keeping the ASP, and the Senate. Democratic Senator Abraham Ribicoff of Connecticut and twelve of his colleagues claimed that Blumenthal lacked the legislative authority to enter into any agreement with the EU involving an exchange of additional EU tariff reductions for abolition of the ASP. The Senate flexed its muscle by passing Senate Concurrent Resolution 83 on June 29, 1966, declaring that the ASP could not be altered in any way without the prior consent of Congress. When chemical talks were suspended, Herter condemned the resolution as an impediment to the success of the Kennedy Round.[76]

In September 1966 the most pressing sector was agriculture. The EU had submitted its offers at the end of July, and they were examined item by item. Both Blumenthal and Herter were unhappy over the initial offers of the EU. The U.S. Department of Agriculture declared that EU agricultural policy would prove counterproductive because it would stimulate agricultural production in member countries and build higher tariff walls against outside products. The United States wanted to export wheat, feed grain, oil seeds, citrus, poultry, and tobacco to the EU. In return, the United States was willing to negotiate a gradual reduction of dairy, rice, sugar, cotton, meat, and wool tariffs, all of which were protected in the United States. However, the EU introduced its concept known as the *montant de soutien*—negotiations based on a ceiling rather than a reduction. The EU's position on agriculture was based on the sacrosanct Common Agricultural Policy (CAP) where stabilization was more important than trade liberalization, and that commodity arrangements and market sharing were the best way of dealing with agricultural problems.[77]

Key farm groups in the United States were so upset with the lack of progress on agricultural tariff reductions that they wanted to terminate the Kennedy Round. Kennedy had promised farmers during the passage of the Trade Expansion Act in 1962 that American farm products would have access to the European market. In fact, the American Farm Bureau supported the Trade Expansion Act only after it was amended to give firm commitments to American farmers. The Senate passed a resolution in 1963 sponsored by Democratic Senator Hubert Humphrey of Minnesota and Senate Republican Minority Leader Everett McKinley Dirksen of

Illinois, with the House concurring, that the U.S. negotiators obtain assurances that American agriculture would have access to the European market. Progress in agriculture was linked to progress in other areas.[78]

Intensive nongrain agricultural negotiations continued through the fall and winter of 1966. A series of bilateral bargaining sessions between the United States and the EU over each point of reduction occurred into the spring of 1967. Concessions were granted on $656 million of the $1,203 million of imports from the United States by linear countries such as the United Kingdom, Japan, and the members of the EU and the EFTA.[79]

In the nongrain area of negotiations the United States became the chief demander of concessions, and the discussions were carried out on a bilateral basis. However, talks in the grain area were multilateral since Argentina, Australia, Canada, and the United States were all exporters, while the United Kingdom, Japan, and the EFTA were importers. EU countries were both importers and exporters of grain. For example, the French exported soft wheat, while all countries in the EU imported hard wheat and feed grain.[80] The negotiators were seeking agreement on regulating trade in wheat and other grains, and lower tariffs were not the key issue. Instead, exporters of grain wanted a fair share of the highly protected EU market and the establishment of minimum prices. The United States wanted to export 17 million tons of grain a year to the EU or have access to 14 percent of its market while the EU had promised only 10 percent. The American negotiators believed that importers like the EU, the United Kingdom, and Japan never would bind (make a commitment that a rate of duty on a product will not be increased) access for imports in order to restrain domestic producers. In fact, importers appeared determined to raise their food output in order to become self-sufficient and to protect their balance of payments.[81]

Though the United States failed to gain what it felt was a fair share of the EU's market in the grain negotiations, it was successful in providing a joint food-aid plan for the poorer countries as part of the grain deal. The American negotiators wanted the wealthier nations to give 10 million tons of grain or food equivalent per year, independent of commercial market conditions, to poorer countries. The combined food aid would be furnished by both food exporters and importers. The food-aid principle was important to the United States as a means of guaranteeing the EU's agricultural market. If the EU and other importers of food participated in the program and shipped grain to poor countries, it would open the way for the United States to export more grain to the EU. Since the plan benefitted exporters of food, the importers like Japan, the Netherlands, the United Kingdom, and West Germany all opposed it. Nonetheless, the United States was able to negotiate an agreement for food aid with the major participants in Geneva. The program provided for a total aid of 4.5 million tons of wheat or an equivalent annually for a period of three years. Japan had the option of giving other aid in substitution for grains.[82]

On December 31, 1966, Herter died of a heart attack at the age of seventy-one. Johnson appointed Herter's chief assistant in the United States, William Roth, as the new special representative for trade negotiations. Roth's first job was to assure certain important members of the Congress that the negotiations were on track. For example, in January 1967 Congressman Curtis worried that the talks were moving too slowly, while Democratic Senator Russell Long of Louisiana, chairman of the Senate Finance Committee and majority whip, declared that the American delegation should take a tough stand and insist on a "quid pro quo" from those countries wanting favors from the United States. On March 10 Roth testified before Long's Senate Finance Committee to assure all in attendance that the United States firmly believed in reciprocity and would work for an equitable trade agreement.[83]

Johnson aided the Kennedy Round negotiations when on January 11 he announced that he would rescind the high tariffs on watches and sheet glass. Both had been raised under the escape-clause provision after the Tariff Commission had declared that these industries had needed protection. The Swiss and Belgian governments had protested the watch and sheet-glass tariff increases in 1954 and 1962, respectively. Now in 1967 the Tariff Commission no longer saw a threat to these industries, and the tariffs were rolled back to their earlier levels. Twelve days later, on January 23, the president once again demonstrated his commitment to liberal trade when he declared in his economic message to Congress that the world must not lose the opportunity to lower trade barriers.[84]

In early February Roth announced that he would travel to Europe to try to speed up the negotiations. The new special representative for trade negotiations set March 26 for the conclusion of the Kennedy Round. He claimed that a later date would leave little time to deal with the administrative details before the Trade Expansion Act expired. He expected that the negotiations would be difficult, but he was respected by the Europeans, who were impressed with his business-oriented and nonpolitical approach to trade liberalization.[85]

Roth's March 26 deadline was unrealistic, as the grain accords held negotiations up until May 10. On May 11 the EU announced that it had reached an agreement with the United States on the grain accords, mentioned earlier, and that other EU tariff reductions were conditional on the U.S. Congress repealing the ASP.[86] By May 15 fifty countries accounting for 80 percent of world trade agreed to an average tariff reduction of one-third. Roth pointed out that the United States had given or received concessions on products involving $16 billion of American trade. The United States also had won concessions on agricultural products accounting for $2 billion of American exports, of which $650 million were in grains.[87]

The nations agreed that the tariff reductions would be implemented in five annual stages, as specified in the Trade Expansion Act. The United States was prepared to make its first two cuts on January 1, 1968, and January 1, 1969. However, the EU decided on July 1, 1968, as the date for the final alignment of its members' tariffs to the common external tariff, and not wanting to revise tariffs three times between January 1, 1968, and January 1, 1969, the EU proposed to make the first two Kennedy Round cuts on July 1, 1968, the first reduction six months later than that of the United States, and the second cut six months earlier. The final three stages of the Kennedy Round cuts would be made simultaneously by all the nations on January 1 of 1970, 1971, and 1972.[88]

On June 30, 1967, forty-six nations signed the final act of the Kennedy Round.

The reductions affected 70 percent of industrial countries' dutiable imports; two-thirds of them were 50 percent or more, and one-fifth of them 25 to 50 percent. After reading a congratulatory wire from President Johnson hailing the agreement, Blumenthal signed the accord for the United States.[89]

The Kennedy Round was the most important tariff-reducing and trade-liberalization agreement up to that time. It would be surpassed only by the Tokyo and the Uruguay accords of the 1970s and 1990s. The major accomplishment of the Kennedy Round was the average tariff reduction of 36 to 39 percent by all major industrial countries. In some areas like iron and steel and textiles, tariff reduction was small. For example, the U.S. government cut tariffs on wearing and cotton apparel and most types of footwear modestly and refused any reductions on woolen goods. The woolen-goods industry was placed on the American exceptions list when the domestic wool industry complained that it was suffering from imports from Japan, Italy, and Great Britain. The tariff on leather goods was reduced only from 10 to 8.5 percent.[90]

Most of the tariff cuts came in the nonagricultural areas. The largest cuts were in machinery, transportation equipment, and chemicals. For instance, 91 percent of the machinery, 93 percent of chemicals, 92 percent of pulp and paper, 83 percent of raw materials and fuels, 81 percent of base metals other than iron and steel, and 81 percent of all other manufactures were affected by the Kennedy Round reductions. These cuts expanded world trade significantly. The dutiable non-agricultural imports of all major industrialized countries, after the final rates were in effect, would be expected to increase by about 10 percent above the level that would have been reached without the Kennedy Round reductions, or by $2 billion to $3 billion per year based on the 1964 levels of trade. U.S. trade with other industrial nations in nonagricultural areas, based on 1964 levels of trade, could be expected to increase by about $500 to $600 million per year for imports and exports.[91]

The Kennedy Round agricultural negotiations were not as successful as those in the nonagricultural areas. In the case of tropical products such as coffee, cocoa, bananas, tea, and tropical oilseeds, $2.6 billion was dutiable, but only $1.1 billion was subject to duty reduction, and two-thirds of these products were reduced by less than 50 percent. In the nontropical category only $3.6 billion out of $7.5 billion of dutiable imports was subject to duty reduction, and over half of these reductions were for 50 percent or less. Negotiations in the special groups on meats and dairy products were unproductive. The joint-food aid commitment, in the grain negotiations, proved to be the most important part of the agricultural talks.[92]

In exchange for additional tariff reductions, the U.S. negotiators made two important nontariff commitments at the Kennedy Round. The first commitment was to eliminate the ASP, which was discussed earlier and the other was to participate in a new GATT antidumping code. The antidumping agreement stated the procedure for countries to take before applying special duties based on the assertion that imports were entering the country at less than fair value, causing injury to domestic producers. Blumenthal and Roth prepared an international antidumping code in early 1967. It was a balanced agreement that brought national policies into closer harmony. The most important change in the United States Antidumping Act of 1921 regulations agreed to was a maximum of ninety days for making appraisement. The United States had been criticized for its long investigations of alleged dumpings and its practice of withholding appraisement during the investigation. When a country withheld appraisement, it delayed the determination of customs duties until the antidumping investigation was completed. Imports could be released under bond pending appraisement, but the amount of duty to be paid remained uncertain.[93]

Just as Congress criticized the president for exceeding his negotiating authority in agreeing to eliminate the ASP, it now attacked him for agreeing to an antidumping code. In 1968 Congress passed legislation stating that the Anti-dumping Act of 1921 should take precedence over the antidumping code of the Kennedy Round. The Antidumping Act of 1921 was part of the Emergency Tariff Act, and it empowered the U.S. International Trade Commission, after protests by domestic producers, to slap duties on foreign goods.[94]

On December 16, 1967, President Johnson signed the proclamation that put the first year of the Kennedy Round into effect beginning on January 1, 1968. The president praised the Kennedy Round reductions, declaring that the average cut of 35 percent over five years would greatly benefit the American economy.[95]

Though the Johnson administration praised the Kennedy Round and was quick to take the credit for its success, there was a growing dissatisfaction in Congress with some of its results. The Congress believed that the administration had failed to obtain enough concessions for the American farmer. Congress also berated the executive for attempting to usurp the legislature's authority to deal with nontariff measures such as the ASP and the antidumping code. Congress would not eliminate the ASP until the Tokyo Round in the 1970s, and as mentioned earlier, it refused to recognize the negotiated antidumping code.[96]

Protectionist sentiment in Congress had begun to grow before the ink on the Kennedy Round agreement had dried. A range of industries, including the textile and apparel manufacturers, petitioned Congress for relief from imports. On October 30 Under Secretary of State Nicholas Katzenback, in a speech in New York City, warned that the four years of hard negotiations would be undone if the protectionists prevailed in Congress. By 1970 organized labor, which had endorsed the Kennedy Round, was arguing that a new competitive situation had made old free-trade concepts obsolete.[97]

Protectionist sentiment in the United States would resurface in the early 1970s, and Congress would try to regain some of its authority over trade policy. The Kennedy Round was the last round that did not have to be ratified by Congress. The Trade Expansion Act of 1962 gave the executive full authority to conduct tariff reductions from 1963 to 1967 without having to return to Congress for approval. As we shall see in the next few chapters, the Tokyo Round would require the Trade Reform Act of 1974 to start it and the Trade Agreements Act of 1979 to conclude it, and both the Uruguay Round and the North American Free Trade Agreement would have to be ratified by Congress.[98]

NOTES

1. Theodore Sorensen, *Kennedy* (New York: Harper and Row, 1965), pp. 410-411.

2. Ernest Preeg, *Traders and Diplomats: An Analysis of the Kennedy Round of Negotiations under the General Agreement on Tariffs and Trade* (Washington, DC: Brookings Institution, 1970), pp. 45-46.

3. *New York Times*, January 2, 1962, p. 1; Ben Seligman, "Tariffs, the Kennedy Administration, and American Politics," *Commentary* 33 (March 1962): 185.

4. Seligman, "Tariffs, the Kennedy Administration, and American Politics," p. 185.

5. *New York Times*, January 7, 1962, p. 64.

6. Ibid., January 8, 1962, p. 1. Sorensen, *Kennedy*, pp. 410-411.

7. *New York Times*, January 28, 1962, sec. 4, p. 1; Preeg, *Traders and Diplomats*, p. 44.

8. *New York Times*, January 8, 1962, p. 117.

9. Arthur Schlesinger, Jr., *A Thousand Days: John F. Kennedy in the White House* (Boston: Houghton Mifflin Company, 1965), p. 847.

10. *New York Times*, January 9, 1962, p. 6; January 26, 1962, pp. 1, 11.

11. Ibid., January 16, 1962, p. 14.

12. Ibid., January 18, 1962, p. 12.

13. Ibid., January 20, 1962, p. 1.

14. Ibid., January 21, 1962, p. 1.

15. Ibid., p. 40; *New York Times*, January 20, 1962, p. 9; January 23, 1962, p. 12; January 24, 1962, p. 8.

16. *New York Times*, January 26, 1962, pp. 1, 11; Preeg, *Traders and Diplomats*, pp. 46-47.

17. *New York Times*, January 26, 1962, p. 11.

18. "Summary of the Trade Expansion Act of 1962," *Current History* 43 (July 1962): 50-51.

19. Preeg, *Traders and Diplomats*, p. 49.

20. *New York Times*, January 26, 1962, p. 30.

21. Sorensen, *Kennedy*, p. 411.

22. *New York Times*, February 1, 1962, p. 37.

23. Preeg, *Traders and Diplomats*, p. 49; *New York Times*, February 4, 1962, sec. 4, p. 5.

24. *New York Times*, February 4, 1962, sec. 4, p. 5; March 21, 1962, p. 1.

25. Seligman, "Tariffs, the Kennedy Administration, and American Politics," p. 192.

26. *New York Times*, March 13, 1962, p. 1.

27. Ibid.; *New York Times*, March 14, 1962, p. 38.

28. *New York Times*, March 14, 1962, p. 1; *Economist*, March 17, 1962, p. 1023.

29. Preeg, *Traders and Diplomats*, p. 51.

30. *New York Times*, March 20, 1962, p. 1.

31. Preeg, *Traders and Diplomats*, p. 53.

32. *New York Times*, April 1, 1962, p. 6.

33. Ibid., May 6, 1962, p. 1.

34. Ibid.; Preeg, *Traders and Diplomats*, pp. 51-52.

35. Preeg, *Traders and Diplomats*, p. 52.

36. *New York Times*, May 11, 1962, p. 1.

37. Ibid., May 18, 1962, p. 1.

38. Ibid., June 5, 1962, p. 1; June 12, 1962, p. 1.

39. Ibid., June 27, 1962, p. 1.

40. Ibid., June 29, 1962, p. 1.

41. Ibid., August 1, 1962, p. 7; August 3, 1962, p. 7.

42. Ibid., August 14, 1962, p. 5.

43. Ibid., August 17, 1962, p. 2; August 24, 1962, p. 1.

44. Ibid., September 15, 1962, pp. 1, 10; September 20, 1962, p. 1; September 22, 1962, p. 28.

45. Ibid., September 27, 1962, p. 1.

46. Ibid., October 12, 1962, p. 20; Schlesinger, *Thousand Days*, p. 848.

47. *New York Times*, November 16, 1962, p. 1.

48. Preeg, *Traders and Diplomats*, pp. 53-54; *Economist*, September 22, 1962, p. 1099.

49. Preeg, *Traders and Diplomats*, pp. 54-57.

50. Ibid., p. 6; *New York Times*, May 17, 1963, p. 44.

51. Preeg, *Traders and Diplomats*, pp. 70-71.

52. Ibid., p. 7.

53. Ibid., pp. 3-4; *New York Times*, May 22, 1963, p. 1.

54. *New York Times*, May 19, 1963, sec. 4, p. 3; Preeg, *Traders and Diplomats*, pp. 3-4.

55. Preeg, *Traders and Diplomats*, p. 8.

56. Ibid., p. 11.

57. *New York Times*, May 23, 1963, p. 12.

58. Ibid., July 17, 1963, p. 37.

59. Ibid., July 19, 1963, p. 2; July 23, 1963, p. 11.

60. Ibid., September 18, 1963, p. 1; October 22, 1963, p. 1; Preeg, *Traders and Diplomats*, pp. 77-78.

61. *New York Times*, November 21, 1963, p. 55.

62. Ibid., December 20, 1963, p. 43.

63. Preeg, *Traders and Diplomats*, pp. 59, 81.

64. *New York Times*, May 5, 1964, p. 1; Preeg, *Traders and Diplomats*, p. 82.

65. Preeg, *Traders and Diplomats*, pp. 81-82; *New York Times*, May 6, 1964, p. 77.

66. *New York Times*, September 8, 1964, p. 14.

67. Ibid., September 15, 1964, p. 14.

68. Ibid., November 17, 1964, p. 1; Preeg, *Traders and Diplomats*, pp. 87-88, 94.

69. *New York Times*, November 19, 1964, p. 64; December 18, 1964, p. 49.

70. Preeg, *Traders and Diplomats*, p. 92.

71. Ibid., pp. 111-114; *New York Times*, July 24, 1965, p. 33.

72. Preeg, *Traders and Diplomats*, p. 122.

73. Ibid., p. 124.

74. Ibid.

75. Ibid., pp. 126-127.

76. Ibid., pp. 127-128; Patrick Low, *Trading Free: The GATT and U.S. Trade Policy* (New York: Twentieth Century Fund Press, 1993), p. 175.

77. Low, *Trading Free*, p. 180.

78. *Congressional Record*, June 25, 1963 (88th Congress), p. 11570.

79. Preeg, *Traders and Diplomats*, p. 150.

80. Ibid., p. 151.

81. Ibid., pp. 157-158; *New York Times*, April 2, 1967, sec. 4, p. 3.

82. *New York Times*, March 27, 1967, p. 49; Preeg, *Traders and Diplomats*, p. 254.

83. Preeg, *Traders and Diplomats*, p. 161; *New York Times*, January 1, 1967, p. 1.

84. *New York Times*, January 12, 1967, p. 1; Preeg, *Traders and Diplomats*, pp. 163-164.

85. Preeg, *Traders and Diplomats*, p. 178; *New York Times*, February 4, 1967, p. 31; February 15, 1967, p. 1.

86. *New York Times*, May 11, 1967, p. 1; May 12, 1967, p. 1.

87. Ibid., May 16, 1967, pp. 1, 20.

88. Preeg, *Traders and Diplomats*, pp. 199-200.

89. *New York Times*, July 1, 1967, p. 1.

90. Ibid., June 30, 1967, p. 1; Preeg, *Traders and Diplomats*, pp. 256-257.

91. Preeg, *Traders and Diplomats*, pp. 246 and 259; *New York Times*, June 30, 1967, pp. 1, 48.

92. Preeg, *Traders and Diplomats*, pp. 250-251, 258.

93. Ibid., pp. 166-167; I. M. Destler, *American Trade Politics: System under Stress* (New York: Twentieth Century Fund Press, 1986), p. 63.

94. Low, *Trading Free*, p. 174; Edward S. Kaplan and Thomas W. Ryley, *Prelude to Trade Wars: American Tariff Policy, 1890-1922* (Westport, CT: Greenwood Press, 1994), p. 101.

95. *New York Times*, November 28, 1967, p. 67; December 17, 1967, p. 20.

96. Low, *Trading Free*, p. 174.

97. Destler, *American Trade Politics*, pp. 38-39; *New York Times*, October 31, 1967, p. 59.

98. Destler, *American Trade Politics*, pp. 17-18, 67.

5

The Trade Reform Act and the Tokyo Round

THE TRADE REFORM ACT OF 1974

Between the end of the Kennedy Round in 1967 and December 1974, when the Trade Reform Act was passed, protectionist sentiment was gaining popularity in the Congress. Both the farmers and labor unions were generally unhappy with some of the Kennedy Round provisions. The farmers complained that both European and Japanese markets remained closed to many of their agricultural products, and labor protectionists, led by the AFL-CIO, lamented that imports caused high unemployment. The trade adjustment assistance program, part of the Trade Expansion Act, did nothing to help American workers because the rules to qualify for assistance were too stringent. In fact, not a single worker or firm met the requirements for help during the entire 1960s.[1]

President Richard Nixon, viewed by many as a conservative on many social and economic issues, was opposed to the protectionist sentiment that began to take root in Congress. On April 10, 1973, he challenged the Congress by sending it a comprehensive Trade Reform Act, calling for the most important changes in more than a decade in the U.S. approach to world trade. Nixon declared that the main purpose of the bill was to reduce the economic conflicts that undermined peace and stability in the world by expanding trade and prosperity for the United States and its trading partners.[2]

The bill would give the president more power over trade policy than any other president before him had had. Nixon asked for the following: (1) He wanted unlimited authority to raise, lower, or eliminate tariff duties on imports as well as to use a variety of techniques to reduce U.S. nontariff barriers in return for similar foreign actions, with either house of Congress having the right to veto the final result. (2) He called for new and more rapid procedures to help domestic industries damaged by increasing imports. Under the previous escape-clause law in the Trade Expansion Act of 1962, to get protection, an industry had to demonstrate that higher imports were the major cause of injury or threat of injury. This act would eliminate the causal link between increased imports and concessions and would require that imports be only a "substantial" cause of injury or threat of injury. (3) Nixon urged Congress to allow the president to offer the most-favored-nation principle to Communist countries, but Congress would have the right to veto any such agreement. As we shall see later, the president had already made such an agreement with the USSR. (4) Nixon wanted new powers to impose restrictions on goods from countries engaging in unfair trade practices such as limiting U.S. imports, a quota system, or subsidizing their own exports. (5) He asked Congress for new authority to impose sweeping import taxes or quotas when serious deficits in the nation's balance of payments occurred and to reduce all or most of the tariffs when the balance of payments was in surplus. (6) The president wanted congressional authority to drop tariffs to zero on most manufactured and semimanufactured goods from most developing countries in order to aid their exports and economic development.[3] The passage of the trade act would allow the President to enter into international agreements for the next five years and pave the way for the Tokyo Round of trade negotiations.

Reaction to the Nixon Trade Reform Act legislation was mixed. Most European officials welcomed the American initiative, and the chief spokesperson of the European Union declared that the bill would help make the trade climate less frigid. However, C. Fujino, president of the Mitsubishi Corporation, in a speech before the Harvard Business Club in New York City, questioned what criteria the United States would use to determine what were "fair or unfair" trade practices.[4]

Protectionist opposition to the bill came mostly from the labor unions, led by George Meany, head of the AFL-CIO. According to Meany, the Nixon trade bill did not meet the problems of trade. There was no specific machinery to regulate the flood of imports, and it did nothing to close the lucrative tax loopholes for American-based multinational corporations. Instead, Meany wanted Congress to pass the Burke-Hartke bill, a protectionist measure that would impose import quotas on goods and increase the taxation of the profits earned by American corporations abroad. The AFL-CIO president denounced the American multinational corporations as exporters of American jobs and a major cause of the growing unemployment in the manufacturing sector.[5]

On April 12 Democrat Wilbur Mills, chairman of the House Ways and Means Committee, informed the president that he supported the Trade Reform Act and would do all that he could to give the president what he wanted. However, Mills warned Nixon that there was considerable protectionist sentiment in Congress as a result of intense labor lobbying. P. DeCico, the president of the International Brotherhood of Electrical Workers, declared that any congressman who supported the Trade Reform Act instead of the protectionist Burke-Hartke bill to restrict imports would not receive any financial support from the union.[6]

The protectionists argued that the Trade Reform Act would give Nixon too much power over the regulation of trade. However, Peter Flanigan, assistant to the president for international affairs, defended the Nixon trade bill in a speech to the Financial Analysts Federation in Washington in early May 1973. He argued that the president's powers contained in the bill were not really new, but rather the renewal of the extension of powers that had been granted to presidents in the past.

Flanigan contended that the powers had been changed on the basis of experience, that tariffs had been substantially reduced under previous presidential negotiating authority, and that the scope for actual reduction was not much different from that granted to President Kennedy in 1962. In concluding, Flanigan warned that the Burke-Hartke bill pending in Congress would impose import quotas on most products and would reduce both exports and imports by $8 billion.[7]

One day after Flanigan's speech supporting the Trade Reform Act, he led a delegation of cabinet secretaries to speak before the House Ways and Means Committee on the merits of the bill. Flanigan told the members of the committee that the new trade bill would not immediately affect the U.S. balance-of-payments problem. He emphasized that the trade bill and the subsequent negotiations would lay the groundwork for more open and fair trading in the future. Many members of Congress were concerned about the balance-of-payments deficit, which would continue to grow into 1974. As we shall see later, the administration would blame imported oil for most of this deficit.[8]

Secretary of State William Rogers followed Flanigan's testimony by praising the trade bill as a major ingredient in a successful foreign policy recipe. He explained that Nixon needed the bill in order to have fruitful negotiations at the upcoming Tokyo Round. He stressed the need for new trading rules that would allow for temporary import restrictions. His main argument was that many countries, such as Japan, had the productive capacity to achieve an outpouring of exports that would disrupt other countries' economies.[9]

Secretary of Labor Peter Brennan and Commerce Secretary Frederick Dent both appeared before the committee the following day. Brennan took the opposite view to that of the labor unions and declared that imports did not cause large-scale unemployment. He noted that the United States had had a record trade deficit in 1972, while total jobs in the economy had grown by 2.6 million. He admitted that imports caused some job displacement, but maintained that adjustment problems should not be confused with large-scale unemployment. Dent pointed out that the new "safeguard" provisions in the bill would make it easier and much faster for American industries and workers damaged by imports to obtain relief.[10]

On June 18 members of the House Ways and Means Committee met with Special Trade Representative W. D. Pearce and other administration spokesmen to begin work on a draft trade bill. The committee voted 15 to 9 to exclude the press and the public from the proceedings. At the same time, Nixon sent a message to the committee stating that he would be willing to compromise on his sweeping bargaining powers in the bill, but he implored the committee to act quickly to give the administration the time it needed to prepare for the upcoming trade negotiations.[11]

Since 1933 liberal trade policies had prevailed for the most part. Now in 1973 protectionists supported by the growing trade deficits were clamoring for import quotas and other protectionist measures. In 1971 the United States had experienced a $2 billion trade deficit, which grew to $6.4 billion the following year—the first trade deficits of the century. In May 1973, with the trade bill before Congress, the deficit totaled $157.9 million, as Japan and Western Europe were now challenging

U.S. trade dominance in the world. This, combined with floating exchange rates as world-wide inflation made it difficult to stick to fixed exchange rates, the need to import expensive fuel, and the need to control food exports, made trade policy more worrisome than it had been in the 1960s. During the Kennedy years the dollar remained strong, fuel prices were low, and trade surpluses abounded. In this type of ambience protectionism in the United States had few followers.[12]

In late June 1973 I. W. Abel, head of the United Steelworkers of America, testified before the House Ways and Means Committee and made an impassioned plea on behalf of all American workers to "slow the massive flood of imports that are sweeping away jobs and industries in wholesale lots." [13] Abel, who was also chairman of the AFL-CIO's Economic Policy Committee, stated that failure to enact the Burke-Hartke bill would cause a decline in the living standards of all Americans and would leave the United States a fourth-rate industrial power.[14]

Prospects for quick passage of the Trade Reform Act dimmed by early July. Mills and other Congressional leaders declared that there was little chance of passage by the House of Representatives before the August 3 summer recess. The administration announced that with or without the bill, American representatives would attend the September GATT meeting in Tokyo.[15]

On July 12 the Nixon administration asked the House Ways and Means Committee to allow the president, without the approval of Congress, to remove two sensitive nontariff barriers. The administration wanted to permit the importation of both benzenoid chemicals and scotch whiskey. Both the American Selling Price and the "proof-gallon" method of valuation made it expensive to import both articles. In both cases Congress refused to grant the administration its request.[16]

Only four days later the protectionists suffered a major defeat when the House Ways and Means Committee rejected 16 to 6 an amendment to Nixon's Trade Reform Act offered by Democratic Congressman James Burke of Massachusetts. The amendment would have provided for quotas on imports of particular articles when foreign-produced goods accounted for as much as 15 percent of the U.S. market. After the vote a disappointed Burke informed the press that there was now little chance of enacting portions of his Burke-Hartke bill in the present session of Congress.[17]

After a brief recess in August, the House Ways and Means Committee on October 3 by a vote of 20 to 5 gave Nixon almost unlimited negotiating authority for the forthcoming international trade talks. Though the bill allowed the president to lower both tariff and nontariff barriers, subject to congressional approval, and to impose higher tariffs or even quotas on countries that maintained unjustifiable or unreasonable restrictions on U.S. goods, it failed to extend to the Soviet Union the most-favored-nation (MFN) clause that Nixon supported so enthusiastically. The committee made it clear to the administration and the Soviet government that any MFN treatment would be tied to Soviet emigration policy toward both Jews and others. This was a crushing blow to the president, who felt the need to reach out to Communist countries through trade agreements. In fact, the administration was so sensitive about denying Russia MFN status that Secretary of State Henry Kissinger asked the House leaders on October 11 to postpone the House vote because of the concern that its anti-Soviet amendment would upset discussions with the Russians on ending the Middle East crisis. (The United States and Russia were cooperating to end the 1973 Middle East war between Egypt and Israel.) The committee split over whether to deny the Soviets export credits—an amendment sponsored by Ohio Democrat Charles Vanik. The House Rules Committee would allow the Vanik Amendment when the bill came to the floor for a final vote.[18]

The brief history of what eventually became known as the Jackson-Vanik Amendment to the Trade Reform Act began in October 1972. Nixon had negotiated the East-West Trade Relations Bill with the Soviet Union. The president hoped that Russia would prove more flexible in the upcoming Strategic Arms Limitation Talks (SALT II) if he could convince Congress to change the trade law that imposed high tariffs on goods from Communist countries. He promised the Soviets that he would urge Congress to grant them MFN status. However, there was concern in the United States over Soviet emigration policies, especially the high taxes the Russian government imposed on Jewish exit visas. On March 15 Democratic Senator Henry Jackson from Washington State, with seventy-three cosponsors in the Senate, attached his amendment to the Nixon East-West Trade Relations Bill tying the grant of MFN status for the Soviet Union to Jewish emigration.[19]

In April, when Nixon finally submitted his Trade Reform Act to Congress, it included the granting of MFN status to Russia. Nixon had committed himself to helping the Russians get the same trade benefits as U.S. allies. On March 20 he convinced the Export-Import Bank to grant a loan of $202 million for the Soviet purchase of American industrial equipment, and eight days after that, a U.S.-USSR Trade Council opened in Moscow, with over three hundred American firms joining its membership.[20] When Jackson told the president that he would oppose MFN status for the Soviets unless they changed their emigration policy, the president criticized the senator and his supporters for their failure to understand the goals of his foreign policy—improved relations with the Soviet Union. Nixon complained that even after the Soviet president Leonid Brezhnev had informed Kissinger in April 1973 that Russia had suspended the exit tax on Jewish emigration, Jackson insisted on a guarantee that the Soviets would issue a minimum number of exit visas as well as ease emigration for other nationalities. The president commented that both liberals and conservatives had joined against him on this issue:

On the one side the liberals and the American Zionists had decided that now was the time to challenge the Soviet Union's highly restrictive emigration policies, particularly with respect to Soviet Jews. On the other side were the conservatives, who had traditionally opposed detente because it challenged their ideological opposition to contacts with Communist countries. My request in April, 1973 for Congressional authority to grant most-favored-nation trade status to the Soviet Union became the rallying point for both groups: the liberals wanted MFN legislation to be conditioned on eased emigration policies; the conservatives wanted MFN defeated on the principle that detente was bad by definition.[21]

From early October until December the Nixon administration continued to delay the House vote on the Trade Reform Act for fear that the anti-Soviet amendment would be passed. On December 2 the president finally decided to ask the House to proceed with the trade bill vote despite the risk of the strong anti-Soviet amendment. However, two days later Nixon, in a letter to Speaker Carl Albert, threatened to veto the Trade Reform Act if it denied the Soviets MFN status. The president was not serious about vetoing the act, but he tried unsuccessfully to bully the House into giving him what he wanted. He wanted the Trade Reform Act because he was firmly committed to the free-trade concept. It was no accident that on December 2 he finally was willing to allow the House to vote on his bill. George Shultz, his secretary of the Treasury, had warned him that continued delay jeopardized the bill, as unemployment was expected to rise in 1974. According to Shultz, the expected higher level of unemployment would support the AFL-CIO's position against the bill in Congress.[22]

Finally, on December 11, 1973, the House of Representatives voted on the Trade Reform Act. Just as the House Ways and Means Committee had, the House voted 272 to 104 to give the president what he asked for in terms of raising and lowering tariff rates and adjustment assistance to unemployed workers, as mentioned earlier.[23] However, Nixon realized that the House would not approve the MFN clause for the Soviet Union, and he hoped that rather than embarrass the Russian government, it would not vote on MFN status at all. New York Republican Barber B. Conable asked that the House drop that amendment, but the House wanted to go on record and voted 298 to 106 not to rescind the amendment.[24] Then it added insult to injury by adding the Vanik amendment, not part of the House Ways and Means Committee bill, that denied the Soviets export credits to buy American machinery. The House voted 319 to 80 to withhold both MFN status and export credits to the Russian government until the Nixon administration could certify that the Soviets no longer restricted emigration by high taxes or other means.[25]

Nixon was devastated by the embarrassing House vote, but in his State of the Union Address on January 30, 1974, he asked the Senate to support the MFN for the Soviets. The president was pleased that the United States had run a foreign trade surplus of $765.9 million for the first eleven months of 1973 and hoped that common sense would prevail in the final version of the Trade Reform Act.[26]

On March 7 Kissinger testified for the administration before the Senate Finance Committee on the trade bill. The secretary of state declared that he would personally recommend that the president veto the bill if Congress continued to refuse to grant trade concessions to the USSR In his opinion, the bill was the wrong vehicle to force the Soviets to make changes in their society. He emphasized that if the United States wanted peaceful relations with the Russians, it must treat them as a normal trading partner.[27]

Democratic Senator Russell B. Long of Louisiana, chairman of the Senate Finance Committee, held open hearings throughout most of March on the Trade Reform Act. He encouraged testimony of varying opinions on the impact of the bill. Senator Abraham Ribicoff, Democrat from Connecticut and a member of the committee, spoke regularly about his concerns that the bill would bring a flood of imports into the United States, especially from European countries that had to offset their higher oil costs.[28]

Meany also spoke before the committee on March 27. He described the House bill as obsolete and urged the committee to pass a more realistic bill. He ridiculed the 1973 trade surplus that the administration emphasized to justify the trade bill. Meany claimed that much of the gain in trade was the result of heavy exports of farm goods and critical raw materials, and that it was the exports of these commodities that caused domestic shortages and brought rapid acceleration of inflation. He called the surplus of 1973 a dangerous illusion since imports continued to flood U.S. markets, eliminating both jobs and industries. He was particularly disturbed by U.S. exports of technology that was used abroad to create jobs to manufacture products that will eventually compete with American goods.[29]

In April passage of the Trade Reform Act looked bleak, as both Senators Vance Hartke, Democrat from Indiana, and Jackson predicted that the bill would not be voted on until 1975. The Senate Finance Committee had completed open hearings in the middle of March with very few senators in attendance. Hartke promised in a speech to the American Marketing Association on April 2 that he would once again try to amend the bill to restrict imports in order to save American jobs. The committee did not begin closed-door considerations of the trade bill until the end of May.[30]

In the middle of June Democratic Senator Adlai E. Stevenson III from Illinois, Jackson, and sixteen other senators introduced amendments in the Finance Committee that would require congressional review of all Export-Import Bank transactions of more than $50 million and limit the Nixon administration's ability to extend government-backed credits to the USSR and other Communist countries, except Yugoslavia and Rumania. This was a blatant attempt by Congress to pass political judgment on important trade transactions.[31]

In late July the Senate Finance Committee made substantial changes during the closed-door session on the controversial House-passed trade bill. The committee agreed to give the administration authority to eliminate lower tariff rates on a country-by-country basis if other countries discriminated against entry of U.S. goods. The panel also agreed to give Congress a stronger voice in deciding any negotiated changes in nontariff barriers that affected U.S. laws. Other changes would give the administration authority to eliminate U.S. tariffs during negotiations if duties were less than 10 percent—a provision that could affect 85 percent of U.S. imports.[32]

On July 29 Senator Long predicted that passage of the Trade Reform Act and other legislation would depend on how long the Nixon impeachment trial distracted senators from their tasks. On August 8 the president announced his resignation, effective August 9, rather than face impeachment over Watergate and the possibility of a long trial in the Senate. Gerald Ford, former Republican minority leader in the House and the first appointed vice president under the Twenty-fifth Amendment to the Constitution, assumed the presidency. Questions now arose over whether the new president would push for the trade bill and participation in the Tokyo Round. European Union officials who were concerned about the president's commitment to free trade (Ford came from Michigan, a strong labor-union state) were pleased when the new president in a speech to Congress on August 13 called for the immediate passage of the Trade Reform Act.[33]

As the trade bill made its way through the Senate Finance Committee, the Commerce Department announced record trade deficits in July and August. Ford's Council of Economic Advisers warned the president that the $728-million trade deficit in July could put downward pressure on the American dollar and cause inflation as foreign goods became more expensive. In August the deficit grew to $1.1 billion, causing even greater alarm. The administration placed the blame for these growing trade deficits on the higher cost of foreign oil and an increase in manufacturing imports.[34]

Finally, on October 18 Jackson announced a breakthrough on the Trade Reform Act. Ford, much less demanding than Nixon that the Soviets be given MFN status, agreed to a compromise. Russia would get MFN status in return for "substantial relaxation" in Soviet emigration laws. Nixon had been unwilling to interfere with the internal policy of the USSR. He had wanted to give it MFN status unconditionally and had hoped that the Russians would then change their emigration and other hostile policies toward the free world.[35]

The Senate Finance Committee voted in favor of the Trade Reform Act on November 20 and then decided to delay sending the bill to the full Senate until Kissinger had the opportunity to testify on the agreement with the USSR regarding Soviet emigration practices. Long declared that the secretary of state would not be able to meet with the committee before early December. At the same time, Long affirmed that he would support the bill on the floor in its present form. The chairman was concerned that the bill would be delayed by unnecessary amendments once it reached the full Senate.[36]

The bill that emerged from the Senate Finance Committee differed from the House version in one significant way. The House bill granted authority to the president to negotiate away nontariff barriers to imports. The House would allow such a change to take place automatically unless it acted within ninety days to veto the president's action. Critics of this version of the bill contended that under such authority the executive could nullify such things as antipollution legislation in the name of eliminating a barrier to trade. On the other hand, the Senate Finance Committee version would require affirmative action by Congress before the president could effect a change in nontariff barriers. Other than that, both bills gave the president the power to negotiate substantial reductions in tariffs, made it easier for U.S. companies to get relief from excessive imports, and gave adjustment assistance to unemployed workers also affected by imports.[37]

Senator Hartke and other opponents of the bill still hoped to make amendments on the Senate floor that had little to do with trade. Their strategy was to clutter up the bill with amendments, such as raising the taxes on foreign earnings of U.S. oil companies, and then allow the bill to die, as Congress would adjourn in two weeks. The strategy of the bill's supporters would be to kill all amendments and riders and cut off debate by a motion to table. Some liberals, such as Democratic Senators Walter Mondale from Minnesota and Gaylord Nelson of Wisconsin, had mixed feelings concerning the vote. Though they favored higher taxation of oil companies, passage of the Trade Reform Act was more important.[38]

On December 13 the Senate approved by a vote of 77 to 4 the Trade Reform Act that had been in Congress for twenty months. It also voted 88 to 0 to authorize trade concessions to the Soviet Union in return for freer Soviet emigration policies. Passage of this bill was made possible by the decision of the Senate to limit further debate and amendments. Cloture was imposed by a vote of 71 to 19, averting a series of popular amendments on taxation and other matters unrelated to the bill.[39] Senator Jackson lauded the bill, declaring that it would liberalize world trade. However, Jackson, in regard to the Soviets, warned that "the basis of trust and confidence that is essential to the whole range of our relations with the Soviet Union would be destroyed if the Russians did not live up to its commitments." The Soviets would immediately benefit from lower tariffs on vodka and other products from the Soviet Union. In addition, the bill would open the way to similar trade agreements with such Communist nations as Hungary.[40]

The House and Senate versions of the bill were quickly reconciled because Congress wanted to adjourn for the Christmas holidays. On December 20 the Conference Committee report was approved by the House by a vote of 323 to 36 and by the Senate, 72 to 4.[41] The final version of the Trade Reform Act included the following:

Tariffs

The president could abolish any tariff that was 5 percent or less and could cut any tariff above 5 percent by three-fifths. An example would be a tariff that was 20 percent of the value of the imported product, which could be reduced to 8 percent.[42]

Nontariff Barriers

The executive was permitted to negotiate to change or rescind nontariff barriers such as quotas, safety standards, and special customs valuation procedures as they existed in the United States in return for similar foreign concessions. However, any agreements made by the president would be subject to the approval of Congress under a speeded-up procedure. The Conference Committee favored the Senate version rather than the House's, much to the disappointment of the administration. The House bill would only have allowed the Congress to veto any such agreement.[43]

Escape Clause

The Trade Reform Act would make it easier for domestic industries to make a case before the newly named United States Trade Commission, formerly called the Tariff Commission, that they had been injured by a flood of imports. The president could grant relief, including import restrictions, if the commission found injury. This House version of the bill was accepted by the Conference Committee over the Senate bill that denied the president the right to grant relief.[44]

Adjustment Assistance

The adjustment assistance provision of the bill would make it easier for groups of workers to make a case that they had lost their jobs because of import competition. If the secretary of labor filed a petition on behalf of these workers, assistance in the form of cash and other benefits would be made available to individual companies and, for the first time, to entire communities showing they had been damaged by import competition.[45]

Section 301—Retaliation and Countervailing Duties

Section 301 gave the president new powers to retaliate by import restrictions against countries that discriminated against the United States. The president also could impose special duties on imports that were subsidized by the exporting government more quickly. However, the bill provided a four-year "grace period" in which imposition of the duties would not be mandatory on the secretary of the Treasury pending proposed international negotiations to establish ground rules.[46]

Trade with Communist Countries

The Conference Committee left the Jackson compromise intact. The bill authorized MFN status for Communist countries, including the Soviet Union. However, in the case of the Soviets, the MFN treatment accorded to them would be withdrawn after eighteen months unless Soviet emigration procedures were liberalized.[47]

Preferences for Less Developed Countries

The act allowed the president to join the heads of other industrial governments to reduce to zero duties on many products from the poorer countries. However, the list contained a number of restrictions, and the process would be carried out at the upcoming Tokyo Round.[48]

The Trade Reform Act of 1974 also changed the status of the special representative for trade negotiations (STR). This position had been created in the

Trade Expansion Act of 1962. After two Nixon administration efforts to weaken or abolish it, the Trade Reform Act of 1974 made the STR a statutory unit in the Executive Office of the President and gave cabinet rank and salary to its chief.[49] This act provided the United States the leverage it needed in the upcoming Tokyo Trade Round. The Ford and Carter administrations were now prepared to take the next step in liberalizing world trade.

THE TOKYO ROUND

The Tokyo Round of multilateral trade negotiations resulted in agreements to reduce tariffs significantly and to eliminate or reduce nontariff barriers. It marked the seventh round of multilateral reductions in international trade barriers that had been negotiated under the General Agreement on Tariffs and Trade (GATT). The Tokyo Round formally opened in September 1973 (bargaining did not begin in earnest until January 1975 after the passage of the Trade Reform Act) and concluded in April 1979.[50]

In September 1973 Nixon pronounced the major objectives of the new trade talks just prior to the opening of the GATT meeting in Tokyo. He explained that the talks were to achieve for Americans benefits of expanding world trade, to work out trade problems, to reform some present trade guidelines and practices that reduced trade opportunities for U.S. producers, and to seek ways to improve trade relationships with both less developed countries and countries with differing economic and political systems.[51]

Delegates from one hundred nations met on September 12 for a three-day GATT meeting welcomed by the Japanese prime minister. Before the conclusion of this three-day conference, the delegates signed what became known as the Declaration of Tokyo—a document providing the guidelines for the first two years of complex negotiations to be held in Geneva beginning in early 1974. Briefly, it called for extensive tariff reductions, the elimination of nontariff barriers, a system of monetary stability, and special consideration for developing countries. France and the United States differed on the importance of monetary stability. French Finance Minister Giscard d'Estaing stated that a new trade agreement would be impossible to achieve unless a new monetary system, built on stable exchange rates, was first established. The U.S. position echoed by Treasury Secretary Shultz was that a stable system could not be built unless goods, including agricultural products, were free to move in international channels.[52]

Though the U.S. representatives attended the opening meeting in Tokyo in the Fall of 1973, nothing of substance was accomplished until after the Congress passed the Trade Reform Act in December 1974. When the GATT trade negotiators opened their talks in Geneva on February 11, 1975, the United States was armed with a new trade agreement and ready to undertake serious negotiations. Harald B. Malmgren, the head of the U.S. delegation that year, in his opening remarks warned that the negotiators should not leave final decisions to "one big burst of energy," as had been the case in the Kennedy Round. He explained to the other delegations that the Ford administration had only a five-year negotiating mandate under the terms of the new Trade Reform Act.[53]

Several days later the ninety nations in attendance approved a timetable to start negotiations on most key issues by March 4. Six days later representatives from the EU, the United States, and Japan, among others, met to discuss how to expand the earnings of developing countries by opening foreign markets to their traditional exports. The United States took the lead by announcing that it accorded priority to tropical fruit imports from developing nations and did not expect anything in return from these nations. The GATT's annual trade study group reported that the developing countries were hard hit by both higher oil and commodity prices and had to increase their exports in order to meet their obligation.[54]

The EU and the United States had some differences to resolve in 1975. On March 21 the United States called for across-the-board tariff cuts, with elimination of tariffs of 5 percent or less. The EU, on the other hand, favored large cuts for only the highest existing tariffs and no outright eliminations. The EU and the United States also disagreed on whether to include agricultural products in the bargaining over tariffs. The U.S. government had promised American farmers that it would make every attempt to open the protected European agricultural market by including agricultural products in tariff reductions. The EU, especially the French, wanted to exclude tariff reduction from discussion of the agricultural sector. The GATT trade session on agriculture ended in deadlock for the remainder of 1975.[55]

On October 16 President Ford's trade negotiator Frederick B. Dent, in a speech in Amsterdam, sought to reassure EU countries that the United States was not moving in a protectionist direction. Dent had been receiving complaints by EU countries that some American industries were asking for protection under the new provisions of the Trade Reform Act. Dent declared that American companies had a right to apply for relief, but it was not automatically granted, and the EU should not use this as an excuse to break off the trade talks.[56]

The EU had been watching closely as American automobile and shoe industries applied for relief from imports at the end of 1975. The Treasury began investigating to see whether foreign cars were being "dumped" in the United States, that is, being sold in America at lower prices than in the home market. The shoe industry had also claimed that it was being hurt by imports, though dumping was not the issue here. The EU was concerned that this would lead to higher duties on both auto and shoe imports and would work against the spirit of the Tokyo Round. The EU, by making a complaint, was putting the Ford administration on notice that any imposition of higher duties would be met by retaliation. The Ford administration, on the other hand, was frustrated by the slow movement of the GATT talks. It wanted the talks speeded up and concluded in early 1977.[57]

In an attempt to take the initiative, the United States, in November 1975, proposed an international accord to curb government subsidies that enabled exporters to unfairly undercut competitors in foreign markets. The United States pushed for an agreement defining those subsidies to be banned and those to be permitted and asked for a clarification on what actions governments could take in response to violations of any accord. American representatives insisted on banning all subsidies that allowed products to be sold cheaper abroad than at home.[58]

On January 19, 1976, the Geneva talks were again threatened by the Ford administration's decision to restrict imports of specialty steels. Paul Luytens, the EU trade negotiator, was concerned that this would lead to a plethora of requests for import quotas in the United States. Though Ford had granted quota relief for specialty steel, he remained sensitive to EU criticism and, several months later, rejected the advice of the International Trade Commission to grant similar relief to the shoe industry.[59]

By the end of March 1976 the Geneva trade talks had accomplished very little. The United States and the EU had not even agreed on a method of cutting tariff rates. The United States still insisted on across-the-board cuts by as much as 60 percent, claiming that they would narrow the spread between low and high tariff rates. The EU charged that the U.S. plan for cutting tariffs would not significantly narrow disparities between high and low rates of duties on imports.[60]

If a change was needed to jolt the trade talks, the presidential election of 1976 was just what the doctor ordered. Jimmy Carter defeated Ford and demonstrated his commitment to liberal trade by appointing free traders as his principal economic advisers. W. Michael Blumenthal became the new secretary of the Treasury and Robert S. Strauss the special representative for trade negotiations.[61] However, it was Vice President Walter Mondale who, in early 1977, took the initiative by flying to Brussels to meet with EU's Executive Committee president, Roy Jenkins, in order to revive the Geneva trade talks.[62]

Blumenthal was an excellent choice as secretary of the Treasury to stimulate the dormant talks. He had headed the U.S. delegation to the 1967 Kennedy Round and had established a reputation for being tough, but knowledgeable, imaginative, and hardworking. He was the first secretary of the Treasury in a long time to appreciate the importance of trade.[63] Strauss, on the other hand, had no prior experience with trade policy. He was a former treasurer and chairman of the Democratic National Committee, and his strength was in political maneuvering. However, the new STR declared at the outset that the United States would not give anything away in the Tokyo Round talks and that free trade must be blended very carefully with economic reality and jobs.[64]

Strauss faced a very difficult task in early 1977. The most difficult issue to resolve was the EU's position on agricultural policy. It continued to demand that farm discussion be handled separately from the rest of the talks, while the United States insisted on a single attack on all trade barriers. Simply put, all tariff reductions, whether on agricultural or manufactured goods, should be discussed together. The EU had a common agricultural policy—it limited imports and subsidized exports and feared that the United States wanted to destroy its policy. The United States believed that the EU continued to look for ways to avoid opening its markets to American farmers.[65]

Strauss flew to Geneva in early July to visit the EU Commission. He hoped to convince it that the United States supported liberal trade and pointed to Carter's compromise on the issue of shoe imports. Strauss declared that the president refused to impose tariffs on shoe imports, even after being criticized by Lane

Kirkland, the secretary-treasurer of the AFL-CIO, and instead asked only for voluntary restraints from foreign nations on their exports. The STR told the EU's leaders that he hoped that all GATT negotiations would be concluded by spring, 1978.[66]

While Strauss worked to reach compromises with the EU, he became concerned about U.S.-Japanese trade relations in late 1977. He specifically complained about Tokyo's growing world trade and current account surplus. He stated that Japanese quotas and restrictive trade policies were igniting protectionist sentiment in the U.S. Congress, and that American-Japanese relations were near the "bursting point." When the Japanese minister for international economic policy flew to Washington in December 1977, Strauss asked the Finance Committee senators to host a luncheon for him and to threaten retaliation if Japan did not liberalize its trade policies. Evidently this tactic worked, as Strauss traveled to Japan the following month and received specific Japanese commitments to reduce their exports of color televisions and steel.[67]

The Carter administration made it clear that raising the import barriers against imported steel would not solve the steel industry's problems, and it was pleased that the Japanese had agreed to reduce their steel exports. In fact, a month prior to this agreement with Japan, the administration had declared that it was seeking additional multinational tariff and trade agreements with the EU. The four-hundred-page computer printout of requests for concessions covered mainly agricultural products. There were some one thousand individual items, from citrus fruits and shelled almonds to beef, representing an annual volume of $11 billion of American exports. Similar lists were presented by the EU and Japan.[68]

With protectionism rising in all countries due to an international recession causing high unemployment, the American position was to accelerate the negotiating schedule at Geneva and try to reach a full agreement by spring 1978. By January 15 the hard bargaining began as negotiating countries responded to each other's tariff and nontariff lists. Alan Wolff, a U.S. deputy special trade representative, asked for greater access to the European market for grains, tobacco, poultry, citrus fruits, and beef. Wolff made it clear that the United States was not asking the EU to eliminate its sacred Common Agricultural Policy, which kept European agricultural prices artificially high. However, he expected that the EU would have to make some concessions to the United States in order to satisfy American farmers.[69]

In December, as economic conditions worsened, the AFL-CIO held its biennial convention in Los Angeles. Meany, speaking to the delegates, called upon the Carter administration to protect American workers from further job losses caused by imports. He claimed that the current trade negotiations in Geneva were based on political expediency and not on the needs of the U.S. economy. He declared that the goal of the administration must be expansion of trade based on "fairness, reciprocity, and mutual benefit." He called for import quotas to put an end to dumping, and countervailing duties against imports subsidized by foreign governments.[70]

The trade talks at Geneva opened in 1978 with a sudden burst of activity when the EU on January 20 offered tariff concessions on at least one hundred agricultural products it imported at the value of $1.3 billion annually. A week later Strauss emphasized the need to work quickly and proposed that the United States would cut industrial tariffs on the average of 40 percent during the next eight to ten years. He warned that the longer it took to conclude the talks, the greater the risk of plunging the world once more into an era of protectionism. Immediately after Strauss spoke, the United States, the EU, and Japan agreed to set July as the date for completion of the GATT talks.[71]

From March 1978 until the end of the year, the media recorded the record trade deficits that gave renewed hope to the protectionists. The trade deficit in March was $2.9 billion for the United States, the fifth-largest monthly deficit on record.[72] The assistant secretary of the Treasury, C. Fred Bergsten, an opponent of protectionism, attempted to put the bad news in the best possible perspective, claiming that the trade deficits of the last two quarters, the last quarter of 1977 and the first quarter of 1978, represented peak deficits that should not be experienced again. He predicted that the deficits would decline in the second half of 1978 and into 1979 as U.S. dependency on foreign oil diminished.[73] However, Bergsten's prediction proved faulty, as the trade deficits continued to rise. The deficit was $2.99 billion in July, up from $1.6 billion in June. In fact, the trade deficit for the first eleven months of 1978 was a record $26.7 billion and brought increased demands for protection.[74]

The major reasons for the steep trade deficits in 1978 were the high rate of inflation in the United States (consumer prices rose at a compound annual rate of 10 percent in October) and a growing demand for imports. The Carter administration was optimistic that slow growth in 1979 would shrink the trade deficit by reducing the demand for imports, making protectionism unnecessary. Leonard Silk, writing in the *New York Times*, blamed the deficit on the huge increase in imports and not, as Bergsten suggested, on oil imports. Silk pointed out that U.S. imports of petroleum products declined by $500 million, or 4.4 percent, in the third quarter of 1978, while other imports rose by more than $7 billion, or 26.7 percent. Most of these imports were finished manufactured goods.[75]

In October 1978 the American textile manufacturers and trade unions asked Congress to exempt them from the Geneva negotiations. The textile industry and its union allies contended that domestic manufacturers were being hurt by "unfair" competitors who hired cheap labor and took advantage of government subsidies. The industry pointed to the trade deficit in textiles and apparels, which stood at $5 billion, a record. Senator Ernest Hollings, Democrat of South Carolina, had worked for months to exclude textiles from the multilateral trade talks, but had never been able to get his bill out of the Finance Committee. However, Hollings, through parliamentary maneuver and the absence of Chairman Long, was able to make his bill an amendment to legislation to renew the Export-Import Bank. Both Carter and Strauss called the Senate action "devastating" to the Geneva trade talks and promised to make every effort to have the amendment dropped in Conference Committee.[76]

While the textile manufacturers and their unions complained about European subsidies, the EU in Geneva began to wonder whether it would be able to continue to export subsidized products to the United States without countervailing duties being imposed by the Carter administration. On November 16 the Western European nations demanded assurances from the United States that no countervailing duties would be imposed on their subsidized exports as the price for concluding the Tokyo Round.[77] On the following day, with the hope of keeping the Tokyo Round in session, the administration assured the EU that it would try to resolve the impasse threatening GATT. Carter's trade representative declared that the problem arose after Congress recessed without renewing the president's authority to waive additional duties on subsidized foreign imports. The Treasury's right to waive imposition of countervailing duties on dairy products, canned hams, leather goods, and other imports expired on January 2, 1979. The administration wanted the waiver extended until August 1 to permit completion of the negotiations. Consequently, the administration was required to impose approximately $700 million in duties on imports by January 3, 1979.[78]

The French refused to participate in any discussions with the United States until the threat of countervailing duties was lifted. Other EU countries agreed to talk, but only after the United States made it clear that it would delay the collection of import duties. Finally, on December 29 a compromise was reached when the United States and its major trading partners agreed on a "fair-trade" charter that limited the effects of government subsidies on trade flows. The new charter or code would ensure that all countries observe international trading rules when temporarily limiting imports that were harmful to domestic industries. It required that countries use fair and open procedures in the adoption of product standards that affected international trade. It allowed for increased opportunities for exporters to bid for sales to foreign governments. It encouraged uniform methods of appraising imports for the purpose of applying import duties. Finally, it promoted cooperation and unified ways to deal with the problem of commercial counterfeiting, such as copying commercial trademarks.[79] It was estimated that the new code would create new markets for American companies abroad with the potential of additional income of $25 billion annually.[80]

In February 1979 Strauss announced that the current GATT negotiations were almost complete. There were still some obstacles to overcome, such as the European demand for greater U.S. tariff cuts, the agreement on a policy toward the less developed nations, and the unsettled tariff issues between the United States and Canada. However, the major stumbling block was finally resolved when the House Ways and Means Committee approved a bill on February 21 permitting the Treasury Department to waive countervailing duties on imports unfairly subsidized by foreign governments. By March 28 the bill had passed both houses of Congress, and it smoothed the way for the finalization of the Tokyo Round.[81]

On February 25 Alonzo McDonald, Strauss's assistant, declared that now only one major obstacle remained for a successful conclusion. The United States and Japan were at odds over access to the Japanese telecommunications market. The Japanese government did not want its telegraph and telephone company covered by the code being drafted to limit discrimination against foreign suppliers in obtaining government procurement contracts.[82] At the end of March U.S.-Japanese trade talks had collapsed because the Japanese government had refused to allow American companies to supply telecommunications equipment in order to protect the Nippon Telephone and Telegraph Company.[83] Strauss threatened to retaliate by denying the Japanese access to American procurement that would be open to all countries that did not discriminate against the United States.[84]

The United States was not alone in having difficulty with Japan. The EU also took a tough stand against Japanese trade policies. The EU Commission complained that the Japanese trade concessions were inadequate and recommended that Western Europe erect trade barriers against all Japanese products if Japan did not take steps to reduce its burgeoning trade surplus by June 1979.[85]

On April 11, 1979, after five years of negotiations, the United States and the world's leading industrial nations finally endorsed the new GATT agreement officially ending the Tokyo Round. McDonald and Strauss called the negotiations the most successful in thirty years.[86] They declared that the agreement would mean slower inflation, reductions in the huge American trade deficit, and increased employment for the United States. President Carter hailed the pact as "the most far-reaching and comprehensive" trade agreement in three decades.[87]

The major provisions of the final agreement can be divided into four categories. First were the nontariff trade barriers such as the various codes on subsidies, standards, customs valuation, and a series of industry agreements, including steel and aircraft. The second part of the package dealt with agriculture, the third with industrial tariff reductions, and the last with the modernization of the GATT system.[88]

The work on the nontariff trade barriers was the most important part of this agreement. The keystone was the body of codes that established guidelines of conduct for nations in areas previously considered untouchable. The GATT Secretariat compiled a list of more than eight hundred specific nontariff distortions of international trade and grouped them into five categories.

The first category dealt with a customs valuation code that prohibited a customs administration from placing fictitious or arbitrary values on imports that would raise duties. The method of valuation used by a country for imported goods could be as important as the rate of the duty. The code would make countries base customs valuation on the actual price paid for a product or its invoice value. If the invoice value could not be determined, countries could use other valuation methods in a manner stipulated by the code.[89]

A government procurement code, the second category of nontariff barriers, opened to foreign competition government contracts for supplies worth more than $195,000. This code was designed to prohibit discrimination against foreign products at all stages of government procurement to encourage more international competition. It detailed rules on drafting the specification of goods to be procured, advertising prospective purchases, time allowed for submission of bids, the qualification of supplies, the opening and evaluation of bids, the award of contracts, and the hearing and review of protests. The code did not apply to the purchase of goods involving national security or agricultural support programs.[90]

A third category of nontariff barriers dealt with eliminating trade-distorting subsidizing of exports, combined with rules governing the use of countervailing duties that governments use to offset the price advantages associated with subsidized imports. American companies had complained that foreign corporations sold goods in the United States more cheaply because these goods were subsidized. The code prohibited outright export subsidies for manufactures and primary mineral products. However, agricultural subsidies were prohibited only when they displaced the exports of other members or undercut prices in a specific market. Criteria were formulated to determine injury resulting from domestic subsidies, and if injury was proven, the countries would be allowed to seek redress through the use of countervailing duties.[91]

The fourth category consisted of the code that prevented product regulations relating to health, safety, and other matters from interfering with trade. This was called the technical barriers to trade code, and it encouraged the use of open procedures in the adoption of international standards.[92]

The final category of codes dealt with simplifying import-licensing procedures. Nations not only were to make licensing procedures easier for importers, but they had to apply them in a nondiscriminatory manner. For example, importers now had to apply to only one administrative body to secure licenses, and the licenses could not be refused for minor errors in documentation.[93]

The accomplishments in agriculture were less spectacular when compared with the nontariff codes. The United States, the world's most efficient agricultural producer, wanted to reduce tariff barriers to give it freer access to both the EU and Japanese markets. However, the EU opposed opening its highly protected agricultural markets and the Japanese resisted pressures to reduce the protection of their high-cost farmers who had political connections. The Americans wanted the Japanese to reduce their import quotas on oranges in order to allow more Florida and California orange imports, but the Japanese refused to accommodate the United States.[94] However, some progress was made in dairy products and meat. The accord set minimum prices for some milk powders and fats and certain types of cheeses. It also established an international dairy-products council to supervise the working of the accord and to keep the market under review. The Tokyo Round created an international meat council to watch the world's supply and demand situation of beef, veal, and live cattle. As it turned out, both the Tokyo Round and the Kennedy Round before it failed to accomplish much in the area of agriculture due to regulation, protection, and subsidies that interfered with free trade.[95]

The Tokyo Round provided for a cut in tariffs on industrial products of 30 percent on trade that amounted to more than $155 billion in 1977 dollars. The average tariff on manufactured goods was reduced from 7 percent to 4.7 percent.[96] Anticipating opposition to these cuts in Congress, American trade negotiators made public that industries plagued by high imports such as textiles, leather, steel, rubber, and autos were being shielded from the brunt of the new tariff cuts under terms of the new GATT accord. Alan Wolff, deputy special U.S. trade representative, indicated that duties for leather imports were being reduced only 4 percent, rubber 21 percent, autos 16 percent, steel 27 percent, apparel 15 percent, and textiles 21 percent, all less than the average of 30 percent. Wolff, in defending the work completed in Geneva, disagreed with the Congressional Budget Office's claim that import-sensitive industries would be big losers under this agreement.[97]

The Tokyo Round also provided for a new framework for world trade, including a set of procedures for examining disputes between GATT partners and new methods to determine whether a country could restrict imports due to a deficit in its balance-of-payments account.[98] There was also a provision that would allow waiving the GATT rule for equal treatment of all member nations in order to allow developing nations more favorable treatment and to extend to them special concessions.[99]

The developing nations, over ninety countries that made up a majority of the ons in the GATT talks, were dissatisfied with the results of the Tokyo Round, claiming that it did not do enough for the world's poor. Led by Petrah Tomic, the Yugoslavian delegate, they boycotted the signing ceremonies. Tomic declared that the agreement did not live up to the industrialized world's commitment to give the developing nations preferential treatment on a regular basis.[100] Delegates from Mexico and Venezuela complained about the growing protectionist barriers imposed by the United States, the EU, and Japan against their exports.[101]

In May, a month after the signing of the pact, the Carter administration began its preparations to send the agreement to Congress in the form of another trade act. Congressional approval was needed for the nontariff agreements. The president explained to congressmen that the bill would provide more jobs for Americans and emphasized that it would help reduce the high inflation rate in the country. The administration actually distributed to Congress an economic analysis showing that the agreement would reduce inflation by at least 0.5 percent annually.[102]

The AFL-CIO worked against the administration, declaring that the new agreement would hurt the U.S. economy. Rudy Oswald, the AFL-CIO research director, wanted the Carter administration to renegotiate the agreement. He declared that foreign nations excluded their key sectors from import penetration, and that the procurement code would not open up vast opportunities for American business, as Carter claimed. He pointed out that the European countries would never apply the code to their agencies that purchased electrical and telecommunications equipment.[103]

On June 19 Carter submitted to Congress the Trade Agreements Act. It included a copy of the nontariff agreements negotiated at the Tokyo Round, a draft of the implementing bill (the Trade Agreements Act), and a statement of administrative action. The major provisions of the trade act had been known for some time, and the legislative process had been responsible for weakening the opposition. For example, beginning on January 4, 1979, the president gave his required ninety-day notice of intent to conclude the Tokyo Round. Both the House Ways and Means Committee and the Senate Finance Committee drew up legislation with the administration's approval by the end of May. All these meetings were closed to the public in order to limit the number of lobbyists who might influence the finished product. The legislation was not permitted to be amended by the full House and Senate, as they could only approve or reject the final product.[104]

The Trade Agreements Act approved the nontariff agreements discussed earlier, including eliminating the American Selling Price that was used for customs valuation. However, the most important change made by Congress on the nontariff agreements dealt with countervailing duties. The House Ways and Means Committee and the Senate Finance Committee had disagreed on criteria relief-seeking firms had to meet. The House committee and the president wanted to maintain what had originally been negotiated at Geneva. However, the Senate Finance Committee wanted to change the wording of the bill in a way that would have weakened it. For example, the Senate wished to use only the word "injury" in order for the government to seek countervailing duties against imports. The House and president wanted the tougher standard, "material injury," which the Senate eventually accepted.[105]

Both houses gave their approval to the Trade Agreements Act in July 1979. On July 11 the House approved the bill 395 to 7; on July 23 the Senate passed it 90 to 4; and Carter signed it on the White House lawn on July 26.[106] Of the bill's 11 opponents, 5 were from Wisconsin, a dairy-producing state. The dairy industry had protested the slight adjustment in cheese import quotas and refused to support the bill.[107]

Congress gave the president the authority to participate in the Tokyo Round by passing the Trade Reform Act in 1974 and then approved the results of the nontariff agreements of the Tokyo Round by passing the Trade Agreements Act in 1979. Strauss, more than anyone else, deserved credit for the smooth passage of the 1979 bill. He averted expected massive industry opposition by having nearly a thousand representatives from every private sector of the economy take part in the talks.[108] The major achievement of the Tokyo Round was the negotiation of codes on nontariff barriers that for the first time subjected them to international agreement. The major failure was the continuation of the agricultural trade barriers. The trading nations of the world would once again try to breach these barriers in the Uruguay Round beginning in 1986.

NOTES

1. Franklin Root, *International Trade and Investment*, 7th ed. (Cincinnati, OH: South-Western Publishing Co., 1994), p. 219.
2. *New York Times*, April 11, 1973, p. 1.
3. Ibid.
4. Ibid., April 12, 1973, pp. 69, 75.
5. Ibid.
6. Ibid., April 13, 1973, p. 62; May 7, 1973, p. 18.
7. Ibid., May 9, 1973, p. 65.
8. Ibid., May 10, 1973, p. 65.
9. Ibid.
10. Ibid.; *New York Times*, May 12, 1973, p. 41.
11. *New York Times*, June 19, 1973, p. 55.
12. Ibid., June 27, 1973, p. 1; July 5, 1973, p. 43.
13. *New York Times*, July 5, 1973, p. 45.

14. Ibid.

15. Ibid., July 9, 1973, p. 51.

16. Ibid., July 13, 1973, p. 54.

17. Ibid., July 17, 1973, p. 55.

18. Ibid., October 4, 1973, p. 65; October 5, 1973, p. 11; October 12, 1973, p. 15.

19. Stephen E. Ambrose, *Nixon: Ruin and Recovery, 1973-1990*, 3 vols. (New York: Simon and Schuster, 1991), vol. 3, p. 170.

20. Ibid.

21. Ibid., p. 171; Richard Nixon, *RN: The Memoirs of Richard Nixon* (New York: Grosset and Dunlap, 1978), pp. 875-876.

22. *New York Times*, December 4, 1973, p. 1; December 5, 1973, p. 71.

23. Ibid., December 12, 1973, pp. 1; 12.

24. Ibid.

25. Ibid.

26. Ibid., January 1, 1974, p. 27; January 31, 1974, p. 1.

27. Ibid., March 8, 1974, p. 1.

28. Ibid., March 6, 1974, p. 51.

29. Ibid., March 28, 1974, p. 55.

30. Ibid., April 3, 1974, p. 59; April 15, 1974, p. 47; May 7, 1974, p. 63; May 24, 1974, p. 43.

31. Ibid., June 18, 1974, p. 3.

32. Ibid., July 30, 1974, p. 54.

33. Ibid.; *New York Times*, August 10, 1974, p. 37; August 13, 1974, pp. 20, 45.

34. *New York Times*, August 16, 1974, p. 29; August 27, 1974, p. 16; September 26, 1974, p. 1.

35. Ibid., October 19, 1974, p. 1.

36. Ibid., November 20, 1974, p. 67; November 21, 1974, p. 71.

37. Ibid., October 27, 1974, sec. 3, p. 5.

38. Ibid., December 11, 1974, p. 65.

39. Ibid., December 14, 1974, p. 1.

40. Ibid., p. 41.

41. Ibid., December 21, 1974, p. 55.

42. Ibid.

43. Ibid.

44. Ibid.

45. Ibid., p. 57.

46. Ibid.

47. Ibid.

48. Ibid.

49. I. M. Destler, *American Trade Politics: System under Stress* (New York: Twentieth Century Fund Press, 1986), p. 91.

50. Alan V. Deardorff and Robert Stern, *An Economic Analysis of the Effects of the Tokyo Round of Multilateral Trade Negotiations on the United States and the Other Major Industrialized Countries* (Washington, DC: U.S. Government Printing Office, 1979), p. 116; Root, *International Trade and Investment*, p. 195.

51. *New York Times*, September 9, 1973, p. 11.

52. Ibid., September 13, 1973, p. 71; September 14, 1973, p. 53; September 16, 1973, sec. 4, p. 6.

53. Ibid., February 12, 1975, p. 51.

54. Ibid., February 14, 1975, p. 51; March 11, 1975, p. 49.

55. Ibid., March 22, 1975, p. 44; March 28, 1975, p. 35.

56. Ibid., October 17, 1975, p. 55.

57. Ibid., November 17, 1975, p. 6.

58. Ibid., November 18, 1975, p. 56.

59. Ibid., January 20, 1976, p. 43; March 21, 1976, sec. 4, p. 16; Destler, *American Trade Politics*, p. 118.

60. *New York Times*, March 24, 1976, p. 1; March 25, 1976, p. 53.

61. Ibid., January 6, 1977, p. 41; March 12, 1977, p. 29.

62. Ibid., January 25, 1977, p. 7.

63. Ibid., January 30, 1977, sec. 12, p. 8.

64. Ibid., March 15, 1977, p. 51; Destler, *American Trade Politics*, pp. 91-92.

65. *New York Times*, January 30, 1977, sec. 12, p. 8.

66. Ibid., April 6, 1977, p. 12; April 7, 1977, p. 22; July 4, 1977, p. 22; July 12, 1977, p. 39.

67. Destler, *American Trade Politics*, pp. 92-93.

68. *New York Times*, November 2, 1977, sec. 4, p. 1.

69. Ibid.

70. Ibid., December 9, 1977, sec. 4, p. 5; December 11, 1977, p. 44.

71. Ibid., January 21, 1978, p. 37; January 27, 1978, sec. 4, p. 5.

72. Ibid., May 27, 1978, p. 25.

73. Ibid., June 6, 1978, sec. 4, p. 2.

74. Ibid., August 30, 1978, p. 24; December 1, 1978, sec. 4, p. 2; December 29, 1978, sec. 4, p. 1.

75. Ibid., December 1, 1978, sec. 4, p. 2.

76. Ibid., October 3, 1978, p. 10.

77. Ibid., November 17, 1978, sec. 4, p. 12.

78. Ibid., November 18, 1978, p. 27.

79. Ibid., December 30, 1978, p. 29.

80. Ibid., January 3, 1979, sec. 4, p. 1.

81. Ibid., February 20, 1979, sec. 4, p. 1; February 22, 1979, sec. 4, p. 1; March 29, 1979, sec. 4, p. 12.

82. Ibid., February 26, 1979, sec. 4, p. 2.

83. Ibid., March 30, 1979, sec. 4, p. 1.

84. Ibid.

85. Ibid., April 2, 1979, sec. 4, p. 1.

86. Ibid., April 12, 1979, p. 1.

87. Ibid., April 13, 1979, sec. 4, p. 1.

88. Ibid., April 12, 1979, sec. 4, p. 2.

89. Ibid.; Deardorff and Stern, *Economic Analysis*, p. 118; Root, *International Trade and Investment*, pp. 197-198.

90. Root, *International Trade and Investment*, p. 197; *New York Times*, April 12, 1979, sec. 4, p. 9.

91. *New York Times*, April 12, 1979, sec. 4, p. 9; Root, *International Trade and Investment*, p. 197.

92. Root, *International Trade and Investment*, p. 197.

93. Ibid., p. 198.

94. Ibid., p. 196.

95. *New York Times*, April 12, 1979, sec. 4, p. 9.

96. Root, *International Trade and Investment*, p. 196.

97. *New York Times*, April 19, 1979, sec. 4, p. 1.

98. Ibid., April 12, 1979, sec. 4, p. 9.

99. Ibid.

100. Ibid.

101. Ibid., April 24, 1979, sec. 4, p. 3.

102. Ibid., May 17, 1979, sec. 4, p. 12.

103. Ibid., May 11, 1979, sec. 4, p. 9.

104. Ibid., June 20, 1979, sec. 4, p. 1; Destler, *American Trade Politics*, pp. 66-67.

105. Destler, *American Trade Politics*, pp. 121-122.

106. *New York Times*, July 12, 1979, sec. 4, p. 1; July 24, 1979, p. 1; July 27, 1979, sec. 4, p. 1.

107. Destler, *American Trade Politics*, p. 67.

108. *New York Times*, August 5, 1979, sec. 3, p. 16.

6

Fair Trade
and the Uruguay Round

THE TRADE AND TARIFF ACT OF 1984

After the election of Ronald Reagan in 1980, both the budget and trade deficits grew rapidly. The Reagan tax cuts and the increase in military spending caused the budget deficit to rise from $74 billion in 1980, Carter's last year in the presidency, to $185 billion in 1984, the end of Reagan's first term. The trade deficit in 1984 was a record $122.4 billion, up from $36.2 billion in 1980.[1] Economists blamed the trade deficit on growing budget deficits. As the budget deficit grew, so did real interest rates, causing the appreciation of the dollar. The high value of the dollar made American products very expensive compared to foreign goods, producing a ballooning trade deficit. However, the unions such as the AFL-CIO and the United Steelworkers of America, among others, refused to recognize this relationship between the two deficits, and instead they called for protectionist legislation to reduce the trade deficit.[2]

Despite the positive results of the Tokyo Round, the United States and other governments were concerned about the growing protectionism in the early 1980s. Only eighteen months after the Tokyo Round, the GATT Consultative Group of Eighteen (CG-18) agreed in June 1981 that a ministerial meeting should be called in Geneva in November 1982 to discuss weaknesses in the trading system. It was clear to the CG-18 that the multilateral trading system was endangered by the economic recession, especially in the United States. The major result of the meeting was that the CG-18 declared that all the contracting parties should "make a determined effort to ensure that trade policies and measures are consistent with GATT principles and rules and to resist protectionist pressures in the formulation and implementation of national trade policy."[3]

At the ministerial meeting in 1982 the United States had wanted to address certain problems that had existed over the years such as opening up world agricultural markets to American farmers and modernizing the GATT by extending it into new areas such as protecting intellectual property against counterfeit goods. However, the other CG-18 members were not interested in pursuing these objectives until a later date. The United States made it clear through its trade representative, William Brock, that the trading system was on the verge of disintegration unless a new round of trade talks was called. In the meantime, the United States pursued its own trade policies.[4]

In the summer of 1984 the slumping American trade performance (total imports rose 26.2 percent to a record $33.5 billion in July, while exports rose only 10.3 percent to $19.4 billion) worried economists, who feared that the imbalance between imports and exports would revitalize the call for protectionism in the U.S. Congress.[5] In fact, members of Congress were already talking about abolishing the Generalized System of Preferences (GSP), a minor provision of the Trade Reform Act of 1974 that was due to expire in January, 1985 whereby industrialized nations gave duty-free access to their markets to less developed nations.[6] Now with the enormous trade deficit, organized labor opposed continuing the GSP, especially for the big three newly industrialized countries (NICs), South Korea, Taiwan, and Hong Kong. Union leaders contended that imports from these countries now were competitive with U.S. products without the need for special treatment. In the House of Representatives at the end of 1983, there was not a single House vote to sponsor the continuation of GSP.[7]

In July 1984, William Brock, the U.S. trade representative, who supported the GSP, urged the Senate Finance Committee to join a bill renewing the GSP with a bilateral free-trade agreement with Israel and several minor trade proposals. On July 30 the committee voted to attach this package as an amendment to a minor tariff-adjustment bill already passed by the House.[8] Senator John C. Danforth, Republican from Missouri and chairman of the Senate Subcommittee on Trade, wanted to take charge of the bill on the floor. He convinced Republican Senate Majority Leader Howard H. Baker, Jr., of Tennessee to give him the necessary floor time. Baker was reluctant to give Danforth time, for he believed that the bill had little chance of passing either house.[9]

On September 17 Danforth began hearings on the bill. Baker had originally given him only one floor day, but as amendments were added to the bill (thirty-two were added in three days' time), the Missouri senator was given additional time.[10] Danforth was aided by Senator Lloyd Bentsen, Democrat of Texas, and Brock. Both attempted to allay the fears of the textile industry over the Israel free-trade agreement.[11] Two other factors worked in favor of the bill's passage: (1) The administration promised to seek negotiated restraint agreements with steel-exporting nations with the aim of reducing imports to about 18.5 percent of the U.S. market. (2) Organized labor proved totally ineffective, almost unaware of what was taking place. Labor could have caused problems such as proposing unfriendly amendments or demanding domestic-content provisions in the final version of the bill. However, the United Auto Workers union was preoccupied with major wage negotiations, and the AFL-CIO was inexplicably inactive. Not a single labor amendment was proposed during the entire four-day debate. On September 20 the Senate version of the Trade and Tariff Act passed by a landslide vote of 96 to 0.[12]

The Senate version of the trade bill incorporated the GSP and the bilateral trade agreement with Israel. However, for the most part, it gave the president additional power to retaliate against restrictive practices in international trade and gave protection to specific interest groups. The president warned the Senate that its version of the trade bill, which restricted, among other things, imports of Chinese shirts and European wines, could bring retaliation against American farm exports.[13] However, the most bitter criticism of the new trade bill came from an editorial in the free-trade-oriented *Washington Post*. The editorial declared:

The losers in every major trade case of the past year—the copper producers, the shoemakers, the wine producers—have managed to insert language to try to win in Congress what they lost in litigation. The wine industry wants protection but can't meet the current law's first requirement—to show that imports are actually hurting it. The bill would change the law to say that the wine makers don't have to show that they are being hurt; they would only have to show that their suppliers—the perennially distressed grape growers—need to sell more grapes. There was originally some good legislation in this bill, but it has long since been grievously outweighed by its burden of bad amendments. If the bill gets to President Reagan, he will have a clear and urgent responsibility to let it go no farther.[14]

On September 27 the House Ways and Means Committee reported out four separate trade bills that were passed by the House on October 3. They included a bilateral trade agreement with Israel, protection of the American steel industry, a five-year extension of the GSP, and a measure extending import relief to domestic wine makers and grape growers.[15] Democrat Richard A. Gephardt of Missouri attempted unsuccessfully to amend the House bill to deny GSP renewal for the big three NICs. The four House bills were attached as amendments to the Senate-passed bill and sent to the Conference Committee for reconciliation.[16]

Danforth chaired the Conference Committee and was able to work out a compromise bill. Most of the protectionist provisions of the bill were either rescinded or watered down. For example, the conferees struck out the protectionist provision aimed at China's textiles and weakened the special benefits designed to help the copper, shoe, ferroalloy, dairy-products, and wine industries. However, it did allow grape producers to challenge wine imports if these imports affected their sales. The final bill included the GSP provision and the bilateral trade agreement with Israel. The steel industry gained the most from the bill, as steel imports were reduced to between 17 and 20 percent of the American steel market. However, this protection was contingent upon the spending of the steel companies to modernize their plants and retrain workers.[17]

President Reagan signed the Trade and Tariff Act into law on October 30, 1984, giving special thanks to those who had guided the fair-trade bill through Congress. He included Bentsen and Danforth in the Senate and Democrat Dan Rostenkowski of Illinois as chairman of the House Ways and Means Committee, but special thanks went to Brock, who worked diligently with Congress to formulate a bill that would temper the complaints of the protectionists, but would not be objectionable to U.S. international trading partners.[18]

THE OMNIBUS TRADE AND COMPETITIVENESS ACT, 1988

The Omnibus Trade and Competitiveness Act (OTCA) was passed by Congress in the summer of 1988. Between 1984 and 1988 the United States decided that a policy of "fair trade" would replace "free trade" as its trade objective. The concern of the American people and government with the growing trade deficit that was becoming both a political and economic issue, and the continuous lobbying by protectionists, made Americans who advocated free trade look like agents of foreign governments. The American government would no longer open its doors to the goods of other countries unless they reciprocated in kind. Instead, it would retaliate swiftly in the future against what it regarded as unfair trade practices. The U.S. trade representative would identify countries that ran persistent trade surpluses with the United States and would attempt to negotiate a solution to the problem. If negotiations failed to remove unfair trade practices, the United States would retaliate by restricting that foreign country's access to U.S. markets.[19]

Work on the OTCA began in 1985 and took almost three years to complete. The House of Representatives finally passed the legislation on April 21, 1988, by a vote of 312 to 107. The most comprehensive trade bill in fourteen years contained the following provisions: (1) Section 301 of the Trade Reform Act of 1974 was substantially modified in the 1988 act. It defined "unfair trade" and transferred from the president to the U.S. trade representative (USTR) the authority both to initiate investigations of "unfair trade" practices and to order sanctions when necessary. However, the president retained control over the timing and method of retaliation. The 1988 act also introduced Super 301 and Special 301. Under Super 301 the USTR had to identify in 1989 and in 1990 U.S. trade-liberalizing priorities for specific countries and practices and then initiate investigations to seek the removal of the measures. The process could take from twelve to eighteen months. Special 301 contained the following provisions: (1) It allowed the USTR to identify the countries that denied adequate intellectual property protection and to impose sanctions against them. (2) It granted trade relief to industries seriously injured by imports. These industries could get protection if they were willing to make "positive adjustment" to foreign competition. (3) It clarified the Foreign Corrupt Practices Act to specify what kind of knowledge made American corporate officials liable if their foreign employees or agents were involved in a bribery. (4) It expanded programs for workers displaced by imports by creating a $1-billion retraining program, with most of the money going to the states. (5) It barred foreign companies from serving as primary dealers in U.S. government securities unless their government allowed U.S. companies to compete abroad in the same manner. (6) It granted the president the authority to continue the negotiations in the Uruguay Round sponsored by GATT. Specifically, the president was to make every effort to negotiate agreements opening markets in the areas of banking, insurance, and other services. (7) It called for a three-year ban on government purchases from the Toshiba Corporation, parent of Toshiba Machine Corporation, which violated export controls with technology sales to Russia. (8) It called for sixty days' notice of plant closings or long-term layoffs by companies employing more than one hundred persons. Notice was required if layoffs affected either one-third of the work force or five hundred persons.[20]

Rostenkowski praised the House for the overwhelming positive vote and declared that the new legislation would make the United States a strong leader for open markets. However, President Reagan was threatening to veto the legislation based on only one provision that he found unacceptable—giving workers sixty days' notice before plant closings or layoffs. Robert H. Michel, House Republican leader from Illinois, echoed the president's sentiments when he said that the proposed requirement "imposes a straitjacket around small business as well as large ones, inhibiting them from making decisions that can save jobs and create new ones."[21] Michel attempted unsuccessfully to have the bill sent back to the Conference Committee, where it could be stripped of this provision. Michel and Reagan accused the House of giving in to organized labor, while the Democratic Senate leadership warned the president that a veto of this bill could jeopardize his free-trade accord with Canada. The stage was set for a presidential veto, and Congress believed that it had enough votes to override.[22]

On April 27 the Senate approved the OTCA by a vote of 63 to 36. However, unlike the House, the vote fell short of the two-thirds majority necessary to override a possible presidential veto. The Democratic leaders stated that the trade legislation was urgently needed by the nation and asked the president not to use his veto power. Michael Dukakis, the governor of Massachusetts and the Democratic candidate for president in November 1988, made a personal plea to Reagan to change his mind about the bill. Senator Bentsen declared that the president should reconsider his veto because there was so much about the bill that Reagan supported.[23]

The Democrats in Congress and their supporters, the labor unions, needed more time to win over votes to override an almost certain Reagan veto. They decided to delay sending the president the trade legislation until they felt secure about override.[24] In the meantime, the AFL-CIO selected New York, California, and other large states as areas where they would attempt to persuade senators to override the president using a major propaganda blitz.[25]

Immediately after Reagan received the bill, he quickly vetoed it. On May 24 the House wasted little time overriding Reagan's veto by a vote of 308 to 113. However, on June 8 the Senate by a vote of 61 to 37 voted to uphold Reagan's veto. The president in his veto message told the Congress that he favored all of the existing trade bill except the part about giving workers sixty days' notice prior to shutdowns. Reagan urged the Congress to pass similar legislation without that objectionable provision, which he would sign.[26] One week later House Democrats, conceding that they could not override a Reagan veto, agreed to take up another version of the landmark trade legislation without the contested provision. However, they made clear that they would attempt to weave the provision into future legislation.[27] In the Senate Bentsen claimed that he had seventy co-sponsors for the revised trade legislation and predicted that the bill would become law before the end of the summer.[28]

The pending trade legislation received mixed reviews from American economists. Most claimed that the United States had to insist that Japan, Korea, Hong Kong, and Taiwan open their markets to American trade if they expected the United States to do the same. However, the consensus concerning the impact of the bill in attaining these goals was that success solely depended on whether the president was an activist, bent on forcing other countries to purchase more American goods. The bill did not force the president to take any action. However, now that the president had a choice on whether to impose trade sanctions or do nothing, he had to be aware that trade would become a major political issue of the 1990s.[29]

The new OTCA passed the House on July 13 by a vote of 376 to 45, and about two weeks later the Senate acted favorably by a vote of 85 to 11. Finally, on August 23 Reagan signed the new bill into law, and the United States now had a "fair-trade" policy.[30] Clayton K. Yeutter, the U.S. trade representative, said that the new bill would bring about a stronger and more aggressive trade policy, and that it would open new market opportunities for American business.[31]

Japan, South Korea, and the EU criticized the passage of the new trade bill. They viewed the bill as protectionist legislation aimed at their markets. They complained that the bill left the judgment of fairness in trade matters to American authorities. Dietrich von Kyau, an economics official at the West German Embassy, said that "the opportunities are there for unilateral action, and this is an open invitation to others to do the same."[32] Senator Bentsen revealed that lobbyists for foreign governments had spent more than $100 million to defeat the bill.[33]

The Japanese government declared that the bill was aimed at its export markets to reduce its large trade surpluses with the United States. Japan's foreign minister, Sosuke Uno, urged Reagan to veto the bill. He said that his country objected to the general retaliatory provisions and also to the provisions against the Toshiba Machine Corporation.[34] Hajime Tamura, the minister of international trade and industry, feared that the United States was once again becoming a protectionist country. He said, "I strongly hope the U.S. Administration will maintain its usual posture of maintaining free trade, and at the same time make efforts not to damage the bilateral U.S.-Japanese relationship in the future. If the bill becomes law, Japan reserves the right to examine the enforcement of the bill within the framework of the GATT."[35]

The rancor that the OTCA caused could have been avoided if the surplus countries had worked with the United States to find a way to reduce their surpluses. Richard Gardner, professor of law and international organizations at Columbia University, urged the United States to try to get the Organization for Economic Cooperation and Development, the GATT, and other institutions to bring about a peaceful solution to the world balance of payments. However, most of the United States' trading partners saw the OTCA as American protectionism, while the American government viewed it as the beginning of the "fair-trade" policy.[36]

THE URUGUAY ROUND

The impetus for a new GATT round came from the United States. As early as 1982, only three years after the end of the Tokyo Round, the United States was calling for more talks to put GATT back on course. The Tokyo Round produced tariff cuts but failed to satisfy the United States. The American economy was stumbling as a result of high oil prices; its exports were made less competitive by high interest rates and the strong dollar. In 1982 Brock had criticized the GATT system, declaring that it was in trouble due to the growth of protectionism in the United States. He concluded that unless the GATT system was reformed to include, among other things, equitable agricultural agreements, the future of multilateral trade was doomed.[37] As mentioned earlier, the trade acts of 1984 and 1988 had demonstrated that the United States had changed its trade philosophy from "free" trade to "fair" trade. The EU and Japan were concerned that fair trade was a euphemism for protectionism, and though neither pushed for new GATT trade talks, they agreed to them in order to deal with the growing protectionist sentiment in the United States.[38]

Delegates from 116 countries met in Punta del Este, Uruguay, from September 15 to September 20 to launch the trade talks known as the Uruguay Round, the eighth in the history of the GATT. The trade negotiations would last until December 1993, seven long years. Like the previous GATT rounds, most of the meetings would take place in Geneva. Clayton Yeutter, the USTR under Reagan, led the American delegation in the early years of the Uruguay Round. By the time it was finished, he would be replaced by Carla Hills, in the Bush administration, and Mickey Kantor, who is currently serving in the Clinton administration. It is Kantor, Clinton's former campaign manager, who deserves most of the credit for concluding the Uruguay Round.[39]

Uruguay's foreign minister, Enrique V. Iglesias, chaired the opening session of the conference. He urged the nations of the world to make the supreme effort to remove the dangers of suicidal trade wars and to embark on a policy of trade liberalization. A Punta del Este Declaration was formulated that established the goals and principles that would guide the Uruguay Round to its conclusion. The declaration was divided into two sections: (1) the Group of Negotiations on Goods (GNG), which negotiated traditional trade issues and new issues relating to investment and intellectual property; (2) and the Group of Negotiations on Services (GNS), which dealt strictly with all services. Both groups were under the jurisdiction of the Trade Negotiations Committee (TNC), which determined the rules and conduct of negotiations.[40]

In the past the GATT had covered only merchandise trade. However, in recent years, trade in services had been growing, and GATT coverage was necessary. Therefore, the Punta del Este Declaration stated that the aim of negotiations of trade in services was to establish a multilateral framework of principles and rules to achieve the "progressive liberalization and expansion of such trade." The Uruguay Round first had to define what constituted international service transactions. For example, should these services include financial services such as banking, insurance, and accounting; professional services such as legal, educational, and medical services; and business services such as advertising, consulting, and design? When the services to be covered in negotiations had been decided, a determination had to be made on the direction and volume of trade in these areas. Finally, the specific barriers to trade in services had to be negotiated, for example, government procurement of services that favored domestic suppliers, outright exclusion of foreign service companies, and discriminatory restraints on the activities of foreign-owned service establishments such as limiting foreign insurance companies to the sale of certain policies.[41]

The GNS had to conclude which government policies toward international trade in services were legitimate and which were not. This was not an easy task, since the GATT had no experience to guide it. However, the United States insisted that services be included in the Uruguay Round since it would benefit the most by the breaking down of trade barriers—it had the comparative advantage in the service area. On the other hand, less developed countries like Brazil and India opposed the idea of service negotiations; they wanted to promote their own service industries and needed protection.[42]

The GNG originally consisted of fourteen negotiating groups covering the following areas: (1) tariffs, (2) nontariff measures, (3) tropical products, (4) natural-resource-based products, (5) textiles and clothing, (6) agriculture, (7) GATT articles, (8) safeguards, (9) most-favored-nation (MFN) agreements, (10) subsidies and countervailing measures, (11) dispute settlement, (12) trade-related industrial property rights (TRIPs), (13) trade-related industrial measures (TRIMs), and (14) functioning of the GATT system. Though all of these areas were important, the United States was especially interested in an agricultural agreement that would open the EU and Japanese markets to American farm goods and in the elimination of subsidies in both agricultural and nonagricultural sectors.[43]

The developing countries were dissatisfied with the results of the Tokyo Round. They wanted assurances that they would be given special treatment. For example, they demanded that the industrial countries implement a policy of both "rollback and standstill." "Standstill" required that countries pledge not to adopt any GATT-inconsistent measures, to exercise GATT rights with restraint and in a GATT-consistent manner, and to refrain from enacting any measures to improve their negotiating position. "Rollback" called for the phasing out of GATT-inconsistent measures by the end of negotiations.

A GATT agenda was agreed upon by the signatories at Punta del Este by September 20 after a compromise was struck on agricultural subsidies and service industries. The inclusion of the farm subsidies on the agenda had been the principal objective of the United States and a group of fourteen agricultural nations called the Cairns Group. They included Argentina, Australia, Brazil, Canada, Chile, Colombia, Fiji, Hungary, Indonesia, Malaysia, New Zealand, the Philippines, Thailand, and Uruguay. These agricultural exporting countries had met in Cairns, Australia, in 1986 and had proposed the elimination of all agricultural subsidies.[44] Though the French vehemently opposed this at Punta del Este, the language was worked to include the phased reduction of the negative effects of direct and indirect subsidized competition on world markets. The United States was also able to include services on the agenda, such as piracy of intellectual property and investment. The meeting ended with most delegates believing that the Uruguay Round would be completed in four years. As we shall see, it would take seven long years before an acceptable agreement was worked out.[45]

The events of the Uruguay Round can be divided into four stages. The first stage began immediately after the Punta del Este meeting and lasted until the conclusion of the ministerial meeting in Montreal, Canada, in December 1988. The second stage began in the fall of 1990 and concluded with the Brussels ministerial meeting in December 1990. The third stage began in January 1991 and ended with a final agreement in December 1993. The fourth and final stage began in April 1994 with the signing of the agreement in Marrakesh, Morocco, and ended with its ratification by the U.S. Congress in December 1994.[46]

THE FIRST STAGE, OCTOBER 1986-DECEMBER 1988

In the first six months following the Punta del Este organizational meeting and throughout most of 1987, no negotiations of substance took place. Most of the meetings dealt only with organizational questions. Negotiations did not begin in earnest until 1988, after the OTCA was passed by the U.S. Congress granting the administration, among other things, new authority to conduct multilateral negotiations based on "fast-track" procedures. This method assured that all new nontariff trade barrier (NTB) agreements reached in Geneva would not be subject to amendments by Congress. As it turned out, the fast track was extended until March 1991 and then twice more before negotiations were completed.[47]

While the negotiations over organizational questions continued to dominate the Uruguay talks in 1987, the United States and the EU were on the verge of a major trade crisis. It began in 1986 when Spain and Portugal joined the EU and reduced American grain imports based on the EU's protectionist system. American farmers protested vehemently to the Reagan administration, and the president responded by threatening to impose a 200 percent duty on some $400 million worth of imports of European food and beverages, including French brandy and cheese, all European white wines, Belgian endives, and British gin. Due to the popularity of these items among affluent young Americans, the conflict was called the "yuppies' trade war."[48] However, after three days of talks, mostly on the transatlantic telephone, the trade war was averted when the Europeans agreed to compensate the United States for its losses of $430 million in sales of corn and sorghum.[49]

In March 1987 the EU and Japan criticized the United States for thinking that the Uruguay Round would resolve its trade problems, mainly its growing trade deficit, which was a $145.1 billion at the end of 1986. Both wanted the United States to concentrate on reducing its budget deficit, which would help the trade deficit.[50] This same opinion was echoed by some leading trade economists such as I. M. Destler. Destler was opposed to the United States continuing in the Uruguay Round while the trade deficit remained so high. He claimed that U.S. trade successes occurred when the trade balance was improving as a result of the declining dollar. He proposed that the United States reduce the value of the dollar by getting its budget deficit under control. This would cause the trade deficit to fall, and when it reached under $100 billion, the United States, once again, could enter multilateral trade negotiations. Destler hoped for the cooperation of the EU and Japan. He hoped that both would agree to stimulate their economies through macroeconomic policy, mainly increased public works programs and lower taxes. This would allow the population of both the EU and Japan to buy more of their own output, and less would be exported to the United States. This did not happen because both the EU and Japan feared that economic stimulation would cause serious inflation.[51]

Throughout most of 1988 negotiations were stalled over agricultural dis-agreements between the EU, mainly France, and the United States. The United States claimed that agricultural import barriers prevented consumers from getting lower-priced food from foreign countries while, at the same time, these consumers paid taxes to finance export subsidies (getting rid of excess production caused by high support prices). The United States had demanded a drastic reform of the EU's Common Agricultural Policy (CAP) with cuts of 70 percent in subsidies. The EU, led by France, instead offered only a 30 percent reduction. The EU spent the most on agricultural support, which amounted to $81.62 billion in 1990, or 48 percent of EU agricultural output. The United States blamed its declining share of the world wheat market on these subsidies. For example, in the 1980s the EU's share of the world wheat market rose from 16 to 21 percent, while that of the United States fell from 46 to 31 percent.[52]

On the eve of the ministerial meeting in Montreal, USTR Yeutter sounded pessimistic when he declared that the trade talks had accomplished very little. He stated that the United States wanted concessions from the EU and Japan on protection for intellectual property and a reduction in agricultural subsidies, and if they were not made, the trade talks would fail. He warned that no agreement would be preferable to a bad agreement.[53]

The TNC met in Montreal from December 5 to December 8 to discuss nontariff measures, GATT articles, subsidies, and TRIMs. All that year the fourteen negotiating groups had worked on texts for the ministers' approval. Six of the fourteen groups reported out clear texts for approval in Montreal. The most important dealt with TRIMs and agriculture.[54]

Though the issues concerning TRIMs had been controversial up to this point, and the text presented to the ministers was a paper of disagreements, the delegates were able to compromise on every issue. A framework was created for the liberalization of $900 billion worth of services that crossed borders and also the $3 trillion worth of services that were provided domestically around the world, such as banking, insurance, and accounting.[55]

Throughout the Uruguay Round the TRIPs remained one of the most intractable issues of all. The United States demanded that standards be established for better international protection of intellectual property rights. However, this provoked deep-seated opposition among developing countries who resisted the idea of standardized intellectual property regulations on the GATT agenda. Representatives from Brazil and India declared that it was imperative that the United States and other advanced countries make their technical knowledge available to combat hunger and disease throughout the world.[56]

All efforts to reach an agreement on agriculture failed. The United States wanted a long-term commitment to the total elimination of all trade-distorting subsidies in agriculture and agreements on some short-term reform measures, including a freeze on internal support, export-subsidy, and import-protection levels. The EU refused to make a commitment to the complete eradication of subsidies. Unlike the United States which had only 2.5 million farmers, and where farming was no longer a major occupation, the EU would not accept the political and social consequences of abandoning its 12 million farmers.[57]

Though the Montreal meeting ended inconclusively as agricultural negotiations failed, an agreement was reached to reduce trade barriers for less developed nations on a variety of tropical products such as bananas, coffee, and tea.[58] The reduction of barriers on tropical products, without reciprocation, had always been a demand of developing nations. Before ending the meeting, Arthur Dunkel, the GATT director-general, promised to continue to pursue areas such as TRIPs and agriculture in order to reach an agreement on them before 1990.[59]

BETWEEN STAGES—JANUARY 1989-SUMMER 1990

When George Bush became president in January 1989, he nominated Carla Hills as the new USTR. For all of 1989 and part of 1990, there were no major ministerial meetings taking place or progress made at the Uruguay Round. The sixteen months between the end of the first stage and the beginning of the second stage were devoted primarily to trade problems between the United States and Japan. The major problem was Japan's failure to open its telecommunications market to American companies.[60]

In May 1989 Hills was formulating a plan to impose duties of 100 percent on some Japanese goods as retaliation for Japan's failure to open its telecommunications market. Hills declared at her confirmation hearings that she would not hesitate to impose sanctions against countries that imposed unfair trade barriers. It became obvious to the Japanese government that the United States intended to take action against it, and Japanese officials immediately protested to the American Embassy in Tokyo that American trade sanctions under the OTCA were a violation of free-trade principles.[61]

On May 25 Hills named Japan, India, and Brazil as unfair traders under the new OTCA, subjecting them to possible sanctions if their import barriers were not lowered within eighteen months. It looked like a trade war was brewing when the Japanese government charged that the United States was undermining international accords by threatening unilateral action against its trading partners. Japanese officials refused to negotiate trade issues with the United States while under threat of unilateral sanctions.[62]

At a GATT meeting on June 21, the Organization for Economic Cooperation and Development (OECD), which had been watching the trade conflict between the United States and Japan, criticized the use of the OTCA to impose trade sanctions unilaterally on Japan, India, and Brazil. The EU had already criticized the unilateral nature of the OTCA and had warned the United States that if it were used against the EU, the EU would challenge it before GATT.[63]

Though the Japanese government refused to accept the blame for American trade problems, (it declared that U.S. trade deficiencies resulted from years of mismanagement in its industrial and educational systems), it agreed in late June to provide foreign companies with greater access to its mobile telephone market. Within ten months, on April 27, 1990, the Bush administration had dropped Japan from the list of countries subject to reprisal tariffs as a result of unfair trade practices.[64]

THE SECOND STAGE, FALL 1990-DECEMBER 1990

By the fall of 1990, the Uruguay Round talks were once again taking place in Geneva. The delegates had wanted to conclude the negotiations by the spring of 1991, but the impasse over the percentage of subsidies to allow threatened the success of the entire round. The United States had favored a 75 percent reduction in border restrictions and domestic support levels and a 90 percent cut in export subsidies on agriculture. These reductions were to be staged over ten years starting from January 1991 and using 1990 as the base year. The EU proposal had been limited to a 30 percent reduction in domestic support levels over five years from a 1986 base level. The United States and other members of the Cairns Group had complained that Germany and France, for political reasons, subsidized inefficient small farmers and encouraged them to dump their products on world markets. Yeutter, the former USTR and now secretary of agriculture, declared that the differences between the United States and the EU on subsidies were so great that they threatened to prolong the negotiations beyond the spring 1991 deadline.[65]

When the Brussels talks opened on December 3, 1990, the United States wanted to concentrate on agricultural negotiations, making them the centerpiece of the talks. The United States had seventy other countries allied with it against the EU on the subsidy issue. However, the EU, led by France, refused to discuss the subsidies, and Hills, not wanting the meeting to end in failure, suggested suspending the Brussels Conference for three to four weeks to give the leaders an opportunity to revive the momentum.[66]

In an attempt to bridge the gap in agriculture, Swedish Agricultural Minister Mats Hellstrom, who had been presiding over the agricultural negotiations, made a compromise proposal. He called for 30 percent cuts in border restrictions, domestic price supports, and export subsidies over a five-year period from a 1990 base. This compromise included elements of both positions, and while the United States accepted it as a basis for negotiations, the EU firmly rejected it.[67]

When the Brussels Conference ended on December 7 without an agreement on agriculture, a feeling of hopelessness and despair prevailed. GATT Director-General Dunkel, realizing the need to maintain momentum, called for a meeting of the TNC on January 15. Dunkel and other GATT officials were also concerned that if the negotiations were not completed by the spring of 1991, and it did not look like they would be, the Bush administration would have to ask Congress by March 1, 1991, for an extension of the "fast-track" authority. If there was progress in the Uruguay Round negotiations, the OTCA had foreseen the possibility of a two-year extension. The question remained whether Congress, which had praised Hills for standing firm at Brussels on the agricultural issue, would agree to the extension.[68]

THE THIRD STAGE, JANUARY 1991-DECEMBER 1993

On March 1, 1991, Bush formally asked the Congress for an additional two years of the "fast-track" authority to negotiate trade agreements. Congress had ninety days to approve or deny the president's request. It debated the issue from March until the end of May, with the majority in favor of the extension. Senator Bentsen became the administration's chief spokesman. He warned those legislators who wavered that any attempt to kill the "fast-track" extension would doom the Uruguay Round. Some legislators favored the legislation, but only if amendments were attached to deal with trade-expansion issues such as environmental protection and uniform labor laws. On May 23 the House of Representatives approved the "fast-track" legislation by a vote of 231 to 192, and a day later the Senate authorized it by a vote of 59 to 36.[69]

From April to December 1991 Dunkel made every attempt to break the stalemate in the Uruguay Round negotiations. He convened the TNC in April, reducing the negotiating structure from fourteen negotiating groups to seven. These groups were to deal with tariffs, nontariff measures, tropical products, textiles and clothing, agriculture, rule making or TRIMs, and subsidies, countervailing duties, antidumping, safeguards, preshipment inspection, or TRIPs.[70] Finally, in December Dunkel, desperate for an agreement after five tense years of negotiations, proposed a compromise. He called for cutting subsidies to farmers worldwide, phasing out import quotas on third-world textiles, and giving more protection to patents and copyrights. The EU criticized the Dunkel compromise, while the United States gave it little support.[71]

In January 1992 Dunkel set the middle of April as his new target for the completion of the Uruguay Round. However, trade negotiators were saying publicly that an agreement by spring was unlikely unless American and European leaders personally intervened to formulate a compromise on farm subsidies, the main problem. By now, most of the EU nations except France wanted to compromise on reducing subsidies.[72]

As the talks continued into 1992, the negotiators faced another problem. The American media were focusing less on the Uruguay Round and more on the importance of the North American Free Trade Agreement (NAFTA) on the American economy. By August 1992 the NAFTA negotiations were completed and were immediately injected into the 1992 presidential election. The Uruguay Round became media irrelevant until 1993.[73]

On April 19 Bush met with EU leaders to try to break the stalemate in global trade talks. These meetings proved futile because the French refused to make any concessions on subsidies. In fact, the trade talks deteriorated further when the EU announced that it would not reduce soybean subsidies.[74] By October trade negotiations had stalled completely as the EU waited for the American presidential election results.[75]

On November 6, three days after Bill Clinton's election to the presidency, the Bush administration, intending to get the attention of France, decided to force the EU into reducing subsidies on agricultural goods.[76] The United States threatened to impose 200 percent tariffs on European wine and other goods on December 6 if the EU would not agree to a compromise on subsidies. Though the EU warned that it would retaliate if Washington went forward with its threat, the German government was working secretly to convince the French to make concessions on the subsidy issue.[77]

On November 10 a breakthrough occurred when President Francois Mitterrand of France announced that his government would accept deep cuts in subsidized grain exports and subsidized production of soybeans and other oilseed crops in order to avoid punitive U.S. tariffs on white wines.[78] Immediately French farmers, who made up only 6 percent of the work force, but held enormous political power, began to organize protests against the reduction in their protective subsidies. It is interesting to note that Jacques Delors, a Frenchman and head of the EU, supported the agreement, but only a day after the compromise announcement the French prime minister, Pierre Beregovoy, called the new farm trade pact unacceptable, though he stopped short of threatening to veto it.[79]

As the year 1992 came to a close, the United States had elected a new president who would take office on January 20, 1993, the Uruguay Round talks were once again on track as the EU and the United States were calling for a final agreement by mid-January 1993, and tens of thousands of farmers from across Western Europe were demonstrating in Strasbourg, France, against the EU-U.S. farm trade accord. On December 26 President-elect Clinton chose Mickey Kantor as USTR to conclude the Uruguay Round talks.[80]

On February 11, 1993, Kantor, realizing that the Uruguay Round could not be concluded prior to June 1, 1993, the date that presidential "fast-track" authority was due to expire, announced that the Clinton administration would notify Congress of its desire to extend the authority by six months until December 1993. Notification of "fast-track" renewal had to be made ninety days prior to June 1.[81]

Peter Sutherland, the new director-general of GATT, who replaced Dunkel in June 1993, declared that he accepted the post believing that a final agreement would be concluded by the end of the year. The basis for Sutherland's optimism was an economic meeting in Tokyo in July that paved the way for concluding the global trade talks. Agreements were made at this meeting to make specific tariff cuts, to curb the Japanese trade surplus, and to resume the Uruguay Round in Geneva on July 12.[82]

The growing optimism in the summer that the talks could be concluded by December came to a sudden halt in the fall. Once again it was the French who were making the waves. In September top American and European officials met in Washington to move to prevent a dispute over farm subsidies from scuttling the Uruguay Round negotiations. Kantor met with Sir Leon Brittan, the EU's vice president, to prevent the new French government, led by Prime Minister Edouard Balladur, from reneging on its 1992 subsidy accord with the United States. Kantor declared that the United States would not renegotiate that agreement. Secretary of the Treasury Bentsen supported Kantor and warned the EU that any attempt to change the subsidy accord could endanger the GATT negotiations and the new December 15 deadline.[83]

Great Britain and Germany both supported the United States against the French. The British were exasperated at the French attempt to change the accord to placate their farmers. Great Britain threatened to boycott EU meetings if the December 15 deadline was not met. Chancellor Helmut Kohl of Germany became America's strongest ally as he quietly worked behind the scenes to get Balladur to agree to the subsidy accord of 1992.[84]

However, Balladur continued to insist that he could not accept the 1992 subsidy accord. He claimed that GATT in France had become a frightening symbol of an American plot to harm the French farmers, crush French culture in Hollywood, and rob France of its identity. Balladur had staked his political future on ensuring that France was not seen to have surrendered in any accord. He stated that he wanted another agreement with the United States that he could take to his countrymen and persuade them that a liberalized GATT would be good for France.[85]

The Clinton administration, realizing that Balladur had committed himself politically to changing the 1992 subsidy accord, reluctantly agreed to compromise on the subsidy issue. However, the French also insisted on limiting the number of American movies and television programs entering Europe. The French were concerned that their culture was being threatened by Hollywood. On the other hand, the United States wanted France to stop subsidizing its own movie industry. Kantor complained that France levied an 11 percent surcharge on all foreign-made movies, which it used to subsidize French film making.[86]

Finally, on December 14 France and the United States put aside their differences to clear the way for a world trade agreement involving more industries in more countries, 117 nations, than any other trade accord in history. The seven years of talks had solved some of the major issues between the nations, notably some of the farm-subsidy disputes, but still left many issues like free trade involving movies, television programs, music, and financial services like banking and stock brokerage unresolved.[87]

Balladur had claimed that France had won a victory in the GATT accord by forcing the United States to be flexible about agriculture. Indeed, France was able to persuade the United States to change the subsidy accord made in 1992. By the terms of that accord, the United States and the Europeans agreed to reduce the tonnage of subsidized grain exports by 21 percent and to limit other farm subsidies.

However, France, Europe's largest agricultural exporter, wanted that agreement changed to enable it to subsidize more grain exports over the next six years, and in return, it agreed to convert some of its quotas on farm imports into low tariffs. This would enable American farmers to export more of their goods to the European market. The French were also happy about the fact that no agreement was made on movies and television.[88]

The United States benefitted from the Uruguay Round in spite of the concessions it made to France and the EU. The U.S. entertainment industry was the big loser, but the Clinton administration could not sacrifice the entire pact for one industry.[89] The American president hailed the pact, claiming that it was the single largest trade agreement in history. He declared that he did not expect the GATT accord to be as difficult to pass in Congress as the NAFTA treaty. Laura D'Andrea Tyson, head of the Council of Economic Advisers, stated that the United States would probably gain $100 billion to $200 billion a year in new output once the GATT accord went into effect on January 1, 1995. Generally, American economists were pleased with the pact, claiming that growth in the world's poor aspiring nations, expected as a result of the concessions made on tropical products, would make those nations bigger markets for U.S. products.[90] The GATT agreement can be broken down into the following areas:

Tariffs

The nations agreed to reduce their tariffs by an average of one-third. The United States and the EU reached this average by cutting their tariffs on one another's goods in half while cutting tariffs on goods from the rest of the world by much less. Agricultural tariffs were reduced by 36 percent in industrial nations and 24 percent in developing nations.[91]

Quotas

The Uruguay Round eliminated most textile and finished apparel quotas. Previous trade rounds had ended most manufacturing quotas. The GATT accord also called for replacing farm import quotas with low tariffs.[92]

Trade-Related Industrial Property Rights (TRIPs)

All countries, including the developing nations, agreed to protect patents, copyrights, trade secrets, and trademarks. In the past the pirating of computer programs, record albums, videocassettes, and prescription drugs had been common policy in many countries, especially developing ones.[93]

Trade-Related Industrial Measures (TRIMs)

The Uruguay Round ended the practice of requiring high local content in some products like cars and of requiring factories to export as much as they import. The new accord would limit the ability of countries to favor domestically owned factories at the expense of foreign-owned ones.[94]

Safeguards

Safeguard methods are used to protect countries against import surges. The GATT accord allowed countries to temporarily raise tariffs or other import barriers when import surges caused severe damage to domestic producers. If a country kept these restrictive measures in place for more than three years, then countries losing sales had the right to retaliate.[95]

The Uruguay Round talks accomplished little in the areas of financial services, shipping, steel, telecommunications, and audiovisual products. The United States limited the activities of many foreign financial services companies in the United States in areas such as banking and insurance because U.S. companies were prohibited access to foreign markets. The same thing can be said about shipping. The United States and the EU could not reach an agreement on reducing subsidies to European steel makers, and both the EU and the United States have agreed to continue talking on allowing telecommunications companies to offer services anywhere. The failure to reach an audiovisual agreement has already been discussed.[96]

The Uruguay Round of talks created the World Trade Organization (WTO), a new trade organization to replace the GATT as of January 1, 1995. The WTO would be a more powerful multilateral organization than the GATT Secretariat, having the power to assess trade penalties against countries by a vote of either two-thirds or three-quarters of the nations. The GATT Secretariat could act only when the members unanimously voted to do so.[97]

THE FOURTH STAGE, APRIL 1994-DECEMBER 1994

On April 15, 1994, four months after agreement was reached on the new GATT accord, the ministers of 109 countries met in Marrakesh, Morocco, to sign the accord, which weighed 385 pounds and ran to more than 22,000 pages. The agreement was expected to stimulate $5 trillion in new trade by the year 2005. Both Vice President Al Gore and USTR Kantor represented the United States at the signing. Kantor was asked how the United States would pay for the lost revenue caused by the tariff reductions. Under budget rules in Congress, any reduction in taxes (tariffs are considered taxes on imports) has to be compensated by either tax increases somewhere else or by spending cuts. It was estimated that the GATT agreement would cost the United States $13.9 billion in tariff collections over the next five years. Kantor expected that the Treasury would collect about three dollars in revenue for every dollar lost in tariffs as a result of the new GATT accord.[98]

The bill to carry out the new GATT accord was not sent to Congress until September 1994. During that time both the media and certain members of Congress questioned the president's commitment to its speedy passage. Both House Majority Leader Gephardt and Democratic Senator Daniel Patrick Moynihan, chairman of the Senate Finance Committee, warned the president that he should not wait until after the November 1994 congressional elections to take action. Gephardt, a critic of free trade as practiced by the United States and an opponent of NAFTA, supported the GATT accord.[99]

If Clinton needed additional incentive after Moynihan accused his administration of foot dragging, the governors of all fifty states urged quick congressional approval of the GATT agreement. The governors were economic realists, knowing that the passage of the GATT accord would increase job opportunities in their states.[100]

Finally, on September 27 Clinton sent to Congress the GATT bill and predicted that it would pass before Congress adjourned. However, Democratic Senator Ernest F. Hollings, a protectionist from South Carolina, a textile-producing state, and chairman of the Senate Commerce Committee, demanded that the bill be amended to tighten restrictions on textile products entering the United States that competed with those of his state. Hollings called the pact a "tremendous danger" to American workers because its free-trade provisions would encourage the flight of low-wage jobs abroad. The senator could block the bill as chairman of the Senate Commerce Committee. Under the "fast-track" rules intended to accelerate the bill's passage, all committees with jurisdiction over the bill, the House Ways and Means Committee, the Senate Finance Committee, and the Senate Commerce Committee, had forty-five working days to review the legislation. Since all the details had been worked out ahead of time under "fast track," both the House Ways and Means Committee and the Senate Finance Committee had agreed to send the bill immediately to the floor for passage. Hollings threatened to use the entire forty-five days for his committee to review the bill, hoping to delay a Senate vote on it until 1995 when the president's "fast-track" authority would have expired. With the expiration of "fast track," the GATT bill would be subjected to numerous amendments that would lead to its almost certain demise.[101]

During the summer the president took little interest in the GATT bill, assuming that he could get it past Congress without much difficulty. He should have followed Moynihan's advice and sent the bill to Congress earlier for its consideration. Obviously he did not expect the mounting opposition to the bill. However, once Clinton made up his mind to seek ratification in September, he used all of his skills as a politician to accomplish this goal. The House Ways and Means Committee passed the bill 35 to 3 on September 28, and the following day the Senate Finance Committee voted 19 to 0 in its favor. Both Clinton and Senate Majority Leader George Mitchell of Maine were finally able to convince Hollings to allow a Senate vote on the bill after the Thanksgiving holiday in a special lame-duck session of Congress called by the president, the first one in twelve years.[102]

As the midterm elections neared, the Republicans appeared to be delaying a vote on GATT until after the election. Most Republicans like Senate Minority Leader Robert Dole of Kansas supported the bill, but the thinking was that if the Republicans won the election, they might be able to get concessions from the president for their vote. During the election campaign the Republican supporters of free trade avoided it as an issue. The Democrats accused the Republicans of pandering to the supporters of Ross Perot and Pat Buchanan, ardent protectionists.[103]

On November 8, election day, the Republicans shocked the Democrats by winning control of both houses of Congress. It was the first time that the country had a Democratic president and both houses of Congress in Republican hands since 1946. The president's position was weakened considerably because the Republicans now chaired and dominated all the committees in Congress and established their own agenda. Nevertheless, Clinton fully intended to get the GATT bill ratified before the new session of Congress began in January 1995. On November 9, just one day after the election, he asked the current House and Senate incumbents to return to Washington to prepare for a vote on the GATT bill scheduled for after Thanksgiving.[104]

On November 13 Dole, the Senate majority leader in the new Congress, began to waver on the GATT bill. He declared his support of the bill, but he wanted assurances that the United States would be able to pull out of the new WTO if American interests were harmed.[105] Two days later Senator Jesse Helms, Republican from North Carolina and the chairman of the Senate Foreign Relations Committee in the new Congress, urged the president to delay the congressional vote on GATT until the new Congress met in January.[106]

The president had no intention of waiting for the new Congress. However, he needed the unequivocal support of Dole if he expected to be successful. The Senate leader, in a meeting with Clinton administration officials held on November 20, stated that he would be more inclined to vote for GATT if Clinton would drop his objections to a cut in the capital gains tax. Dole had been pressing the president since his election in 1992 to support a cut in the capital gains tax, but Clinton had refused on the grounds that it would benefit only the wealthy. Dole saw the GATT bill as an opportunity to force the president to change his mind, but the president stood firm in opposing any capital gains tax reduction.[107]

Dole's behavior on the GATT was strictly political. The future Senate majority leader did support GATT, but he wanted to run for the Republican nomination to the presidency in 1996 and needed the support of the conservative wing of the Republican party, many of whose members opposed the GATT bill and supported a cut in the capital gains tax. In order to placate the right wing of the Republican party, Dole had to make it look like he was getting something they wanted for his support.[108] When Clinton refused to bargain on a cut in the capital gains tax, the Senate leader was still able to say publicly on November 23 that he made the president agree to a "trigger mechanism" that would enable the Congress to vote to withdraw from the WTO if it proved detrimental to the interests of the United

States.[109]

On November 29 the House of Representatives overwhelmingly approved the GATT accord on tariffs and trade by a vote of 288 to 146. It was passed by a bipartisan vote after only five hours of heated debate. In the breakdown of the vote, Republicans voted for GATT 121 to 56, while Democrats voted for it 167 to 89, and 1 independent voted against it. It should be noted that the future Speaker of the House, Newt Gingrich, voted for the agreement. It is interesting that 89 Democrats voted against their president on such an important issue as GATT, and that Clinton had to depend on the Republican party for his victory. However, many of the Democrats contended that forty years of free-trade agreements, including NAFTA, were costing their constituents jobs and resulting in lower salaries for blue collar workers. Congresswoman Marcy Kaptur, an Ohio Democrat, who voted against the bill, argued that the GATT had not proven beneficial for the American worker in the last forty-seven years. She stated that "real wages for American workers have gone down. You don't have to be a mental giant to figure out that there is a relationship between declining living standards for our workers and our families, and our massive trade deficit."[110]

On December 1 the Senate approved the GATT accord by a vote of 76 to 24. Earlier that same evening a very important procedural vote to waive Senate rules against any bill that adds to the federal deficit was passed by a vote of 68 to 32. Since the trade bill would cost several billions of dollars in tariff revenues and add to the deficit, the vote to waive the rules had to precede the vote on the GATT accord. Voting in favor of the bill were 41 Democrats and 35 Republicans, and voting against it were 13 Democrats and 11 Republicans.[111]

One week later, on December 8, Clinton signed the GATT accord making the United States a member of the new WTO.[112] The majority of countries refused to send the GATT accord to their legislative bodies for ratification until the U.S. Congress approved it. WTO President Sutherland echoed the sentiments of the participants of the Uruguay Round when he warned the U.S. Congress in November 1994 that its failure to approve the accord would destroy the existing world trade order.[113]

NOTES

1. U.S. Department of Commerce, *United States Trade, Performance and Outlook* (Washington, DC: U.S. Government Printing Office, October 1986), p. 111.
2. *New York Times*, September 5, 1984, sec. 4, p. 2.
3. Patrick Low, *Trading Free: The GATT and U.S. Trade Policy* (New York: Twentieth Century Fund Press, 1993), pp. 192-193.
4. Ibid., pp. 204-205.
5. *New York Times*, August 30, 1984, sec. 4, p. 1.
6. I. M. Destler, *American Trade Politics: System under Stress* (New York: Twentieth Century Fund Press, 1986), p. 78.
7. Ibid., p. 224.
8. Ibid.

9. Ibid., pp. 224-225.

10. Ibid., p. 225.

11. Ibid., p. 226.

12. Ibid., pp. 226-227; *New York Times*, September 21, 1984, sec. 4, p. 2.

13. *New York Times*, October 1, 1984, sec. 4, p. 2.

14. Destler, *American Trade Politics*, p. 228.

15. *New York Times*, October 4, 1984, sec. 4, p. 1.

16. Ibid., Destler, *American Trade Politics*, pp. 228-229.

17. *New York Times*, October 5, 1984, sec. 4, p. 2; October 6, 1984, sec. 1, p. 29; October 15, 1984, sec. 4, p. 1.

18. Ibid., October 31, 1984, sec. 1, p. 1.

19. Franklin Root, *International Trade and Investment,* 7th ed. (Cincinnati, OH: South-Western Publishing, Co., 1994), p. 221.

20. *New York Times*, April 22, 1988, sec. 4, p. 5.

21. Ibid.

22. Ibid., April 27, 1988, sec. 4, p. 2.

23. Ibid., April 28, 1988, sec. 1, p. 1; April 29, 1988, sec. 1, p. 16.

24. Ibid., May 5, 1988, sec. 4, p. 6; May 6, 1988, sec. 4, p. 2.

25. *New York Times*, May 6, 1988, sec. 4, p. 2.

26. Ibid., June 9, 1988, sec. 4, p. 1.

27. Ibid., June 16, 1988, sec. 4, p. 1.

28. Ibid.; *New York Times*, June 24, 1988, sec. 4, p. 1.

29. *New York Times*, July 14, 1988, sec. 1, p. 1.

30. Ibid., July 14, 1988, sec. 4, p. 1; August 4, 1988, sec. 4, p. 1; August 24, 1988, sec. 2, p. 6; August 24, 1988, sec. 4, p. 1.

31. Ibid., August 4, 1988, sec. 1, p. 1.

32. Ibid., August 4, 1988, sec. 4, p. 19.

33. Ibid.

34. Ibid.

35. Ibid.

36. Ibid., August 7, 1988, sec. 4, p. 4.

37. "GATT: The Eleventh Hour," *Economist*, December 4, 1993, p. 24.

38. Ibid.

39. Low, *Trading Free*, p. 212.

40. Ibid., p. 213.

41. Root, *International Trade and Investment*, pp. 203-205.

42. Ibid., p. 205.

43. Ibid.

44. Ibid., p. 279.

45. *New York Times*, September 20, 1986, sec. 1, p. 1.

46. Low, *Trading Free*, pp. 215-216.

47. Ibid., p. 222; Destler, *American Trade Politics*, p. 209.

48. *New York Times*, January 29, 1987, sec. 4, p. 1.

49. Ibid., January 30, 1987, sec. 4, p. 1.

50. Ibid., March 27, 1987, sec. 4, p. 7.

51. Destler, *American Trade Politics*, pp. 209-211.

52. Root, *International Trade and Investment*, pp. 207-209.

53. *New York Times*, November 30, 1988, sec. 4, p. 1.

54. Low, *Trading Free*, pp. 216-217.

55. Ibid.

56. Ibid.; *New York Times*, December 7, 1988, sec. 4, p. 2.

57. *New York Times*, December 5, 1988, sec. 4, p. 1; Low, *Trading Free*, p.
217.

58. Low, *Trading Free*, p. 217.

59. Ibid., p. 218.

60. *New York Times*, January 28, 1989, sec. 1, p. 7.

61. Ibid., May 2, 1989, sec. 4, pp. 1, 8; May 16, 1989, sec. 4, p. 1.

62. Ibid., May 26, 1989, sec. 1, p. 1; May 26, 1989, sec. 4, p. 1.

63. Ibid., May 20, 1989, sec. 1, p. 35; June 22, 1989, sec. 4, p. 1.

64. Ibid., June 29, 1989, sec. 1, p. 1; April 28, 1990, sec. 1, p. 33.

65. Ibid., November 13, 1990, sec. 1, p. 1; November 19, 1990, sec. 4, p. 4.

66. Ibid., December 4, 1990, sec. 4, p. 1; December 5, 1990, sec. 4, p. 7;
December 7, 1990, sec. 4, p. 1.

67. Low, *Trading Free*, pp. 220-221.

68. Ibid., p. 221; *New York Times*, December 8, 1990, sec. 1, p. 1; December
18, 1990, sec. 4, p. 14.

69. *New York Times*, March 2, 1991, sec. 1, p. 42; April 25, 1991, sec. 1, p. 25;
May 24, 1991, sec. 1, p. 1; May 25, 1991, sec. 1, p. 35.

70. Low, *Trading Free*, p. 223.

71. *New York Times*, December 21, 1991, sec. 1, p. 33; December 24, 1991,
sec. 4, p. 2.

72. Ibid., February 28, 1992, sec. 4, p. 2; Low, *Trading Free*, p. 224.

73. Low, *Trading Free*, p. 224.

74. *New York Times*, April 20, 1992, sec. 4, p. 1; April 23, 1992, sec. 4, p. 1;
May 1, 1992, sec. 4, p. 2.

75. Ibid., October 22, 1992, sec. 1, p. 1.

76. Ibid., November 7, 1992, sec. 1, p. 1; November 10, 1992, sec. 4, p. 1.

77. *New York Times*, November 10, 1992, sec. 4, p. 1.

78. Ibid., November 11, 1992, sec. 1, p. 1; November 12, 1992, sec. 1, p. 11.

79. Ibid., November 21, 1992, sec. 1, p. 1; November 22, 1992, sec. 1, p. 1.

80. Ibid., December 2, 1992, sec. 1, p. 11; December 22, 1992, sec. 4, p. 9;
December 27, 1992, sec. 1, p. 1.

81. Ibid., February 12, 1993, sec. 4, p. 2.

82. Ibid., July 2, 1993, sec. 4, p. 1; July 6, 1993, sec. 1, p. 6; July 9, 1993, sec.
1, p. 1.

83. Ibid., September 14, 1993, sec. 4, p. 3.

84. Ibid., September 21, 1993, sec. 4, p. 1.

85. Ibid., December 4, 1993, sec. 1, p. 49; December 6, 1993, sec. 4, p. 1.

86. Ibid., December 7, 1993, sec. 4, p. 1; December 8, 1993, sec. 1, p. 1;
December 13, 1993, sec. 1, p. 1.

87. Ibid., December 15, 1993, sec. 1, p. 1.

88. Ibid.

89. Ibid., December 16, 1993, sec. 4, p. 1.

90. Ibid., December 15, 1993, sec. 1, p. 1; December 19, 1993, sec. 3, p. 7.

91. Ibid., December 15, 1993, sec. 4, p. 18.

92. Ibid.

93. Ibid.

94. Ibid.

95. Ibid.

96. Ibid.

97. Ibid.
98. Ibid., April 14, 1994, sec. 4, p. 1; April 15, 1994, sec. 4, p. 1; April 16, 1994, sec. 1, p. 35.
99. Ibid., December 22, 1993, sec. 4, p. 2; July 13, 1994, sec. 4, p. 2.
100. Ibid., July 19, 1994, sec. 4, p. 5.
101. Ibid., September 29, 1994, sec. 4, pp. 1, 6.
102. Ibid.; *New York Times*, September 30, 1994, sec. 1, p. 1.
103. *New York Times*, October 16, 1994, sec. 4, p. 3.
104. Ibid., November 10, 1994, sec. 2, p. 6.
105. Ibid., November 14, 1994, sec. 4, p. 5.
106. Ibid., November 16, 1994, sec. 1, p. 1.
107. Ibid., November 21, 1994, sec. 1, p. 1.
108. Ibid., November 18, 1994, sec. 1, p. 1.
109. Ibid., November 24, 1994, sec. 1, p. 1.
110. Ibid., November 30, 1994, sec. 1, pp. 1, 10.
111. Ibid., December 2, 1994, sec. 1, pp. 1, 22.
112. Ibid., December 9, 1994, sec. 1, p. 30.
113. Ibid., November 22, 1994, sec. 1, p. 20.

7

The North American
Free Trade Agreement

THE U.S.-CANADA FREE TRADE AGREEMENT

In March 1985 President Reagan, during a visit to Quebec, proposed a free-trade agreement to Canadian Prime Minister Brian Mulroney that would eliminate all tariffs and nontariff trade barriers (NTBs) between the two countries.[1] What became the U.S.-Canada Free Trade Agreement (FTA) was the precursor to the North American Free Trade Agreement (NAFTA).

Though the FTA was initially proposed in 1985, serious negotiations began only in October 1987 because widespread opposition to the FTA existed throughout Canada. Canadian business leaders were generally enthusiastic about the new markets that would open up to their products and services. However, most Canadian labor unions, led by the Canadian Labor Congress, did not want to open the Canadian market to U.S. goods. They were concerned that the United States would flood Canada with cheaply made goods, resulting in further job losses. Canada, at the time of these negotiations, was mired in a deep recession that made it difficult for Mulroney to sell the FTA to the Canadian people.[2]

By early December 1987 the final details of the FTA had been worked out, and Mulroney announced that he would introduce legislation in the Parliament in May 1988 ratifying the agreement. Mulroney and his Progressive Conservative party wanted the House of Commons to approve the bill before the end of the year so that the FTA could go into effect on January 1, 1989, the date agreed to by both the United States and Canada.[3] However, the Liberal and New Democratic parties opposed the FTA; they were successful in blocking a vote on the agreement and forcing Mulroney to call for early general elections if he expected to meet his January deadline. John Turner, the leader of the Liberal party, wanted to become the new prime minister of Canada, and he hoped to use the FTA, which he called a threat to Canada's sovereignty, as his major issue.[4]

While the Canadians were preparing for a new election, the FTA easily made its way through both the House of Representatives and the Senate in the United States by September 1988. The United States had recognized the importance of

Canada as a trading partner. After all, trade between the United States and Canada exceeded $150 billion a year in 1987, the world's largest bilateral trading relationship. Now with the FTA in effect, it was expected that the volume of trade between the two countries would only increase.[5] On October 2 Reagan signed the FTA with Canada and awaited the outcome of the Canadian general election, which was scheduled for November 21.[6]

Mulroney, a very popular prime minister, had a ten-point lead in the public opinion polls by the middle of October. However, by early November his lead began to shrink as Turner and his Liberal party accused Mulroney of selling out Canada to the United States. Turner claimed that the FTA would allow the United States to dominate Canada both culturally and economically. The *Toronto Star*, Canada's largest-circulation newspaper, reinforced Turner's statements by crusading against the FTA.[7]

Mulroney and his Progressive Conservatives defended the FTA, declaring that its passage would not alter the U.S.-Canadian trade relationship drastically since more than 80 percent of U.S.-Canadian trade was already duty free. Mulroney echoed the sentiments of most of the Canadian business community that passage of the FTA would provide increased income and jobs for the majority of Canadians.[8]

On November 21 Mulroney and his Progressive Conservative party won a major victory, securing 169 seats, 21 more than a majority in the House of Commons. The Liberals won 82 seats and the New Democrats 44.[9] On December 24 the Canadian House of Commons gave final approval to the FTA, only one week before it was due to take effect.[10] The Free Trade Agreement between Canada and the United States included the following areas:

Tariffs

The agreement for the elimination of all tariffs between the two countries within ten years. In 1987 Canadian tariffs on U.S. goods averaged 9.9 percent, while U.S. tariffs on Canadian goods averaged 3.3 percent. Approximately 75 percent of U.S. goods entering Canada were duty free. The FTA placed the remaining tariffs on three lists, depending on whether duties would be eliminated in 1989, 1993, or 1998.[11]

Rules of Origin

While tariffs were eliminated on products originating in Canada and the United States, they continued to be imposed on products originating in third countries. The rules of origin established the percentage of Canadian or U.S. content for the products to qualify for duty-free treatment.[12]

Government Procurement and Foreign Investment

The FTA incorporated the GATT requirement that purchases by specified government agencies valued at more than $171,000 be open to free competition, and it lowered, in selected cases, the dollar threshold to $25,000. The FTA liberalized Canada's foreign investment structure by providing nondiscriminatory access to Canadian energy supplies; eliminating discrimination confronting U.S. financial institutions operating in Canada; ending the current Canadian embargo on imports of used motor vehicles and aircraft; allowing owners of U.S. television programs to be compensated for the retransmission of their programs in Canada; and eliminating all Canadian export subsidies on agricultural trade to the United States.[13]

Business Services

The FTA prohibited either government from placing restrictions on business services. It provided the principle of "national treatment," which required the governments to treat each other's service providers as they would treat their own. The major achievement of this provision was allowing access to the telecommunications networks of both countries.[14]

Dispute Settlement

The FTA established a Canada-U.S. Trade Commission to supervise the implementation of the agreement. It dealt with all disputes except in the areas of anti-dumping and countervailing duties. The countries continued to follow their own anti-dumping and countervailing-duty laws, but established an independent bilateral panel to mediate differences pertaining to these areas.[15]

THE BEGINNING OF THE NORTH AMERICAN FREE TRADE AGREEMENT

On December 17, 1992, the United States, Canada, and Mexico signed the treaty that created NAFTA. This agreement eliminated all trade and investment barriers among the three countries and linked the United States to its largest trading partner, Canada, and its third-largest, Mexico. NAFTA rivals the European Union (EU) as the world's biggest single market, with $6 trillion in GDP and over 360 million consumers.[16] However, the differences between NAFTA and the EU are greater than their similarities. Though both eliminate tariffs and NTBs, the EU, unlike NAFTA, seeks a common currency as well as political, social, and economic integration. The economies of the countries in the EU are more equal to each other than in NAFTA, where the United States dominates. The Canadian and Mexican economies are much smaller than that of the United States, and Canada and Mexico often feel that they will be negotiating from a position of weakness. The U.S. economy accounts for nearly 90 percent of NAFTA's GDP and is about ten times the size of Canada's and twenty-five times the size of Mexico's.[17]

NAFTA began because of the concerns and efforts of Mexican President Carlos Salinas de Gortari. On February 1, 1990, the Mexican president made a speech to the World Economic Forum in Switzerland where he voiced his concern that the industrialized countries, in their rush to help the newly emerging democracies of Eastern Europe, would forget the economic needs of Mexico and the rest of Latin America. Sometime between February and June 1990 Salinas de Gortari realized that it would be in Mexico's best interest to break away from its long tradition of economic nationalism and to conclude a free-trade agreement with the United States and Canada. On his trip to Washington, D.C., in June 1990, Salinas de Gortari met with Bush to announce jointly their intention to work on a free-trade agreement and to include Canada.[18] Canada agreed to join in the NAFTA discussions in January 1991, officially making North America a continentwide free-trade zone, and all agreed to begin discussions in Toronto in June 1991.[19]

All the countries had their reasons for entering the pact. The U.S. negotiators wanted guarantees that Asian and European rivals in textiles, steel, and computers would not bombard the U.S. market from bases in Mexico. The United States also wanted to wipe out the remaining constitutional restrictions on foreign investment in Mexico and to persuade the Mexican government to open up its undercapitalized oil industry to American investment. The Mexican government hoped that the United States would eliminate its quotas on textiles and steel and open U.S. markets to Mexican fruits and vegetables, especially avocados, which were excluded from the United States because screwworms had been found in them forty-five years ago. Canadian banks were anxious to gain toeholds in both Mexico and the United States. The Canadian government also wanted to increase its export opportunities to Mexico in such areas as services, automobiles, and government procurement.[20]

In early February 1991 the Senate Finance Committee began hearings on NAFTA. Many lawmakers were concerned that NAFTA would prove detrimental to the American economy. For example, NAFTA's critics warned about job losses as American companies moved to Mexico to take advantage of low Mexican wages. They declared that NAFTA would lead to a flood of cheap imports from Mexico into the United States, and that only the southern border states and California would benefit from the pact. They warned about the pollution on the Mexican-American border and how it would undermine U.S. environmental standards. Bush's desire to negotiate an agreement with Mexico would be endangered by the rampant pollution caused by maquiladoras, or American-owned factories in Mexico along the U.S.-Mexican border. These U.S. companies could import materials from the United States duty free into Mexico for processing, provided that the output was exported from Mexico. The United States would apply duty only on the value added in Mexico. In order for any NAFTA agreement to pass Congress, the administration would have to respond to NAFTA's critics.[21]

In early April 1991 Salinas de Gortari arrived in the United States on a campaign trip to win support for NAFTA in the United States. The Mexican president was very concerned about the mounting opposition to the agreement in the Congress. Bush held a joint news conference with Salinas de Gortari and promised his Mexican counterpart that he would fight organized labor and those environmental groups who opposed NAFTA. Bush told Salinas de Gortari that he believed that NAFTA would provide increased benefits for everyone, and that he would work hard to convince Congress of its importance.[22]

Bush recognized the need to compromise with Congress, and he supported a bill that would retrain workers displaced by the NAFTA accord. He also promised Congress that he would seek environmental and health safeguards in the agreement. By early May Congress proved much more receptive to NAFTA than it had at the beginning of the year. On May 14 both the Senate Finance Committee and the House Ways and Means Committee voted overwhelmingly to endorse the upcoming negotiations on NAFTA with Mexico and Canada. On May 23 the House of Representatives by a vote of 231 to 192 extended the fast-track provisions for two years for the Uruguay Round and applied it to NAFTA. The Senate affirmed the House vote the next day, 59 to 36. Congress was giving up its right to amend NAFTA and was allowing itself to vote only for or against the administration's accord.[23]

As the NAFTA negotiations continued through the summer and into the fall of 1991, the Bush administration provided its first assessment of the environmental impact of the free-trade agreement. In a statement made to the press, the administration claimed that NAFTA would not lead significant numbers of American manufacturers to move operations across the Mexican border to escape environmental regulations. On the other hand, the administration warned that if the pact was not approved, air and water pollution could get worse along the U.S.-Mexican border because no additional environmental safeguards would be put in place.[24]

The negotiations agenda that was established toward the end of 1991 called for the elimination of import tariffs, reductions in NTBs, protection for intellectual property rights, fair and expeditious dispute-settlement procedures, and a means to improve the flow of goods, services, and investment from country to country. Unfortunately, as 1991 came to a close, disagreements in such areas as energy, banking, autos, and textiles delayed any settlement. President Salinas de Gortari met Bush at Camp David in early December to discuss the progress of the negotiations. Bush was now concerned that if an agreement was not concluded and sent to Congress well before the 1992 election campaign, the chances of Congress supporting it were remote. The support for NAFTA on Capitol Hill remained uncertain because labor, most environmental groups, and consumer advocates opposed it.[25]

In February 1992 the delegates of the three countries met in Dallas for the sixth major round of talks. USTR Carla Hills declared that the trinational agreement would be modeled along the lines of the U.S.-Canadian Free Trade Agreement. She stated that the United States, Mexico, and Canada had agreed to allow any of the three nations to bar all imports that failed to meet its health and environmental standards. However, corn exports emerged as the chief stumbling block in the negotiations because U.S. corn growers wanted more access to the highly protected Mexican market. Mexico was willing to provide access to its banking and securities industries for both the United States and Canada, but it wanted to continue to protect its corn growers.[26]

As the three countries continued to work on the language of NAFTA, Governor Bill Clinton of Arkansas, the leading contender for the Democratic nomination for the presidency, refused to take a position on the free-trade agreement in the summer of 1992. Clinton found himself in a delicate position on this issue. He considered himself an intellectual and a supporter of free-trade principles, like many academics and economists who supported NAFTA. However, the governor was also the consummate politician, and he was concerned that his support of the free-trade agreement would cost him the backing of labor and environmental groups. Clinton knew that by July 1992 the Democratic party was divided on NAFTA. On July 27 Richard Gephardt, the Democratic House majority leader from Missouri, attacked the free-trade agreement, declaring that it did not include adequate safeguards for workers or contain environmental or public health standards. [27]

On August 12 the United States, Canada, and Mexico announced that they had reached an agreement on free trade. Labor groups immediately attacked the accord as a "no-win situation" for the American worker. They talked about enormous job losses and vowed to fight the bill in Congress. On the other hand, many economists believed that NAFTA would have less of a negative impact on American workers than many would believe. A University of Michigan study concluded that as few as 15,000 to 75,000 Americans could lose their jobs over a ten-year period and that these losses were likely to be dispersed across many states and industries.[28]

In the fall of 1992 the presidential campaign heated up as Bush and Clinton, the Democratic nominee, attacked each other on a number of important issues. The president questioned Clinton's leadership qualities, declaring that the Democratic nominee refused to take a stand on NAFTA. Bush claimed that Clinton had to be either for or against NAFTA because "he couldn't have it both ways." The president released the NAFTA text, began lobbying for ratification, and declared that he considered NAFTA a major achievement of his administration. Bush made it very clear where he stood on this issue and was challenging Clinton to do the same.[29]   Clinton responded by accusing the president of using the free-trade agreement as an election-year wedge to split his party and portray him as indecisive. The Democratic nominee stated that he had endorsed the NAFTA talks in 1991, but now he needed more time to study the finished document before he would make a decision to either support or reject it.[30]

On September 10, two days after Clinton said that he needed more time to study the free-trade agreement, he stated that NAFTA appeared to be lacking substantive provisions on job retraining for American workers and environmental cleaning up in Mexico.[31]   Clinton, who had the support of the labor unions, wanted to protect displaced American workers who would be affected by NAFTA. Bush's secretary of labor, Lynn Martin, had testified before the Senate Finance Committee in early September that 150,000 Americans could lose their jobs as a result of the new free-trade accord. Martin tried to assure the committee that the administration would set aside $330 million to $750 million a year for five years to retrain unemployed workers. The secretary of labor claimed that the figure of 150,000 jobs lost was based over ten years and that this was the highest job-loss figure among the twenty studies her department had reviewed. The Democrats believed that these figures were too low and demanded more protection for labor.[32]

On September 14 the Bush administration received some good news when two environmental groups came out in support of NAFTA. Both the National Wildlife Federation and the World Wildlife Federation declared that the administration's environmental and health and safety standards were more than adequate to satisfy their concerns. Bush had promised to prevent Mexican products that did not meet U.S. health and safety standards from entering the United States and to put in place an integrated environmental plan for the border between Mexico and the United States. The president would appoint representatives of environmental organizations to official trade advisory bodies.[33]

However, the most famous of environmental organizations, the Sierra Club, continued to oppose NAFTA on the grounds that it would create increased factory production on the Mexican side of the U.S. border—an area that the American Medical Association referred to as "a virtual cesspool and breeding ground for infectious diseases." The Sierra Club denounced the Bush environmental plan as inadequate because it failed to give consideration to imports that would result from increases in logging, mining, and other extractive industries under NAFTA. Furthermore, the Bush plan did not examine the relationship between NAFTA and environmental-protection capabilities of Canada, Mexico, and the United States.[34]

On October 4, one month prior to the presidential election, Governor Clinton endorsed NAFTA, but not in its current form. The Democratic nominee wanted the agreement to include provisions that would toughen environmental and worker-safety standards in Mexico and allow the American president to establish commissions to monitor the agreement's impact. By supporting NAFTA with conditions, Clinton hoped to gain additional support from free traders and keep his labor backing. USTR Hills saw through the Clinton statement and criticized him by declaring that the omissions identified by the Democratic nominee had already been alleviated by the agreement.[35]

BILL CLINTON AND THE NORTH AMERICAN FREE TRADE AGREEMENT

After Clinton's election to the presidency in November 1992, Salinas de Gortari stopped pushing for quick adoption of NAFTA. The Mexican president realized that he needed Clinton's support when the pact went to the Congress, but that Clinton saw NAFTA and other trade accords as part of a larger national economic strategy, including changes in the tax system and health-care reform. He believed that NAFTA would produce stronger regional ties, and that other Latin American countries, like Chile, might join in the agreement. In any event, the president-elect had told Salinas de Gortari that he supported NAFTA, but refused to push for its passage in Congress or sign it into law until he had negotiated side agreements to protect American workers. Clinton had offered to meet the Mexican president to discuss the side agreements he wanted negotiated.[36]

The NAFTA text was ready for signing by the leaders of the United States, Canada, and Mexico. Bush, embittered by his loss to Clinton, had no intention of allowing Clinton to play any part in the signing ceremony and did not even inform the Clinton transition team of the signing date until it was publicly announced. The president considered this one of the most important agreements of his administration; he also realized that if he signed the accord before the Clinton administration took office on January 20, 1993, the new president would have a more difficult time making changes in the agreement. On December 17 the leaders of all three countries, Bush, Mulroney, and Salinas de Gortari, met in their respective capitals to sign the NAFTA text. Since NAFTA was signed before the fast-track provisions of the U.S. trade law expired, there was no statutory deadline for submitting the implementing legislation. However, the implementing legislation had to be submitted to Congress by the summer of 1993 if NAFTA was expected to go into force in January 1994, the deadline established by Bush and his counterparts.[37]

On January 8 President-elect Clinton met with Salinas de Gortari in Austin, Texas, to assure him that his administration would move quickly to put NAFTA into effect, but only after Mexico accepted side agreements to protect U.S. workers and the environment. Clinton had enumerated five unilateral measures that the United States should enact before NAFTA could go into effect: (1) worker adjustment assistance, including training, health-care benefits, and income supports; (2) environmental funding for cleanups; (3) assistance to farmers to help shift them to alternative crops; (4) assurances that NAFTA did not override the democratic process including giving U.S. citizens the right to challenge objectionable environmental practices in Mexico and Canada; and (5) assurances that foreign workers would not be brought to the United States as strikebreakers.[38]

On February 2 the International Trade Commission, formerly known as the U.S. Tariff Commission, assessed the effects of NAFTA on the U.S. economy. It determined that job losses would occur in the auto, household-appliance, and apparel-manufacturing industries, but it stated unequivocally that the overall effect would be a slight increase in employment and output in the United States. The reason for this expected modest increase in employment and output was the very large integration of Mexico and the United States resulting from a continuous flow of Mexican labor to the United States. In 1990 there were 4.6 million Mexican workers in the U.S. labor force, about 3.6 percent of the total labor force. Integration would also be caused by the large number of U.S. firms already operating in Mexico that exported their products to the United States. However, NAFTA should create some big winners, mostly the multinational corporations that would increase their investments in Mexico, hoping to buy valuable state-owned enterprises such as the telephone company and airlines at reasonable prices. Foreign investors would also be attracted to Mexico in order to produce for the neighboring U.S. market. These investment opportunities lay behind business support for NAFTA, but it would result in higher incomes for the Mexican people, who would now buy capital goods coming mainly from the United States. Simply put, higher growth and income in Mexico would cause an increase in American exports to Mexico and provide more jobs in the United States.[39]

Clinton's USTR Mickey Kantor led the administration's efforts in getting NAFTA through Congress. He brought Mexico and Canada together and pushed them to accept the side agreements pertaining to labor and the environment. On March 16 Kantor testified before the Senate Committee on Environment and Public Works that the environment and labor commissions would have real power. He was referring to the Environmental Protection Commission, which would be headed by Vice President Al Gore. This commission would be granted the powers and resources to both prevent and clean up water pollution and would encourage the enforcement of a country's own environmental laws through education, training, and commitment of resources as well as provide a forum to hear complaints. The Labor Commission would have powers similar to the Environmental Protection Commission. It would protect worker standards and safety; it would have the power to educate and train workers and develop minimum standards as well as dispute-resolution power.[40]

On March 24, 1993, H. Ross Perot, billionaire businessman and third-party presidential candidate in 1992, vehemently attacked NAFTA before the House Small Business Committee. He reiterated what he had said during the 1992 election campaign, that NAFTA would create enormous job losses in the United States because American firms would relocate in Mexico, where labor was cheaper. Perot told the House Small Business Committee that the accord should only be tried on an experimental basis because of the big gap in workers' wages between the two countries. He claimed that imports by a rich country (the United States) from a poor country (Mexico) would reduce the standard of living in the rich country. This was called the "pauper-labor" argument used by protectionists to support high tariffs.[41]

This argument used by Perot and other protectionists (Perot claims that he is not a protectionist, but was only against NAFTA) mistakes the connection between trade and wages. When wages are viewed without taking productivity into account, they have little meaning. For example, on the average, high U.S. labor productivity pays for high U.S. wages. U.S. workers earn more because of their high output, work skills, and superior capital equipment. According to most economists, U.S. wages will continue to increase as a result of higher productivity levels and not because of the erection of tariff barriers to exports from developing countries.[42]

On April 22 Perot testified before the Senate Banking Committee, declaring that the side agreements on the environment and labor would do nothing to improve NAFTA. He told the committee that NAFTA had to be completely revised or defeated in its present form.[43] One week later the majority of Republican senators told Clinton in a letter that they favored the passage of NAFTA. Though the president was pleased by the letter, it came as no big surprise. Clinton knew that he had enough support in the Senate to pass NAFTA, but the crucial battle would take place in the House, where the vote of many pro-labor Democrats remained uncertain.[44]

On May 27 NAFTA cleared its first legislative hurdle when Canada's House of Commons approved NAFTA's implementing legislation by a vote of 140 to 124.[45] The Canadian government supported NAFTA, as mentioned earlier, because it saw investment opportunities in Mexico. However, Canadian critics of NAFTA claimed that Canada had little choice but to join. Simply, it was a choice between a NAFTA in which Canadians could play some role in preventing the erosion of their bilateral FTA or a U.S. hub-and-spoke approach to bilateralism with Mexico and other countries in the hemisphere.[46]

In late May the Clinton administration began attacking Perot's anti-NAFTA statements. At first, Clinton tried to ignore Perot, hoping that his influence and press coverage would fade. However, the closer the NAFTA bill came to a vote in Congress, the more vociferous and misleading Perot's attacks became. Perot had made a television commercial attacking NAFTA in which he used inaccurate information in charging that NAFTA would cost Americans more jobs than it would create. Kantor, Robert Reich, secretary of labor, and Laura D'Andrea Tyson, chairperson of the Council of Economic Advisers, all attacked Perot as irresponsible. They charged that Perot had little understanding of the fundamental proposition in international trade, that in the long run, imports are paid for by exports, and any restriction on imports leads to a reduction in exports.[47]

On June 30 the Clinton administration suffered a major setback in meeting the 1994 NAFTA implementation deadline. The Sierra Club, Friends of the Earth, and other environmental groups were successful in getting federal judge Charles Richey to order the government to prepare a lengthy study of the environmental impact of NAFTA before it could be sent to Congress. The president had hoped to submit the NAFTA bill to Congress by September; he immediately asked the Justice Department to appeal Judge Richey's decision. If the administration was forced to comply with an environmental impact study, NAFTA would be delayed well beyond 1994 or might not get started at all.[48]

Throughout July and August the Clinton administration continued to work on the side agreements affecting labor and the environment in order to sell NAFTA to Congress. One of the agreements proposed by the administration was the establishment of a binational authority with Mexico to issue up to $8 billion in bonds to pay for cleanup of the Rio Grande and other border-area rivers.[49] USTR Kantor promised that the side agreements would be ready by the beginning of August. He told the press that most of the side accords were resolved except the crucial issue of how to bring sanctions against countries when they failed to punish companies that persistently violated environmental and labor standards.[50]

On August 13 the Clinton administration announced the conclusion of the side agreements made with Canada and Mexico. The three countries agreed to set up two North American commissions that would ensure the enforcement of labor and environmental laws as NAFTA eliminated barriers across the continent. The Mexican government had agreed to trade sanctions for violations of labor and environmental laws that it had previously opposed. President Salinas de Gortari even promised to seek a higher minimum wage for Mexican workers.[51] However, on the same day that these side accords were announced, Gephardt and other Democrats in the House refused to support NAFTA. If a vote were taken on NAFTA in the House in August, most Democrats, fearing the loss of labor and environmental support, would oppose the free-trade agreement. It appeared that Clinton would have to rely on the Republicans to back him in the House.[52]

Now that the side accords were in place, the proponents of NAFTA attempted to get the support of the public. One would think that most Americans knew about NAFTA and had an opinion on the subject. However, a *New York Times*/CBS poll taken in early July 1993 found that 49 percent of Americans had heard nothing about NAFTA.[53] If the supporters of NAFTA expected it to pass the Congress, the public had to know what NAFTA would do for its economy. Beginning in the middle of August, NAFTA's proponents talked about all the jobs that it would create in the United States, especially in the high-technology areas. Former Senator Lloyd Bentsen of Texas, who became Clinton's secretary of the Treasury in 1993, was an ardent proponent of NAFTA. He had written an article for the *Dallas Morning News* stating that NAFTA would increase American exports to Mexico, creating more jobs for both the Texas and American economies. Bentsen had stressed the benefits to the Texas economy by declaring that 30 to 40 percent of those jobs created by NAFTA would go to Texans.[54]

On August 16 former USTR Hills made a passionate plea for NAFTA support. She urged Clinton to demonstrate presidential leadership not only by giving lip-service support to NAFTA, but by making every effort to see that it passed Congress before the end of October so that the accord would enter into force on January 1, 1994, as agreed upon by all the parties involved.[55] Three days after Hills's speech on NAFTA, Clinton appointed William M. Daley as special counselor to the president on NAFTA to head the administration's task force to sell the free-trade agreement on Capitol Hill and to the public. Daley, who was well connected in Democratic politics, was a Chicago banker and brother to former Mayor Richard M. Daley. He might be able to influence many of these anti-NAFTA Democratic members of the House.[56]

NAFTA's opponents wasted no time in stepping up their attacks. On August 19 Ross Perot's book entitled *Save Your Job, Save Our Country* began circulating among trade specialists. Perot intended to release his anti-NAFTA book to the public on Labor Day to remind workers that the free-trade agreement would cost them their jobs.[57] Patrick Buchanan, the columnist, television commentator, and very conservative Republican presidential aspirant in 1992, denounced both the free-trade agreement and his fellow Republicans who supported it. Buchanan had especially harsh words for Senator Robert Dole of Kansas, an ardent supporter of the agreement. He said that Dole could not expect to be the Republican party's nominee in 1996 if he supported a treaty that would cost his country jobs. As of this writing, both Dole and Buchanan, among others, have already announced their candidacy for the Republican presidential nomination in 1996.[58]

In order to gain both public and bipartisan support for NAFTA, Clinton invited the five surviving former presidents, Nixon, Ford, Carter, Reagan, and Bush to

Washington on September 14 for a pro-NAFTA ceremony in the White House. Though all five former presidents supported NAFTA, only Bush, Carter, and Ford were able to attend. All the former presidents spoke in favor of the treaty, but Bush and Carter also attacked Perot, with Carter referring to him as a "demagogue " who was careless with the truth and preyed on the fears of American labor.[59] Clinton also used the White House ceremony to sign NAFTA's side agreements on labor and the environment, hoping that this would attract additional Democratic supporters in the House.[60]

One day after Clinton, Carter, Bush, and Ford gave their unequivocal support for NAFTA, Perot went on television to attack the free-trade agreement. He warned the American people that NAFTA would throw 5 million Americans out of work, destroy the American middle class, and wreck the federal government's tax base. It is interesting to note that Perot was supported by Ralph Nader, a leading consumer advocate, Jesse Jackson, a black minister and very liberal Democrat, who had run unsuccessfully for the Democratic presidential nomination in 1984 and 1988, and Pat Buchanan, mentioned earlier. These people had nothing in common politically except their opposition to NAFTA.[61]

On September 16 over three hundred economists from Keynesian liberals like Paul Samuelson to conservative monetarists like Milton Friedman, scholars who hardly agree on anything, signed a letter sent to Clinton praising NAFTA. They condemned protectionism and declared that the free-trade agreement would provide more job opportunities and income in all three countries. NAFTA would allow the United States to export more capital goods and high-technology products to Mexico, and it would meet U.S. foreign policy objectives by promoting economic growth and political pluralism in Mexico. Mexico would increase its exports to the United States as well as become a haven for foreign investment. Canada would have unfettered access to both the U.S. and Mexican markets.[62]

Democratic House Majority Leader Gephardt was not convinced that NAFTA was good for the country. On September 21 he publicly announced that the free-trade agreement was not sound and the U.S. economy was not ready for it. Gephardt, a close ally of labor, had been leaning against the agreement for the past six months, and his defection came as no big surprise to Clinton. The president was confident that NAFTA would pass the House without Gephardt's support.[63]

On September 24 the Clinton administration received some good news when a federal appeals court removed a large obstacle from Clinton's efforts to pass NAFTA. It ruled that the government could submit the free-trade agreement to Congress without an environmental impact statement. This ruling overturned the federal district court ruling made on June 30, 1993, and opened the way for congressional action.[64]

In August the Mexican president had promised the U.S. government that Mexico would raise the minimum wage for Mexican workers in order to make them more competitive with American workers. His pledge, however, lacked sufficient detail to satisfy members of the U.S. Congress who were still uncertain about how to vote on NAFTA. On October 2 Salinas de Gortari, recognizing the importance of the U.S. congressional vote on free trade to his country's economic future, hastily detailed his plan of tying wage hikes to increases in the productivity of Mexican workers.[65]

In late October the Clinton met with congressional leaders to discuss the prospects of NAFTA in Congress. The president was told that many members of the House either opposed the bill or remained undecided. The undecided congressmen offered a solution to the question of whether NAFTA was good or bad for the American economy. They proposed, as Perot had done several months previously, that the United States should accept NAFTA on an experimental basis for three years to see if the agreement would lead to widespread layoffs or lower wages. Clinton rejected this idea, pointing out that NAFTA already allowed each country to withdraw unilaterally with six months' notice.[66]

Also in late October the U.S. and the Mexican governments received a shock when Jean Chretien of Quebec, the Liberal party candidate, won a major victory over the incumbent Kim Campbell of the Progressive Conservative party in Canada's general elections. The Progressive Conservatives had led Canada for nine years and were ardent supporters of NAFTA. On the other hand, the Liberal party had opposed NAFTA, and Canadian Prime Minister-elect Chretien had told both Clinton and Salinas de Gortari that he wanted to renegotiate the free-trade agreement as soon as he took office in early November.[67] Though Canada's House of Commons had already approved NAFTA's implementing legislation in May, Chretien was looking to make changes to satisfy his Liberal party constituents.[68]

In November Clinton began the stretch drive to get congressional approval of NAFTA. The free-trade agreement occupied most of his time during the first ten days of the month. On November 1 he addressed a Chamber of Commerce conference where he called upon corporate America to support his campaign to win NAFTA approval in Congress.[69] However, corporate America did not need convincing when it came to the pact with Mexico. It was already impressed by what Salinas de Gortari had accomplished with the Mexican economy. For example, the Mexican president had reduced Mexico's fiscal deficit from 16 percent of the GNP in 1987 to 0.5 percent of the GNP in 1990. Inflation over the same period of time had declined from 200 percent to 30 percent. However, the most important statistic for potential business investors in Mexico was the reduction in state-owned companies. Mexico had sold off 85 percent of the more than 1,200 state-owned companies, including national airlines, mining companies, the telephone company, and industrial plants. The Mexican government had eliminated all but 2 percent of its import-license requirements and had slashed tariffs on many imports to an average of 10 percent, just slightly above the average in Canada.[70]

After working to convince the business community, Clinton called a White House conference on November 2 where he tried to sway undecided congressmen to vote for free trade. He decided to appeal to their patriotism and to stress the economic importance of NAFTA. The president declared that rejection of NAFTA would be a profound economic setback for American foreign policy. To emphasize that point, Clinton had in attendance former President Carter, James Baker, Bush's secretary of state, and Henry Kissinger, Nixon's secretary of state. Clinton invited Paul Samuelson and other Nobel-laureate economists to attest to the importance of the economic side of the free-trade agreement.[71]

When Clinton declared that failure to ratify NAFTA would undermine American foreign policy, he was hoping to gain the support of the public and the Congress. Both groups generally tend to defer to the president more often when foreign policy issues are at stake. However, Clinton was taking a political risk by making this a foreign policy matter. If he had lost the NAFTA fight in Congress, he would have failed on what had now become a major foreign policy issue, and his credibility in that area would have been undermined.[72]

While campaigning for the free-trade accord in Lexington, Kentucky, on November 4, Clinton decided to issue a challenge to Ross Perot to debate Vice President Gore on NAFTA. The president hoped that Gore, an excellent debater, would make Perot appear as the irresponsible "demagogue" that Carter had called him previously. It was an opportunity to gain support for the agreement before the vote scheduled in Congress in two weeks. Perot quickly accepted the challenge, calling it a "desperate move" by the administration, knowing that its free-trade agreement had little chance of passing Congress. Perot's only regret was that Clinton was sending Gore; he had hoped to debate the president and taunted Clinton for sending a substitute.[73]

On November 9, Gore and Perot debated NAFTA on the Cable News Network, hosted by Larry King. Gore accused Perot of opposing the agreement to win political and financial advantage for himself. He stated that Perot's family obtained special free trade privileges for its development near Cargo Airport in Fort Worth, Texas. Gore claimed that Perot had favored NAFTA until he began running for president. Perot responded by asserting that he favored free trade in general, but opposed NAFTA because it would cause high unemployment in the United States. Perot declared that he would never put his financial interests ahead of those of the United States.[74]

Public opinion polls taken right after the debate and columnists like Anna Quindlen of the *New York Times* credited Gore with doing a better job than Perot because he stayed closer to the facts, while Perot tended to exaggerate the issues. Quindlen praised Clinton for arranging the debate, stating that the president was right to think that he could "kill two birds with one stone"—the debate won friends for NAFTA and revealed Perot as a crank.[75]

Perot's major accomplishment in his debate with Gore was to incense the Mexican government and its people. He described Mexico as an impoverished, third-world country, "a destitute, authoritarian, and unjust place where 36 families own over half the country and virtually everyone else lives in poverty."[76] Perot was trying to show that under these circumstances the United States could not possibly gain anything from a free-trade agreement with Mexico. He had claimed that NAFTA would destroy American sovereignty and worsen Mexican poverty.[77]

Two days before the debate, Clinton accused the labor unions opposing NAFTA of applying "naked pressure" to destroy the pact in Congress. Both Ron Carey, the Teamsters' Union president, and Lane Kirkland, head of the AFL-CIO, blasted Clinton for blaming the unions for his problems. They contended that Clinton did not have the votes in the House, and that he was resorting to desperate tactics. The president admitted that he was thirty votes short of winning House passage, but he remained optimistic that he would be able to convince Congress of NAFTA's importance to both foreign policy and the American economy.[78]

Clinton began intensive lobbying on behalf of NAFTA. He met with small groups of Democratic members of Congress and explained to them how the free-trade agreement would help their constituents. He knew that he needed 218 votes in the House in order to win passage of the free-trade agreement.[79] The president urged the business community to step up its lobbying campaign. Businessmen began mailings, took out newspaper ads, made speeches, and placed telephone calls to congressmen urging them to support NAFTA. Hundreds of business executives and factory workers, who were given time off, went to lobby on Capitol Hill. Lawrence A. Bossidy, chairman of Allied Signal, Inc., and head of U.S.A.-NAFTA, an umbrella coalition of thousands of companies and trade organizations backing the pact, asserted, "I think we have done more on NAFTA than on any legislative issue in history."[80]

With the vote on NAFTA five days away, its critics fought back by warning Americans that they would lose their jobs if the United States eliminated its trade barriers to Mexican imports. NAFTA's critics were labor-union leaders, workers, farmers, small-business people, the clergy, civil rights groups, and environmentalists.[81] A *New York Times*/CBS News poll just two days before the vote found that Americans were evenly split over NAFTA and were uncertain whether it would create jobs or cost them. Of those polled, 41 percent opposed it, while 37 percent favored it.[82]

On November 15, two days prior to the vote, supporters of NAFTA felt confident that they had won commitments from enough members of the House to give them victory. The president remained cautiously optimistic that NAFTA would prevail in the end. AFL-CIO President Kirkland denounced Clinton for supporting the Republicans and NAFTA and thus abdicating his role as leader of the Democratic party.[83]

On November 17 the House of Representatives voted 234 to 200 to approve NAFTA, giving President Clinton the biggest triumph of his presidency. Clinton proudly declared that "America has chosen to compete, not retreat."[84] It is interesting to note that 60 percent of the Democrats voted against the free-trade agreement, including House Majority Leader Gephardt. Newt Gingrich, the Republican House minority leader from Georgia, and his fellow Republicans in the House gave Clinton his margin of victory.[85] Three days later the Senate voted 61 to 38 in favor of NAFTA, but the vote in the Senate, unlike that in the House, was never in doubt. In the upper chamber the Democrats split about evenly, with 27 voting for it and 28 against. Again, the Republicans, led by Robert Dole, the Senate minority leader, came to Clinton's rescue, voting to support NAFTA 34 to 10.[86] However, Clinton deserved most of the credit for the passage of NAFTA. It was he, in the manner of the late Democratic President Lyndon Johnson in the 1960s, who was relentless in working the Congress to secure the votes for the passage of NAFTA.[87]

The Mexican Senate was only waiting for the U.S. Congress to act first. On

November 23 it approved NAFTA by an overwhelming vote of 56 to 2.[88]   The Chretien government in Canada had dropped its objections to NAFTA after receiving minor concessions from the United States such as codes defining what constituted dumping of goods at below fair market value and what constituted unfairly subsidized exports.[89]

On December 8 President Clinton signed NAFTA into law, and the agreement was implemented as planned on January 1, 1994. It was a great victory for all those who supported free trade and a major setback for advocates of protectionism.[90]

THE PROVISIONS OF THE NORTH AMERICAN FREE TRADE AGREEMENT

The following are the main provisions of the NAFTA Treaty. This document runs almost two thousand pages and is very similar to the U.S.-Canada Free Trade Agreement discussed earlier.

Trade

NAFTA calls for the phased elimination of tariffs and most NTBs on regional trade within ten years. The U.S.-Canada bilateral tariffs will continue to be phased out by January 1998.[91]

Rules of Origin

Goods are considered North American if they originate in North America or are transformed in the NAFTA region to undergo a specified change in tariff classification. In certain cases goods must contain a specific percentage of North American content in addition to conforming to the tariff-classification require-ment.[92]

Agriculture

Mexico and the United States agreed to eliminate immediately all NTBs in agriculture trade, converting them to tariff quotas or ordinary tariffs. Most tariff barriers between Mexico and the United States will be eliminated within ten years after January 1, 1994. Mexico and Canada agreed to gradually eliminate all barriers to agricultural trade.[93]

Automotive Goods

All barriers to trade and investment restrictions in automotive parts will end over a ten-year transition period. In order for automotive goods to qualify for preferential treatment, they must contain at least a specific minimum percentage of North American content ranging from 60 to 62.5 percent, depending on the item.[94]

Textiles and Apparel

All tariffs and quotas on regional trade in textiles and apparel manufactured in North America will be immediately eliminated. Canadian apparel that does not meet the strict regional rules of origin will be subject to a U.S. quota.[95]

Government Procurement

A significant portion of the government procurement market in the NAFTA region will be open suppliers of member countries. No member country of NAFTA can discriminate against private companies doing business in the North American region.[96]

Financial Services

Financial service providers in NAFTA can establish financial operations such as banking, insurance, and securities in any NAFTA country. Each country must allow its residents to purchase financial services in another member country.[97]

Investment

All investment barriers are removed for NAFTA investors, and a mechanism has been established to settle disputes between investors and a NAFTA country. National treatment is given to NAFTA investors in each country.[98]

Intellectual Property

All intellectual property is protected within NAFTA. Each country provides protection and enforcement of intellectual property rights on the basis of national treatment.[99]

Environment

NAFTA members must agree to protect the environment throughout the free-trade area. An environmental commission has been established to ensure that all countries comply with the environmental standards.[100]

THE FUTURE OF THE NORTH AMERICAN FREE TRADE AGREEMENT

In early December 1994, with the free-trade agreement almost a year old, NAFTA's supporters praised its success. Clinton, Chretien, and the new Mexican president, Ernesto Zedillo Ponce de Leon, met in Miami on December 11 to celebrate NAFTA's success and to invite Chile to become its newest member.[101]

The *Economist*, a British newspaper, a supporter of NAFTA and free trade in general, wrote about NAFTA's success in its December 10, 1994, issue. It declared that U.S. trade with both Canada and Mexico had expanded at about twice the rate of trade with non-NAFTA countries in the first nine months of 1994 compared with the same period in 1993. U.S. exports to Mexico grew by 22 percent, and imports from Mexico rose 23 percent. The U.S. surplus on this trade edged up to $1.8 billion. Sales to Mexico and Canada accounted for 60 percent of U.S. export growth in 1994.[102]

The *Economist* mocked Ross Perot and anti-NAFTA groups that had warned that workers throughout the United States would lose their jobs. The British newspaper specifically pointed to the auto industry to make its point. It turned out that in the first eight months of 1994 American car exports to Mexico had increased by nearly 500 percent. The Commerce Department had estimated that the surge in exports to Mexico in 1994 had created 130,000 new jobs in the United States.[103]

The *Economist* wrote how NAFTA had benefitted Mexico in the first nine months of 1994. For example, foreign investment in Mexico increased by 20 percent over what it had been in the same period of 1993. Perhaps NAFTA's greatest contribution to Mexico's economy was that it slowed the rate of capital flight from the country.[104]

About ten days after the *Economist* article appeared, the Mexican peso crisis occurred. On December 20 President Zedillo devalued the peso, which many investors considered overvalued. He had no choice, because the Mexican government could not continue to prop up its value in the currency market. Zedillo declared that the Mexican government would allow the peso to float against the dollar, causing predictions by financial analysts that the peso could fall by as much as 30 percent. This shocked the Mexican economy as desperate Mexicans attempted to sell their pesos for other currencies. The United States and Canada could not afford to watch the Mexican economy unravel. Already Mexican stocks had dropped 12 percent, and the peso had declined by almost 30 percent for the week. Both Canada and the United States recognized that this threat to Mexico's economy could destroy NAFTA. On December 21 Mexico's NAFTA partners provided $7 billion in emergency credits to the Mexican government to help bring the situation under control.[105]

The United States continued to watch the Mexican crisis with great concern. By Christmas Day the steep decline in the value of the Mexican peso had resulted in potential losses of $8 billion to $10 billion for U.S. investors in Mexican stocks and bonds.[106]   Both foreign investors and Mexican businessmen dumped their pesos, driving the currency's value further down. The peso lost nearly 40 percent of its value in less than a week's time.[107]

On December 29 a desperate President Zedillo outlined an emergency plan to stabilize the economy by reducing the $30-billion trade imbalance by more than half. He called for an austerity program that included wage concessions from labor, deep cuts in public spending, and high interest rates, with the Bank of Mexico raising its short-term rate to 50 percent. This program would reduce economic growth and bring misery to the Mexican people in the immediate future. However, in the long run it would reduce the large trade imbalance, stabilize the peso, and bring back foreign investors.[108]

As the peso continued to fall in January 1995, the Clinton administration, worried about the Mexican economy and the future of NAFTA, endorsed the Zedillo austerity plan and proposed a $40-billion aid package for Mexico. However, congressional leaders refused to consider spending any American money to save Mexico, or as many saw it, spending money to bail out American investors who had made big profits on Mexican stocks they knew were risky. Many congressmen also felt that they could not justify spending money on Mexico when they were asking the American people to make sacrifices to balance the budget. [109]

The Clinton administration could not allow the Mexican economy to sink. On February 21, 1995, the United States and Mexico reached an agreement on a rescue plan to keep Mexico's private banks from collapsing, while effectively giving Washington veto power over much of Mexico's economic policy for the next decade. The agreement called for an international loan package of $50 billion to Mexico, of which $20 billion came from U.S. Treasury funds—funds that did not require legislative approval.[110]

The peso crisis and the Mexican austerity plan will affect the U.S. trade balance with Mexico, at least temporarily, and give NAFTA's critics like Perot additional ammunition to use against the supporters of the free-trade agreement.[111] The steep plunge in the Mexican peso has made Mexican goods cheaper than American goods, and the cuts in public spending, the reduction in wages, and the high interest rates have reduced economic growth in Mexico. This will mean that in the immediate future U.S. exports to Mexico will decrease considerably, while imports from Mexico will increase. NAFTA is not responsible for any of this, but somehow NAFTA's critics will find a way to blame it.

NOTES

1. *New York Times*, March 19, 1985, sec. 1, pp. 1, 12.
2. Ibid., April 6, 1987, sec. 4, p. 1.
3. Ibid., December 12, 1987, sec. 1, p. 41; May 23, 1988, sec. 4, p. 1.
4. Ibid., July 21, 1988, sec. 1, p. 3.
5. Ibid., August 10, 1988, sec. 4, p. 1; September 20, 1988, sec. 4, p. 1; July 18, 1988, sec. 4, p. 1.
6. Ibid., October 2, 1988, sec. 1, p. 5; October 3, 1988, sec. 1, p. 26.
7. Ibid., November 17, 1988, sec. 1, pp. 1, 18.
8. Ibid., November 20, 1988, sec. 1, p. 1.
9. Ibid., November 22, 1988, sec. 1, p. 1.
10. Ibid., December 25, 1988, sec. 1, p. 6.
11. William McGaughey, Jr., *A U.S.-Mexico-Canada Free-Trade Agreement: Do We Just Say No?* (Minneapolis: Thistlerose Publications, 1992), p. 10.
12. Ibid.
13. Ibid., pp. 8-10.
14. Ibid., p. 10.
15. Ibid., p. 11.
16. Gary C. Hufbauer and Jeffrey J. Schott, *NAFTA: An Assessment* (Washington, DC: Institute for International Economics, 1993), p. 1.
17. McGaughey, *U.S.-Mexico-Canada Free-Trade Agreement*, pp. 3-4.
18. *New York Times*, February 2, 1990, sec. 4, p. 12; June 12, 1990, sec. 1, p. 1.
19. Ibid., January 30, 1991, sec. 4, p. 1; February 6, 1991, sec. 4, p. 2.
20. Hufbauer and Schott, *NAFTA*, p. 5; McGaughey, *U.S.-Mexico-Canada Free-Trade Agreement*, p. 6.
21. *New York Times*, February 7, 1991, sec. 4, p. 5.
22. Ibid., April 7, 1991, sec. 1, p. 6; April 8, 1991, sec. 4, p. 1.
23. Ibid., April 27, 1991, sec. 1, p. 38; May 2, 1991, sec. 4, p. 2; May 15, 1991, sec. 1, p. 1; May 24, 1991, sec. 1, p. 1; May 25, 1991, sec. 1, p. 35.
24. Ibid., October 18, 1991, sec. 4, p. 2.
25. McGaughey, *U.S.-Mexico-Canada Free-Trade Agreement*, p. 5; *New York Times*, December 14, 1991, sec. 1, pp. 5, 18.
26. McGaughey, *U.S.-Mexico-Canada Free-Trade Agreement*, p. 7; *New York Times*, July 8, 1992, sec. 4, p. 2; July 14, 1992, sec. 1, p. 1.
27. *New York Times*, July 24, 1992, sec. 1, p. 12; July 28, 1992, sec. 4, p. 7.
28. Ibid., August 13, 1992, sec. 1, p. 1; August 17, 1992, sec. 4, p. 3.
29. Ibid., September 7, 1992, sec. 1, p. 9; September 9, 1992, sec. 1, p. 1.
30. *New York Times*, September 9, 1992, sec. 1, p. 1.
31. Ibid., September 11, 1992, sec. 1, p. 3.
32. Ibid., September 11, 1992, sec. 4, p. 1.
33. Ibid., September 15, 1992, sec. 4, p. 1; McGaughey, *U.S.-Mexico-Canada Free-Trade Agreement*, p. 31.
34. McGaughey, *U.S.-Mexico-Canada Free-Trade Agreement*, pp. 35-36; *New York Times*, September 15, 1992, sec. 4, p. 1.
35. *New York Times*, October 5, 1992, sec. 1, p. 1.
36. Ibid., November 18, 1992, sec. 4, p. 1; December 4, 1992, sec. 4, p. 1.
37. Ibid., December 4, 1992, sec. 4, p. 1; December 18, 1992, sec. 4, p. 1; Hufbauer and Schott, *NAFTA*, p. 1.

38. Hufbauer and Schott, *NAFTA*, p. 8; *New York Times*, January 9, 1993, sec. 1, p. 8.

39. *New York Times*, February 3, 1993, sec. 4, p. 1; McGaughey, *U.S.-Mexico-Canada Free-Trade Agreement*, pp. 24-25.

40. *New York Times*, March 17, 1993, sec. 4, p. 1; Hufbauer and Schott, *NAFTA*, p. 8.

41. *New York Times*, March 25, 1993, sec. 4, p. 4; Hufbauer and Schott, *NAFTA*, pp. 11-13.

42. Hufbauer and Schott, *NAFTA*, pp. 11-13.

43. *New York Times*, April 23, 1993, sec. 1, p. 22.

44. Ibid., April 30, 1993, sec. 4, p. 2.

45. Ibid., May 28, 1993, sec. 4, p. 4.

46. Stephen J. Randall, ed., *North America without Borders? Integrating Canada, the United States, and Mexico* (Calgary, Alberta, Canada: University of Calgary Press, 1991), p. 28.

47. *New York Times*, May 29, 1993, sec. 1, p. 45; Hufbauer and Schott, *NAFTA*, p. 14.

48. *New York Times*, July 1, 1993, sec. 4, p. 1; July 2, 1993, sec. 4, p. 1.

49. *New York Times*, July 29, 1993, sec. 4, p. 1.

50. Ibid., July 23, 1993, sec. 4, p. 5.

51. Ibid., August 14, 1993, sec. 1, pp. 1, 45.

52. Ibid.

53. Ibid., July 12, 1993, sec. 1, p. 1.

54. McGaughey, *U.S.-Mexico-Canada Free-Trade Agreement*, p. 28.

55. *New York Times,* August 17, 1993, sec. 1, p. 17.

56. Ibid., August 20, 1993, sec. 1, p. 20.

57. Ibid., August 26, 1993, sec. 4, p. 2.

58. Ibid., August 27, 1993, sec. 4, p. 2.

59. Ibid., September 15, 1993, sec. 2, p. 12.

60. Ibid.

61. Ibid., September 16, 1993, sec. 1, p. 20.

62. Ibid., September 17, 1993, sec. 1, p. 1; Hufbauer and Schott, *NAFTA*, p. 8.

63. *New York Times*, September 22, 1993, sec. 1, p. 1.

64. Ibid., September 25, 1993, sec. 1, p. 1.

65. Ibid., October 4, 1993, sec. 4, p. 1.

66. Ibid., October 23, 1993, sec. 1, p. 9.

67. Ibid., October 24, 1993, sec. 1, p. 9; October 26, 1993, sec. 1, p. 1.

68. Ibid., October 28, 1993, sec. 1, p. 20.

69. Ibid., November 2, 1993, sec. 2, p. 9.

70. Randall, *North America without Borders?* p. 10.

71. *New York Times*, November 3, 1993, sec. 1, p. 8.

72. Ibid., November 7, 1993, sec. 1, p. 1.

73. Ibid., November 5, 1993, sec. 1, p. 1; November 8, 1993, sec. 4, p. 9.

74. Ibid., November 10, 1993, sec. 1, p. 1.

75. Ibid., November 11, 1993, sec. 1, p. 27.

76. Ibid., p. 1.

77. Ibid., November 8, 1993, sec. 4, p. 9.

78. Ibid., November 8, 1993, sec. 1, p. 1; November 9, 1993, sec. 1, p. 1.

79. Ibid., November 9, 1993, sec. 1, p. 1.

80. Ibid., November 12, 1993, sec. 1, p. 1.

81. Ibid., November 13, 1993, sec. 1, p. 10.

82. Ibid., November 16, 1993, sec. 1, p. 1.

83. Ibid., sec. 2, p. 10.

84. Ibid., November 18, 1993, sec. 1, p. 1.

85. Ibid.

86. Ibid., November 21, 1993, sec. 1, p. 1.

87. Ibid., November 18, 1993, sec. 1, p. 1.

88. Ibid., November 24, 1993, sec. 1, p. 4.

89. Ibid., December 3, 1993, sec. 4, pp. 1, 17.

90. Ibid., December 9, 1993, sec. 1, p. 20.

91. Hufbauer and Schott, *NAFTA*, p. 2.

92. Franklin Root, *International Trade and Investment*, 7th ed. (Cincinnati, OH: South-Western Publishing Co., 1994), p. 279.

93. Ibid.

94. Ibid.

95. Hufbauer and Schott, *NAFTA*, p. 3.

96. Root, *International Trade and Investment*, p. 279.

97. Ibid.

98. Ibid., p. 280.

99. Ibid.

100. Ibid.

101. "Happy Ever NAFTA?" *Economist*, December 10, 1994, pp. 23-24.

102. Ibid.

103. Ibid.

104. Ibid.

105. *New York Times*, December 21, 1994, sec. 4, p. 1; December 22, 1994, sec. 4, p. 1.

106. Ibid., December 26, 1994, sec. 1, p. 35.

107. Ibid., December 28, 1994, sec. 1, p. 1.

108. Ibid., December 30, 1994, sec. 4, p. 1.

109. Ibid., January 12, 1995, sec. 4, p. 1; January 30, 1995, sec. 1, p. 1.

110. Ibid., February 22, 1995, sec. 1, p. 1.

111. Ibid., December 23, 1994, sec. 4, p. 4.

8

A Return to Unilateralism

With the passage of the Omnibus Trade and Competitiveness Act in 1988 (OTCA) and its Super 301 section, the United States appeared to be turning away from multilateralism and, once again, toward unilateralism. In the late 1980s America had become disenchanted with GATT, even though it still belonged and participated in its proceedings. The United States has claimed that the WTO, the successor to GATT, has failed to address the fundamental differences that divide countries. For example, the WTO has not defused the trade disputes between Japan and the United States that threaten its very existence. The WTO has been unable to convince Japan to open its markets, not only with the United States but with other countries, and to reduce its enormous trade surpluses. Perhaps it was the failure of the Brussels ministerial meeting to end the Uruguay Round in December 1990 that convinced the United States that it could no longer count on the multilateral system to solve its trade problems. During that meeting the United States the European Union (EU), and Japan refused to cooperate with one another, and it took another three years to complete the trading round.[1]

In the 1990s the United States has presented two contrasting faces of trade policy. It professes solid support for the WTO, as seen in the multilateral initiatives undertaken. On the other hand, it unilaterally attacks countries like Japan, China, India, and Brazil that establish barriers against U.S. goods. The Congress, the bastion of revived protectionism, has provided the president with the battering ram to force closed markets open. Section 301 of the Trade Act of 1974 allows the president to ask the U.S. trade representative (USTR) to identify the countries that maintain the most flagrant trade barriers against the United States and to eliminate those barriers. The president's authority lasts for two years. If the United States asks the offending country to eliminate its trade barrier, and it refuses to do so, the president has the authority to retaliate by blocking an equivalent amount of the offending country's exports to the United States. The president has twelve to eighteen months to negotiate with the offending country before retaliation takes effect. In 1988 the OTCA amended Section 301, calling it Super 301, to allow sanctions to be imposed quickly. Under Section 301 some cases have carried on for a decade.[2]

Super 301 has once again put politics back into trade policy as America leans toward sectoral interests in the 1990s more than at any time since the 1920s. There is great pressure now on Congress to respond to the pleas of its constituency for action against countries that keep American exports from entering their markets. Many members of Congress, like Richard Gephardt of Missouri, want to placate their constituents and get reelected. They resent being called protectionists because they denounce free trade. They assert that free trade does not really exist, and that the playing field (the trade arena) is not really level, as it favors Japan, Korea, China, and Taiwan, among others, all of whom flood the United States with their goods. They demand "fair trade" as the new U.S. policy and have put pressure on both presidents Bush and Clinton to use Super 301 to get a "level playing field."[3]

Since 1990 the trade disputes between the United States and Japan have threatened the close political relationship these countries have enjoyed since the end of World War II. Both countries belong to the WTO and have negotiated multilateral trade agreements in the Kennedy, Tokyo, and Uruguay rounds. However, the disputes between these countries have grown worse since the passage and use of Super 301 against Japan. The Japanese government claims that the United States practices managed trade, while the United States denounces Japan's unfair trade practices.[4]

In March 1990 the Bush administration placed Japan on a list of countries subject to reprisal tariffs due to unfair trading. Bush, a firm believer in free trade, met with the Japanese prime minister, Toshiki Kaifu, in Palm Springs, California, to try to prevent the trade strife from undermining the political and economic ties between the two countries.[5] After two days of talks, Prime Minister Kaifu pledged to ease the trade tensions between the United States and Japan by making Japan's markets more accessible to American products.[6]

On April 5, one month after the Bush-Kaifu meeting, Japan cut restrictions on large retail stores doing business in Japan and altered Japanese tax policies so that more land would be made available for commercial and residential use.[7] On April 27 Bush's USTR, Carla Hills, dropped Japan from the list of countries subject to trade reprisals under Super 301.[8]

Throughout 1991 the Bush administration was constantly fighting with Japan over its trading policies. On January 25 Japan and the United States failed to reach an agreement on requests by Washington for greater American access to Japanese construction projects. Under the 1988 agreement between the two countries, Japan had pledged to open seventeen important public areas to U.S. construction companies by establishing new bidding processes. In June 1991, under the threat of American trade sanctions, Japan agreed to establish numerical targets for its government's financial and construction projects to American companies.[9]

When Secretary of State James Baker visited Japan in November 1991, he urged the Japanese to assume a more active role in advocating free trade. During that visit the Japanese government announced a new program to encourage Japanese companies to buy more components and material from the United States and to enter into more strategic alliances with American business.[10]

In January 1992 Bush traveled to Japan with the heads of the big three American automobile companies, who complained about their inability to sell cars and car parts in Japan due to Japanese restrictive trade policies. The president returned to the United States with a Japanese agreement to buy more American cars and $10 billion more in auto parts. The big three American automobile executives, led by Lee Iacocca, denounced the agreement as inadequate. It is interesting to note that Bush, unlike Clinton, did not relish using numerical targets and only did so one time in 1991.[11]

On March 2, 1992, the tables were turned when the United States shocked Japan with its own trade restriction. The United States imposed a tariff on Japanese Hondas made in Canada and imported into the United States. The U.S. government claimed that the Honda Civics did not contain enough North American parts to qualify for duty-free treatment under the U.S.-Canada Free Trade Agreement. This action, costing the Japanese millions of dollars, led to a Japanese statement that it would begin its own investigation to determine whether the Bush administration was discriminating against Japanese interests.[12]

In 1993, when the Clinton administration took office, the United States criticized Japan's trade practices even more vehemently. In January 1993 the U.S. trade-deficit figure with Japan for 1992 became available. Japan's trade surplus with the United States had risen from $38.22 billion in 1991 to $43.67 billion in 1992, an increase of 14 percent.[13] The Democratic Clinton, who had the support of the American labor movement in the 1992 election, used these figures as evidence that Japanese markets, for the most part, remained closed to American goods. In order to force these markets open, Clinton, his chief economic adviser, Laura D'Andrea Tyson, and USTR Kantor became supporters of "managed trade." The United States would insist that the Japanese establish numerical targets for American goods to show that their markets were open. If Japan refused, the United States would use Super 301 to try to force the issue. Tyson claimed that free trade was ideal, but unrealistic. She contended that the best way to expand commerce was through managed pacts and aggressive unilateralism.[14]

On March 31 the United States charged forty-four countries with establishing significant tariffs and other trade barriers, and it identified Japan as the biggest offender.[15] Japan reacted harshly to the tough trade talk from the Clinton administration. It emphatically rejected the contention that its markets were closed to foreign imports and threatened legal action against the United States if it imposed higher tariffs on Japanese goods.[16]

Relations between the United States and Japan deteriorated when Clinton met with Kiichi Miyazawa, the Japanese prime minister, at the White House on April 16, 1993. Instead of trying to work out a settlement of their trade differences, they scolded each other on trade.[17] The president's combative statements on trade struck the Japanese like a series of earthquakes, leaving officials in Tokyo irritated over his insistent demands that Japan reduce its trade surplus by opening its markets.[18]

In February 1994 extensive trade talks between the Japanese government and the Clinton administration broke off after the Japanese refused to accept American demands to set numerical targets for telecommunications, insurance, automobiles and auto parts, and medical equipment. One month later Clinton decided to sign an executive order reinstating his broad legal authority to impose trade sanctions on Japan. The president firmly believed that only credible threats would get Japan to lower its trade barriers.[19]

A few days after the Clinton administration had declared that it would impose trade sanctions on Japan, Peter Sutherland, the director-general of GATT, vehemently criticized the American president for engaging in "managed trade" and resorting to unilateralism. He wanted the Clinton administration to renew the U.S. commitment to a rules-based set of multilateral trading arrangements founded on nondiscrimination.[20] Kantor denounced Sutherland's remarks as unwarranted. He stated proudly that Japan and the United States had made progress in agreeing to increase Motorola's access to the lucrative Japanese cellular telephone market, and for now, this would avert threatened sanctions. However, Kantor made it clear that the cellular telephone issue did not resolve the overall trade dispute concerning numerical targets.[21]

On May 1 the Japanese Ministry of International Trade and Industry (MITI) denied that it engaged in unfair trade practices. Japan's bureaucracy was growing more combative against the constant American attacks on its trade policy. MITI condemned the United States for using Japan's trade surplus with the United States to prove that Japan's markets were closed. MITI contended that most of America's trade problems were internal. For example, it pointed to both the large budget deficit and the low savings rate that contributed to the American trade deficit. If the United States wished to reduce its trade deficit, it should save more and spend less. MITI also criticized the United States for blaming the problems of its domestic industries on trade alone. It declared that the United States could become more competitive if it improved its secondary educational system and spent more money on research and development.[22]

As the United States continued to argue with the Japanese government over trade, statistics began to show a shift in U.S. trade emphasis away from Japan. Since 1990 many American companies had been lured by the faster-growing and less developed markets in China, Korea, Hong Kong, and Taiwan. Japan was already viewed by American industry as a mature and expensive market in which to operate, with strong domestic competitors and strict regulations. American direct investment in Japan in which an American company purchased a Japanese company or built a factory was down in 1994. For example, in the fiscal year that ended in March 1994, there were 317 cases of U.S. direct investment totaling $930 million. This was down from 363 cases worth $1.3 billion in 1993 and only about half the 727 cases in 1990, when American direct investment totaled $1.6 billion. The number of American electronic companies established in Japan declined from a high of 48 in 1991 to 25 in 1993.[23]

Since 1990 U.S. trade with China had been growing rapidly. However, on February 4, 1995, the Clinton administration, under Super 301, imposed punitive tariffs on more than $1 billion of Chinese goods, including plastic goods like picture frames, bikes, answering machines, cellular telephones, and sporting goods, such as fishing rods and surfboards.[24] Unlike Japan, the trade dispute with China had nothing to do with closed markets. For the last two years Chinese factories had been pirating or illegally copying American software and movie and music videos. The Chinese government had ignored this blatant violation of copyright laws, while U.S. businesses were losing millions of dollars as the illegal copies were sold in international markets. Kantor had demanded that the Chinese government close the twenty-nine factories, many of them state owned, that were producing these counterfeit goods, and had given it until February 26 before penalties of 100 percent tariffs would be imposed.[25]

The Chinese government denounced these punitive tariffs and, as expected, threatened to retaliate by imposing tariffs against American goods. However, Chinese trade officials recognized that their country had the most to lose from a trade war against the United States. Through the first eleven months of 1994 the United States had imported $36 billion of Chinese products while only exporting $8.5 billion of goods to China.[26]

On February 26, the day the punitive tariffs took effect, the United States and China signed an accord to end the piracy of software and other goods, and the United States dropped its plan to impose trade sanctions. The agreement, calling for an intensified six-month crackdown on the copyright violators, depended on enforcement by the Chinese government—a government that had been unwilling to act on these issues previously.[27]

Within three months of the settlement of the U.S.-Chinese counterfeiting trade dispute, a major confrontation between the United States and Japan occurred. The United States had been pushing Japan to make its dealers sell more American cars in their showrooms, and to make its car makers buy more of their parts from American firms. The United States claimed that Japanese car makers had colluded to keep most American cars from being sold in Japan.[28] The Japanese MITI refused to yield to American demands, claiming that the Clinton administration was violating all the free-market principles in trying to micromanage trade down to telling Toyota how many American-made parts it must buy.[29]

On May 10 the Clinton administration announced that it was moving against Japan on two fronts. It would file a broad legal challenge against Tokyo's trading practices with the WTO and abide by its decision, but it would also impose unilateral sanctions against the Japanese auto industry. This left the United States open to the charge that it was administering a penalty before the WTO had heard its argument.[30]

Six days later the United States announced that it was placing 100 percent tariffs on thirteen top models of Japanese cars, including such popular models as Toyota's Lexus and Nissan's Infiniti. The tariff, the largest ever against a trading partner, went into effect on May 20, but the sanctions would be rescinded if Japan and the United States reached an agreement by June 28.[31] Customs inspectors would be instructed to double the wholesale prices of Japanese luxury cars selling for more than $26,000 instead of imposing the current 2.5 percent tariff, and this would represent $5.9 billion in car sanctions. This action would make it virtually impossible for Japan to sell these cars in the United States.[32]

Ryutaro Hashimoto, the head of the MITI, denounced the Clinton administration's action of imposing punitive tariffs as a violation of free trade principles. He immediately asked the WTO for a ruling against the American government and declared that Japan would never surrender to America's illegal trade tactics. It is interesting to note that Hashimoto, who hopes to become the next Japanese prime minister, could not appear as giving in to the Clinton administration's demands. The Japanese economy was recovering from a severe recession, and its government and people were in no mood to be lectured by the United States on trade policies. Hashimoto was tired of hearing from USTR Kantor that Japan does not play the trade game fairly. The USTR takes the position that in the 1950s and 1960s the United States could afford to open its market since it controlled 40 percent of the world economy, but in the 1990s its share of the market declined to 20 percent, and it could no longer allow Japan to maintain its sanctuary market.[33]

At the annual meeting of the Organization for Economic Cooperation and Development (OECD) in Paris on May 23, Renato Ruggiero, the first director-general of the WTO, spent much of his time listening to complaints by both Japanese and American officials regarding their respective positions on the trade sanctions. Though it was not the intent of WTO to rule on this matter so early (it could take as long as two years to hear the review and appeals), both sides received some encouragement from WTO trade officials. Japan was told that U.S. unilateral trade sanctions against it violated the rules of the organization, but at the same time, the U.S. counterclaim, that the Japanese regulations and the sales practices of Japanese car makers made it difficult for foreign manufacturers to compete on equal terms in the Japanese market, also received support.[34]

However, on June 13 Ruggiero claimed that the threatened U.S. sanctions against Japan could seriously weaken or destroy the WTO, and he hoped that the two countries could settle their own problems through intensive discussions. Ruggiero spoke at an hour-long interview in Washington where he made it clear that the dispute was a "delicate matter with nationalist implications" in each country. He declared that there were both legal and political considerations, and he hoped that the WTO would not have to make a legalistic ruling. Though both the United States and Japan had declared that they would abide by the ruling of the WTO, Ruggiero was concerned that an unfavorable ruling by this new organization against either country would be ignored and that this would destroy the effectiveness of the organization.[35]

Though the WTO shied away from the Japanese-American trade dispute, the EU took a strong position in favor of Japan. Sir Leon Brittan, the EU's vice president stated that numerical import targets amounted to managed trade and violated international trade rules. Brittan warned that the EU nations would sue both countries if the Japanese agreed to U.S. demands to set numerical targets for increased imports of American cars without including the EU.[36]

On June 15 the leaders of the world's seven industrial countries, the United States, Great Britain, France, Japan, Germany, Italy, and Canada, met in Halifax, Nova Scotia, to discuss economic and foreign policy issues, among others. Though it was agreed prior to the meeting that they would not discuss the Japanese-

American trade dispute due to other pressing matters, Prime Minister Tomiichi Murayama told President Clinton that he hoped to resolve the issue when trade officials of the two countries met in Geneva the following week.[37]

When Japanese and American negotiators met in Geneva on June 22, they accomplished little, and the situation appeared hopeless. Finally, Kantor met with his counterpart Hashimoto on June 26, just two days prior to the sanctions going into effect. They continued to bargain into June 28, only hours before the punitive tariffs were to be implemented, when an agreement was announced between the two countries that settled the two-year automobile dispute and canceled the trade sanctions.[38]

After all the excitement and tension leading up to the June 28 deadline, the trade-dispute resolution was both anticlimactic and inconclusive, as both sides claimed victory. For example, the United States declared that it would be able to sell more U.S. car parts in Japan, and the Japanese agreed to buy more American parts, but no numbers were agreed upon, and there were no enforcement tools to carry this out.[39] The United States wanted the Japanese to agree to sell more American-produced cars in Japan's car showrooms, and Japan agreed to work toward this goal. However, it remains to be seen how much demand there is for American-made cars in Japan. Once again, no numbers were mentioned by the Japanese.[40] The United States also wanted to get the Japanese auto makers to increase their purchases of U.S. repair parts, and the Japanese government promised to try to accomplish this task, without numerical targets. However, the chances of this happening are slim, since the Japanese auto makers would be reluctant to release their grip on the repair market.[41] The final U.S. goal was to get the Japanese government to raise its output and purchases in the United States, and Toyota, Honda, and Mitsubishi agreed to do so. Again, no numerical targets were established, leaving it to the Japanese auto firms to decide how much expansion should take place.[42]

Both Clinton and Kantor claimed that the agreement was a victory for both American business and Japanese consumers. American business would have more access to Japanese markets, and Japanese consumers, due to increasing competition, would have lower prices for both automobiles and auto parts selling in Japan. Both Kantor and Clinton claimed that the agreement was quantifiable. Kantor said that the "agreement is a significant step to fundamental change. It is broad, detailed and quantifiable."[43] Clinton asserted that "the agreement will lead to an increase in purchases of American parts of almost $9 billion or 50 percent in three years."[44]

The Japanese government declared that it avoided numerical targets, its major goal in the talks. Though Clinton mentioned specific figures in his speech to the Congress and the American people, the Japanese government insisted that it had made no commitment to such figures. This could lead to further trade confrontations between Japan and the United States.[45]

American trade policy has changed in the Clinton administration. The United States today appears more protectionist than at any other time since the 1920s and early 1930s, during the period of high protective tariffs. From Franklin Roosevelt to Bill Clinton the United States supported the reduction of trade barriers through multilateral trade negotiations and most-favored-nation clauses. It became an active member of GATT and participated in the major rounds of both tariff and nontariff reductions. However, in 1988, with the passage of the OTCA and Super 301, this began to change, especially in the Clinton administration.

When Clinton became president, he talked about the importance of free trade and gave his support to the GATT by concluding the Uruguay Round in 1994 and backing NAFTA the year before. However, at the same time, he gave hope to protectionists by taking a tough stand against the Japanese government if it did not open its markets to American goods. Clinton's supporters praise the president's strong-arm tactics against Japan. They declare that the Japanese government should begin taking responsibility for the global economic system and must recognize that its trade barriers, its structural surpluses with the rest of the world, and its failure to stimulate its economy undermine the world trading system.[46]

Though Clinton supporters within and outside the administration make a valid point about how Japan is not playing by the rules, and that the president is only trying to level the playing field, the administration's methods may undermine the world trading system that took more than fifty years to build. In attacking Japan unilaterally, Clinton is ignoring the WTO that was created to settle these kinds of disputes. The American president publicly bullied Japan into making a settlement concerning automobiles and auto parts at the end of June 1995 while disregarding the role of the WTO. The WTO was reluctant to get involved in this dispute because of the hostility that was already created between the two countries by Clinton's unilateral action. In early July the Clinton administration was threatening once more to ignore the WTO and pursue its own policy against Japan. This time the Eastman Kodak Company was charging that the Fuji Photo Film Company and the Japanese government were conspiring to keep Kodak film out of the Japanese market. Though the Japanese government ridiculed these charges by Kodak, USTR Kantor will begin an investigation. If Kantor finds any truth in Kodak's assertions and acts unilaterally, there will be another American-Japanese trade confrontation.[47]

Both the EU's Brittan and the WTO's Ruggiero are concerned about the Clinton administration's commitment to free trade in light of its unilateral disputes with Japan. However, Brittan also criticized the Clinton administration's refusal to participate in a global pact on financial services. On June 29 the American government announced in Geneva that it will not open the American market to all financial service companies seeking entry unless the fast-growing Asian and Latin American economies offer greater access to their own markets to American banks, insurance companies, and brokerage houses. By taking this position, the United States is refusing to cooperate with the majority of the WTO in writing global rules for one part of the $1-trillion-a-year market in internationally traded services.[48] In this case the EU is very critical of the Clinton administration, declaring that its negotiating strategy is flawed because developing nations in Asia and Latin America do not really want access yet to the American market since they are still developing their own financial service industries and prefer protection to deregulation. The EU admonishes the Clinton administration for negotiating special access deals and claims that this is undermining a pillar of the post-World

War II trading system known as the "most-favored-nation" clause where what is given to one nation is extended to others in good standing.[49]

If the United States continues its unilateral approach to trade policy by choosing which countries it will challenge with trade sanctions and which countries it will allow access to its markets, the WTO will soon cease to exist and unilateralism and protectionism will return as trade policy. The United States must once again, as it did in the 1930s, show the world that it believes in free trade by practicing it.

NOTES

1. Patrick Low, *Trading Free: The GATT and U.S. Trade Policy* (New York: Twentieth Century Fund Press, 1993), p. 243.

2. *New York Times*, March 2, 1994, sec. 1, p. 1.

3. Low, *Trading Free*, pp. 239-244.

4. *New York Times*, May 8, 1995, sec. 4, p. 1.

5. Ibid., March 3, 1990, sec. 1, p. 31.

6. Ibid., March 4, 1990, sec. 1, p. 22; March 25, 1990, sec. 1, p. 24.

7. Ibid., April 6, 1990, sec. 1, p. 1.

8. Ibid., April 28, 1990, sec. 1, p. 33.

9. Ibid., January 26, 1991, sec. 1, p. 42; June 4, 1991, sec. 3, p. 15.

10. Ibid., November 12, 1991, sec. 1, p. 1; sec. 4, p. 2.

11. Ibid., January 10, 1992, sec. 1, p. 1.

12. Ibid., March 3, 1992, sec. 4, p. 1; March 4, 1992, sec. 4, p. 6.

13. Ibid., January 23, 1993, sec. 1, p. 37.

14. Ibid., March 30, 1993, sec. 1, p. 1; Low, *Trading Free*, p. 244.

15. *New York Times*, April 1, 1993, sec. 4, p. 2.

16. Ibid., March 25, 1993, sec. 4, p. 1.

17. Ibid., April 17, 1993, sec. 1, p. 1.

18. Ibid., April 20, 1993, sec. 4, p. 1.

19. Ibid., March 2, 1994, sec. 4, p. 1.

20. Ibid., March 10, 1994, sec. 4, p. 1.

21. Ibid., March 11, 1994, sec. 4, p. 2.

22. Ibid., May 2, 1994, sec. 4, p. 1; Franklin Root, *International Trade and Investment*, 7th ed. (Cincinnati, OH: South-Western Publishing Co., 1994), pp. 229-233.

23. *New York Times*, November 4, 1994, sec. 4, p. 1.

24. Ibid., February 5, 1995, sec. 1, p. 1.

25. Ibid.

26. Ibid.

27. Ibid., February 27, 1995, sec. 1, p. 1.

28. "Buy My Cars or Else," *Economist*, May 13, 1995, pp. 16-18.

29. *New York Times*, May 8, 1995, sec. 4, p. 1.

30. Ibid., May 11, 1995, sec. 4, p. 1.

31. Ibid., May 17, 1995, sec. 1, p. 1.

32. Ibid.

33. Ibid., May 18, 1995, sec. 4, p. 5.

34. Ibid., May 24, 1995, sec. 4, p. 1; May 30, 1995, sec. 4, p. 4.

35. Ibid., June 14, 1995, sec. 4, pp. 1, 5.

36.   Ibid., May 25, 1995, sec. 1, p. 1.
37.   Ibid., June 16, 1995, sec. 4, p. 1.
38.   Ibid., June 24, 1995, sec. 1, p. 1; June 25, 1995, sec. 1, p. 1; June 29, 1995, sec. 1, p. 1.
39.   *New York Times*, June 29, 1995, sec. 1, p. 1.
40.   Ibid.
41.   Ibid.
42.   Ibid.
43.   Ibid.
44.   Ibid., June 29, 1995, sec. 4, p. 6.
45.   Ibid.
46.   Ibid., June 21, 1995, sec. 1, p. 19.
47.   Ibid., July 5, 1995, sec. 4, p. 4.
48.   Ibid., June 30, 1995, sec. 4, p. 1.
49.   Ibid., July 4, 1995, sec. 1, p. 47.

Bibliography

BOOKS

Ambrose, Stephen E. *Nixon: Ruin and Recovery, 1973-1990*. Vol. 3. New York: Simon and Schuster, 1991.

Baldwin, Robert E. *Nontariff Distortions of International Trade*. Washington, DC: Brookings Institution, 1970.

Bhagwati, Jagdish. *Protectionism*. Cambridge: MIT Press, 1988.

Bhagwati, Jagdish. *The World Trading System at Risk*. Princeton, NJ: Princeton University Press, 1991.

Bovard, James. *The Fair Trade Fraud*. New York: St. Martin's Press, 1991.

Brock, William, and Robert Hormats, eds. *The Global Economy*. New York: W. W. Norton and Company, 1990.

Chernow, Ron. *The House of Morgan: An American Banking Dynasty and the Rise of Modern Finance*. New York: Simon and Schuster, 1990.

Dam, Kenneth. *The GATT: Law and International Economic Organization*. Chicago: University of Chicago Press, 1970.

Deardorff, Alan V., and Robert Stern. *An Economic Analysis of the Effects of the Tokyo Round of Multilateral Trade Negotiations on the United States and the Other Major Industrialized Countries*. Washington, DC: U.S. Government Printing Office, 1979.

Destler, I. M. *American Trade Politics: System under Stress*. New York: Twentieth Century Fund Press, 1986.

Dudley, James. *1992: Understanding the New European Market*. Chicago: Dearborn Financial Publishing, 1991.

Finger, Michael, and Andrzej Olechowski, eds. *The Uruguay Round: A Handbook on the Multilateral Trade Negotiations*. Washington, DC: World Bank, 1987.

Galbraith, John Kenneth. *The Great Crash, 1929*. Boston: Houghton Mifflin Company, 1979.

Garraty, John A. *The Great Depression*. New York: Harcourt Brace Jovanovich, 1986.

Gianaris, Nicholas V. *The European Community and the United States: Economic Relations*. New York: Praeger, 1991.

Hicks, John D. *Republican Ascendancy, 1921-1933*. New York: Harper and Row, 1960.

Hufbauer, Gary C., and Jeffrey J. Schott. *NAFTA: An Assessment*. Washington, DC: Institute for International Economics, 1993.

Hull, Cordell. *The Memoirs of Cordell Hull*. 2 vols. New York: Macmillan Company, 1948.

Humphrey, Don D. *The United States and the Common Market: A Background Study*. New York: Frederick A. Praeger, 1963.

Jackson, John. *Restructuring the GATT System*. New York: Council on Foreign Relations Press, 1990.

Jones, Joseph M. *Tariff Retaliation: Repercussions of the Hawley-Smoot Bill*. Philadelphia: University of Pennsylvania Press, 1934.

Kaplan, Edward S., and Thomas W. Ryley. *Prelude to Trade Wars: American Tariff Policy, 1890-1922*. Westport, CT: Greenwood Press, 1994.

Kindleberger, Charles P. *The World in Depression, 1929-1939*. Berkeley: University of California Press, 1986.

Krugman, Paul. *The Age of Diminished Expectations*. Cambridge: MIT Press, 1990.

Leuchtenburg, William E. *Franklin D. Roosevelt and the New Deal*. New York: Harper and Row, 1963.

Lincoln, Edward J. *Japan's Unequal Trade*. Washington, DC: Brookings Institution, 1990.

Low, Patrick. *Trading Free: The GATT and U.S. Trade Policy*. New York: Twentieth Century Fund Press, 1993.

Lustig, Nora, Barry P. Bosworth, and Robert Z. Lawrence, eds. *North American Free Trade*. Washington, DC: Brookings Institution, 1992.

Markusen, James, and James Melvin. *The Theory of International Trade*. New York: Harper and Row, 1988.

McGaughey, William, Jr. *A U.S.-Mexico-Canada Free-Trade Agreement: Do We Just Say No?* Minneapolis: Thistlerose Publications, 1992.

Nixon, Richard. *RN: The Memoirs of Richard Nixon*. New York: Grosset and Dunlap, 1978.

Preeg, Ernest. *Traders and Diplomats: An Analysis of the Kennedy Round of Negotiations under the General Agreement on Tariffs and Trade*. Washington, DC: Brookings Institution, 1970.

Randall, Stephen J., ed. *North America without Borders? Integrating Canada, the United States, and Mexico*. Calgary, Alberta, Canada: University of Calgary Press, 1991.

Reich, Robert B. *The Work of Nations*. New York: Vintage Books, 1992.

Root, Franklin. *International Trade and Investment*. 7th ed. Cincinnati, OH: South-Western Publishing Company, 1994.

Schlesinger, Arthur, Jr. *The Coming of the New Deal*. Boston: Houghton Mifflin Company, 1958.

Schlesinger, Arthur, Jr. *The Crisis of the Old Order, 1919-1933*. Boston: Houghton Mifflin Company, 1957.

Schlesinger, Arthur, Jr. *A Thousand Days: John F. Kennedy in the White House*. Boston: Houghton Mifflin Company, 1965.

Schott, Jeffrey J. *The Global Trade Negotiations: What Can Be Achieved?* Washington, DC: Institute for International Economics, 1990.

Sorensen, Theodore. *Kennedy*. New York: Harper and Row, 1965.

Stern, Robert M., ed. *U. S. Trade Policies in a Changing World Economy*. Cambridge: The MIT Press, 1987.

Taussig, F. W. *The Tariff History of the United States*. 8th ed. New York: G. P. Putnam's Sons, 1931.

Thurow, Lester. *Head to Head: The Coming Economic Battle among Japan, Europe, and America*. New York: William Morrow and Company, 1992.

Tsoukalis, Loukas. *The New European Economy: The Politics and Economics of Integration*. New York: Oxford University Press, 1993.

Vousden, Neil. *The Economics of Trade Protection*. New York: Cambridge University Press, 1990.

Weintraub, Sidney, ed. *U.S.-Mexican Industrial Integration: The Road to Free Trade.*
  Boulder, CO: Westview Press, 1991.
Yeager, Leland B., and David Tuerck. *Foreign Trade and U.S. Policy.* New York: Praeger
  Publishers, 1976.

ARTICLES

"Background to Peace: Cordell Hull and the Trade Agreement Policy." *Fortune* 16
  (September 1937): 90.
Baldwin, Robert E. "The Political Economy of Trade Policy." *Journal of Economic
  Perspectives* (Fall 1989): 119-136.
Berglund, Abraham. "The Reciprocal Trade Agreements Act of 1934." *American Economic
  Review* 25 (September 1935): 411-425.
Berglund, Abraham. "The Tariff Act of 1930." *American Economic Review* 20 (September
  1930): 467-479.
"Buy My Cars or Else." *Economist*, May 13, 1995, pp. 16-18.
Callahan, Colleen M., Judith A. McDonald, and Anthony Patrick O'Brien. "Who Voted for
  Smoot-Hawley?" *Journal of Economic History* 54 (September 1994): 683-690.
Carson, Joseph G. "Why GATT Is Important to the United States." *Measuring Success,*
  August 1994, p. 1.
"Congress Gives the President More Time." *Newsweek*, March 6, 1937, p. 11.
Eichengreen, Barry. "The Political Economy of the Smoot-Hawley Tariff." *Research in
  Economic History* 12 (1989): 1-43.
"The European Union." *Economist*, October 22, 1994, p. 22.
"The GATT and Its Origin." *Congressional Digest* 33 (January 1954): 6.
"GATT: The Eleventh Hour." *The Economist*, December 4, 1993, p. 24.
"Happy Ever NAFTA?" *Economist*, December 10, 1994, pp. 23-24.
Klein, J. "The Tariff and the Depression." *Current History* 34 (July 1931): 497-499.
"Mickey Kantor's Outrageous Gamble." *Economist*, May 20, 1995, p. 59.
"The 1947 Multilateral Agreement—GATT." *Congressional Digest* 37 (April 1958): 104.
"Opportunity Knocks for U.S. Business." *Time*, August 11, 1958, p. 64.
"Putting a Stop to Trade." *Economist*, May 27, 1995, pp. 18-20.
Seligman, Ben. "Tariffs, the Kennedy Administration, and American Politics." *Commentary*
  33 (March 1962): 185.
"Summary of the Trade Expansion Act of 1962." *Current History* 43 (July 1962): 51-52.
"The Tariff and the Farmer." *Literary Digest*, July 19, 1930, pp. 8-9.
Taussig, F. W. "The Tariff Act of 1930." *Quarterly Journal of Economics* 45 (November
  1930): 1-21.
"Trade Expansion Act of 1962." *America*, February 10, 1962, p. 616.
U.S. Department of Commerce. *United States Trade, Performance and Outlook.*
  Washington, DC: U.S. Government Printing Office, October, 1986, p. 111.
Villard, Oswald Garrison. "The New Cuban Reciprocity Pact." *Nation*, September 12, 1934,
  p. 287.
Weiss, L. "The Trade Expansion Act of 1962." *Department of State Bulletin*, December 3,
  1962, pp. 847-851.

Index

About the Author

EDWARD S. KAPLAN, a professor with the Social Science Department at New York City Technical College of the City University of New York, teaches Macroeconomics, Microeconomics, Money and Banking, and his speciality, Economic History of the United States. He has coauthored *Prelude to Trade Wars: American Tariff Policy, 1890–1922* (Greenwood Press, 1994) and has written several articles on twentieth century U.S. economic history.

ISBN 0-313-29480-1

HARDCOVER BAR CODE